Edwardian Architecture
Style and Technology

Richard Fellows

*

Edwardian Architecture

Style and Technology

Lund Humphries   London

First published in 1995 by
Lund Humphries Publishers Limited
Park House, 1 Russell Gardens
London NW11 9NN

British Library Cataloguing in Publication Data
A catalogue record for this book is available from
the British Library

ISBN 0 85331 653 8

House Editor: Lucy Myers
Designed by Alan Bartram
Typeset by Nene Phototypesetters Ltd, Northampton
Made and printed in Great Britain by The Bath Press, Bath

Frontispiece:
The North Eastern Railway Company headquarters building, York,
seen from the city walls.

Contents

Acknowledgements   6

Part One   Introduction   7

Chapter 1
Edwardian Architects   9

Chapter 2
Change and Development   30

Chapter 3
Technology, Form and Style   49

Chapter 4
New Buildings in Edwardian Britain   74

Part Two   Introduction   85

Chapter 5
Civic Splendour   86

Chapter 6
Palaces of Business   100

Chapter 7
Function and Form   115

Chapter 8
Local Landmarks   127

Chapter 9
The Artistic House   141

Conclusion   155

Bibliography   157

Index   160

Acknowledgements

I would like to thank those people who have helped me to develop the theme of this book by listening sympathetically to my ideas, particularly Dr Dean Hawkes, Dr Jeremy Taylor, and Elizabeth Williamson. As ever, Margaret Richardson provided moral and intellectual support.

Those who have contributed in a more tangible way are Pamela Armitage and her colleagues in the University of Huddersfield Library; Sue Pritchard, whose work with photographic tasks has been invaluable; and Richard Buxton, who has constructed the index. I must also thank friends and colleagues who have transmitted useful pieces of information.

The owners and users of many of the buildings referred to in the text have allowed me to explore their property, and in some cases were able to furnish contemporary documents. Particularly helpful were Christine Hopper at Cartwright Hall; Mr Alan Moorby and Mr Ian Page of the railway companies at York; Ray Linforth of the Gilling Dod Partnership (formerly Willink and Thicknesse), Liverpool; the senior librarian at the University of Birmingham; Mrs V. Chapman and her staff at Wolverhampton Central Library; Mr G. Wyles of Technical Services, Wolverhampton MBC; Elizabeth Hickman; Mrs Long of Thornfield Hall (formerly Home Place); Major Lane; Joan Moss at Banney Royd; and Mrs Pedloe at Ditton Place. Local history librarians in many places have been friendly and co-operative, as have RIBA staff. Mr Bill Kings provided interesting background information on the Bromsgrove Guild.

Finally, I would like to thank my family for their patience and tact.

Richard Fellows

Photographic Acknowledgements

The Architectural Review: pp.14, 21, 22, 26, 27, 45, 47, 66, 67, 78, 79, 90, 106, 107, 115, 119, 122, 135, 142, 146, 153, 154, 155
Author: pp.11, 15, 21, 23, 24, 25, 34, 35, 38, 41, 43, 50, 56, 64, 71, 74, 76, 77, 83, 87, 89(ii), 94, 97, 101, 103, 104, 116, 121, 125, 127, 129, 137, 145, 147, 148, 151, 152
Bradford Art Galleries and Museums: p.98
The British Architectural Library, RIBA, London: pp.16,17,46
City of Cardiff, Public Relations Department: p.89
The Gilling Dod Partnership: pp.109, 111, 112
The Illustrated London News: pp.29, 44
Lancashire County Libraries: p.81
Sue Pritchard: cover, Frontispiece, p.150
Karen Shaw: pp.54, 55
Wolverhampton Public Libraries: p.133

Part One
Introduction

The images of Edwardian architecture are alluring: a lofty gable projecting high above the street, rising from a wall of warm red brick striped with bands of creamy coloured stone; a richly carved frieze running below; a bay window framed in stone and set about with allegorical figures; over all a copper-clad dome with lantern and gilded weather vane. In the country, the image is of a quiet house, combining local materials and crafts, sitting snugly in the folds of the landscape, complementing the surrounding fields and woods with a neat, formal garden of shady walks and clipped yew hedges.

The Edwardian era itself is suffused with the kind of golden glow which has transmuted late medieval times into 'Merrie England'. This is surprising, as it is so close to us in time, yet it represents a lost world with qualities that, it seems, will be impossible to recapture. What is more, its associations are usually agreeable, in contrast to the immediately preceding Victorian period, the world of Dickens and Doré. This is, of course, an illusion, and a close investigation presents a complex and unsettled picture. In architecture itself there are many strands of development and expression, overlapping and intertwined, which are not easy to disentangle.

The use of the term 'Edwardian' may pose some problems. British history makes convenient use of the names of its kings and queens, but architecturally this is not always helpful, as the time-span of a reign can be quite arbitrary in the context of aesthetic and social trends. Edward VII was king for only nine years (1901-10), but the era that bears his name is usually thought of as extending up to 1914, the outbreak of the First World War. This marks a convenient termination because of the length of the conflict itself and the social watershed which the war is supposed to have brought about. Greater problems, however, exist in identifying a starting point. Some commentators have chosen to include the last decade of the nineteenth century, and this makes sense because the architectural linkage is very strong. On the other hand, the passing of Queen Victoria in 1901 was coincident with the demise of several of her leading subjects and the rise to prominence of a new generation. In addition, the enthusiasms of the new monarch were not without effect, and the timing of his accession at the beginning of the century may have given a subliminal signal for change. In writing this book, I have chosen to regard 'Edwardian' as meaning 1900-14, but I have had to include much comment on the 1890s.

In an attempt to identify some of the characteristics of Edwardianism, it is necessary to look back before the turn of the century. The closing decades of the Victorian era had seen a relaxation in social outlook. In architecture, the aggressive and assertive Gothic Revival, with its moralistic theorising, was replaced for almost all but church design by the quaint and picturesque 'Old English' and 'Queen Anne' of Richard Norman Shaw and Ernest George. Both architects continued to be active and influential into Edwardian times. Social conditions improved through the agency of central government, local government and philanthropy. Life was still unpleasant for those born into the lower stratum of society, but reforms which were set in train in the 1880s and 1890s continued during the Edwardian era, and the agencies bringing these about established themselves more soundly.

In carrying forward movements begun in the late nineteenth century, the Edwardians helped to establish important aspects of twentieth-century life, particularly those of a socio-political nature. There were, however, some very unsettling developments at the time. Most of these were confined, for the moment, to the intelligentsia, or to narrow sectors of society, but they were to have profound consequences. Changes in philosophical outlook, the development of psychology, and radical ideas about the physical sciences, for instance, fostered a new uncertainty. Various dangerous political theories and ideas about social engineering were in the air. In addition, rapid technological developments, such as the beginnings of powered flight, the increasing refinement of the motor car, and the growth of wireless telegraphy and the cinema, set the scene for the communications explosion which has helped to characterise this century.

Thus there is an ambiguity within the Edwardian period, which may account for much of its fascination. It is evident that the seeds of social and technological change were already sown by 1914, and it can be maintained that the war merely hastened the process. On the other hand, the feeling that the years from the turn of the century up to the First World War were somehow a coda to the nineteenth century – a glorious sunset following a day of hard work – is not without foundation.

Architecture did not stand outside these conflicting trends, but it must be said that in Britain a simple division between advanced and conventional work cannot be made. The picture is further complicated by the fact that the individual practitioner was still dominant, and that very young men and very old men, and a whole age range in between, contributed to the architectural scene. In other words, personal creativity and taste, shaped by any number of potential influences, was dominant, rather than consensus architecture conforming to a strong, universally held theory.

One characteristic that helps to distinguish Edwardian architecture, then, is its diversity. At least this was so during the first decade of the century. Gradually, change was effected by a number of factors, such as the adoption of new technology and the advent of full-time architectural education, so that by 1914 architectural design was very different in both theory and execution from what it had been ten years earlier.

The book sets out to explore these issues in its first half, by looking at the leading architects of the time, and the nature of their practice, as well as the reasons for change. Rapidly developing constructional and services technology is also discussed, and recurs as a theme throughout, because the interaction between design intention and the means by which it is realised is a vital aspect of architecture. A subsequent chapter deals with the demand for buildings in the Edwardian period, which must have been as broad as at any time during history. Not only were new types such as telephone exchanges and electricity generating stations being built, but company headquarters, department stores and a whole range of buildings for civic and municipal enterprise were being commissioned. Private houses achieved an unprecedented degree of comfort, with an architectural expression that was often personal to the architect or his client, and could be eccentric.

Overwhelmingly what is seen, in all but private houses, is architecture with a public face. The large number of municipal buildings constructed – public libraries, town and county halls, swimming baths, art and technical colleges, fire stations and so on – provided a welcome to their clientele, whilst expressing civic dignity, enhancing the towns in which they were built, and becoming well-loved local landmarks. National businesses were concerned that they should project a wealthy and well-founded image, and that their buildings should give an appropriate physical manifestation to otherwise anonymous bodies. All of this was done at no small expense, and the contribution of artists other than the architect helped to emphasise the idea of large urban palaces, built with the best materials and displaying the work of the most accomplished sculptors, painters and craftsmen, which were accessible to the humblest customer.

The second part of the book is devoted to examples of these buildings: civic and commercial palaces; complex types reflecting new uses and possibilities; libraries, colleges and other public buildings which are major elements in the urban fabric; and private houses built at the height of Britain's 'domestic revival'.

The adoption of these themes sets out to define the special nature of Edwardianism in a way that attempted stylistic, chronological or basic typological categorisation might not.

Viewed from our own, cynical times, it may be that the quality that is most admired in Edwardian architecture is a kind of innocence or naivety, swept away by the cataclysm of the First World War, and made hopelessly irretrievable by its sequel. The naivety has little to do with a want of sophistication in artistic expression, but is concerned with optimism and openness. Even the most pompous Edwardian building engages our sympathy by displaying with pride the materials and crafts that are brought together to make the whole. There is a genuine attempt to create a public art, and an evident delight in the process of doing so.

Chapter 1
Edwardian Architects

Edwin L. Lutyens (1869-1944) and his Scottish contemporary Charles Rennie Mackintosh (1868-1928) are the two best-known Edwardian architects. Lutyens achieved celebrity for his inventive and witty manipulation of architectural elements, whether in country houses or large urban edifices; Mackintosh was famed for his capacity to produce novel and sophisticated design motifs, and his ability to integrate them into a satisfying architectural whole. Although they stand out as highly talented designers, their works have already been well documented, and they represent a fraction of the large number of creative individuals who were busy with different types of architectural practice at the time. It is as though Victorian Britain had produced a brood of particularly gifted children who flourished around the turn of the century.

Attempts to categorise Edwardian architects have proved something of a struggle for even the most perceptive architectural historians. There is certainly no convenient list of characteristics that can be ascribed to all of the period's practitioners. For instance, the age range of those producing important designs around 1900 was wide. At one end of the scale, there were architects like Richard Norman Shaw who had achieved success over the last three decades of the nineteenth century, and were still active and influential. Then there were the great majority of middle-aged men whose practices had become firmly established in the 1890s. In addition, some very young architects managed to break into practice, either by winning competitions or by entering into partnerships. Consequently, it was possible to find important buildings designed by people who had been born nearly fifty years apart. This phenomenon was obviously not exclusive to the Edwardian period, but it does seem to have been more pronounced at that time.

Practice, too, was diverse. There were those accomplished metropolitan practitioners who had private patronage, designing and renovating country houses for the gentry, for instance, and regarding themselves as 'artist architects'; and there were those who entered competitions or worked for commercial clients, and who had to seek work actively. In addition, a number of architects were entering public service as an alternative to private practice. Many continued with the stylistic eclecticism that they had adopted in the 1880s, modifying an essentially visual approach in accordance with changes in fashion. Others maintained their interest in the philosophy of the Arts and Crafts movement, inspired by William Morris and taken up since the 1880s by the more thoughtful members of the profession. Even this is not a clear-cut stylistic distinction, however, as architects of either background chose styles which they thought were appropriate to each particular project. Increasing this confusion further,

changes occurred throughout the period which resulted in a very different design approach being adopted by many before the outbreak of the First World War.

A clearer understanding may, perhaps, be gained by looking first at the older generation who were influential in some way on the leading lights of the 1900s. They were born in the decade 1830-40, and were too young to have been involved in the intensity of the Gothic Revival at its height. As practitioners, they belonged to the more relaxed years towards the end of the century, and although some of them continued to work in Edwardian times, the oldest were around seventy years of age when the King ascended the throne. Richard Norman Shaw (1831-1912) had the most direct effect upon the Edwardians, but Philip Webb (1831-1915) and Alfred Waterhouse (1830-1905) were also important, in different ways. In addition, mention must be made of Ernest George (1839-1922) and John Belcher (1841-1913), but perhaps these mere sexagenarians had the status of 'elder brothers' rather than father figures.

Progenitors
At first sight, Waterhouse would seem to be an unlikely model for the architects who rose to the head of their profession in the first decade of the century. His red-brick and terracotta architecture appeared dated to sophisticated metropolitan practitioners by 1900, and it gradually became the subject of loathing. Waterhouse's influence was not stylistic, though. By building up an enormous practice, which designed hundreds of buildings, he showed how to be an artist and a businessman at the same time; by coping with very complex buildings such as Manchester Town Hall (designed 1868) and the Natural History Museum in South Kensington (begun 1873), he demonstrated how to design a new generation of buildings where a complicated 'programme' of functional requirements was dominant as a generator of form. Finally, as the assessor of many important competitions, he was responsible for launching young architects on successful careers. What is more, the youngsters, such as Edwin Rickards, of Lanchester, Stewart and Rickards, were careful to pander to Waterhouse's preferences and prejudices when submitting designs.

Philip Webb's influence was at the opposite pole. Webb was a friend of William Morris, and had designed the Red House for him as early as 1859. His practice was small. He resolutely avoided publicity during his long career, and in his buildings he rejected prettiness, superficial charm and the latest stylistic trends. He believed that architectural features should not be imposed, but should stem from the materials and constructional techniques used, and although he was willing to

Norman Shaw's New Scotland Yard, Westminster, 1887-90. Shaw's mixture of elements from French Renaissance, English Baroque and Scottish baronial seems singularly appropriate for the building's purpose. Such a combination could easily have fallen apart in lesser hands; instead a very powerful image is produced.

employ a variety of architectural styles, he did not produce a 'Philip Webb' style that his admirers could adopt. His strong theoretical and moral stance made him popular with Arts and Crafts architects and those who wished to avoid the vulgarity of commercial work. He was particularly influential upon William Richard Lethaby (1857-1931), one of the most thoughtful of Edwardian architects, who carried forward Webb's design ideals in his practice, but who was also involved in writing about architecture and teaching design and construction.

Lethaby, when young, was employed by Richard Norman Shaw as his chief assistant between 1879 and 1889. Many of the most distinguished architects of the period were either ex-pupils and assistants of Shaw, or part of his circle. A number of them were responsible for the instigation of the Art Workers' Guild and the Arts and Crafts Exhibition Society, founded

in the 1880s, which gave form and direction to the Arts and Crafts movement. Shaw himself was rather bemused by this activity among his young followers, but continued a practice begun in the 1860s up to his death in 1912. During most of these five decades he was in the forefront of design, and he became one of the few architects whose name was familiar to the layman.

Shaw's work must be discussed a little more fully, because his part in the shaping of Edwardian architecture is paramount. In the 1860s and 1870s, together with his erstwhile partner, W. Eden Nesfield, he led the way away from the intensities of the Gothic Revival and the ponderous Italianate classicism that had dominated English architecture towards a more relaxed style. In a sense, he emphasised features of a traditional English attitude to design which had become partially submerged, but which was still alive. This was concerned with

One of Ernest George's houses in Harrington Gardens, South Kensington, 1882. This one was constructed for W. S. Gilbert, and is a particularly successful fantasy based on a Dutch burgher's house.

visual responses and references to landscape, context and tradition. The architect's ability as a pictorial artist, or at least his sensitivity to picturesque qualities, became all-important. The 'Old English' style which Shaw used for domestic buildings in the countryside drew on the vernacular and Tudor architecture of the Weald of Kent and Surrey, using tile hanging, warm red brick and local stone. There were mullioned windows with leaded lights, cosy inglenooks and tall chimneys. In the city, Shaw used elements from seventeenth-century artisan classicism – the sort of thing one might find in important buildings in old market towns, such as rather clumsy pediments and pilasters, white-framed sash windows and oriels, and roofs topped with leaded lanterns and weather vanes. This quaint concoction was confusingly known as 'Queen Anne'. Shaw did it well, and these eclectic approaches became very popular, but theory was completely lacking. Good results depended entirely upon the sensitivity of the architect as artist.

Ernest George, for whom the young Lutyens worked, expanded this quaint style and made frequent use of German and Dutch elements. Thus the sketch book became all-important to both the practising architect and the student. They took trips to the Continent, visiting towns like Delft and noting street architecture. At home, they went on bicycle rides around country districts, drawing farms and manor houses. A catalogue of picturesque references could be built up. In the hands of an accomplished architect such as George, in the 1880s, this produced delightful, humane buildings; the lesser practitioner produced mundane, sometimes shoddy work, or a vulgar jumble of ill-assorted details. Some commercial architects, especially in the provinces, pursued this approach even after the turn of the century.

This stylistic free-for-all was the context within which many of the leading lights of the Edwardian era were trained. Although the 'Old English' and the 'Queen Anne' were gradually falling out of favour, for most Edwardian architects the approach to design continued to be visual rather than theoretical. Some of the more talented and thoughtful London practitioners considered themselves 'artist architects'. Indeed, in the 1890s, there was a controversy in which many of them, including Shaw and his circle, and also painters such as Alma Tadema and Holman Hunt, confronted the Royal Institute of British Architects over its proposal to introduce registration. Their arguments were presented in a 'Memorial' to the RIBA opposing the proposal, which were then summed up in a volume of essays appearing in 1892 entitled *Architecture: A Profession or an Art?* The RIBA's position implied an examination system for entry and the protection of the professional title. It had been promoted largely by worthy provincials who were in

competition with tradesmen who used the title 'architect', despite their lack of training. The 'artist architects' pooh-poohed the RIBA's position, as they felt that it was impossible to examine art, and that professionalism implied a dull and routine approach. Reginald Blomfield (1856-1942), a member of the Shaw circle, spoke for many when he said that 'architecture should be at the head of the arts, not at the foot of the professions'.[1] Shaw himself always shunned the RIBA, but was proud to be a member of the Royal Academy.

The influence of the Arts and Crafts movement was still to be found in the thinking of most artist architects throughout the Edwardian period. Some continued to design buildings, particularly middle-class houses, in a manner that embraced simplicity, constructional honesty and the need for materials to 'speak for themselves' without the elaboration of unnecessary frippery. However, some of the organisations which had been set up in the first flush of enthusiasm, seeking to implement the socio-political ideas of the movement in a practical way, were in decline. C. R. Ashbee's Guild of Handicraft, for instance, established in 1888 in the East End of London, had removed itself to Chipping Camden in 1902 and five years later ceased to exist. Nevertheless, Arts and Crafts designs were still in demand for decorative purposes, and many architects of grand urban buildings specified work from artist craftsmen, as well as remaining members of bodies such as the Art Workers' Guild.

Artists and architects

The world of the architect in the 1890s and the first decade of the new century was therefore closely linked with that of the artist. In the first place, as we have seen, architectural design was regarded as a visual rather than a theoretical process; secondly, leading architects wished to be associated with painters and sculptors rather than with accountants and solicitors; finally, through their association with the Arts and Crafts movement, architects expected to include the work of other artists in their buildings. Architecture was the 'mistress art', and one of the aims of the movement was to break the arts out of what Reginald Blomfield called their 'watertight compartments'. This attitude was not confined to those architects who designed country houses for enlightened clients: it permeated the world of public and commercial buildings too.

A major building which began this trend towards the inclusion of the arts was John Belcher's Institute of Chartered Accountants. It set the seal on his career and made him one of the foremost architects of the period. The building was constructed in Great Swan Alley, Moorgate, in the City of London, and was completed in 1893. Two leading exponents of the 'new' sculpture, then helping in the revival of the art in

A drawing of part of a stable court designed by John Belcher in the 1890s. This picturesque scheme could have grown from the drawing, instead of the drawing being a mere representation of the design.

Britain, contributed to Belcher's building, and the architect saw it as his responsibility to provide a setting for their work. These two, Hamo Thornycroft (1850-1925) – a family friend of Belcher and, with him, one of the founders of the Art Workers' Guild – and Harry Bates (1850-99) produced copious and distinguished work. At second-storey level, for instance, below the line of windows, was a series of carved relief panels stretching for over forty-two metres, representing 'crafts', 'shipping' and other relevant subjects, executed by Thornycroft. Bates was responsible for several of the figure sculptures, and the abundance of the whole testified to a new attitude to the partnership between architect and artist.

The development continued for at least the next twenty years, fading out towards the end of the Edwardian period, when different design priorities had evolved. Much Edwardian architecture, though, includes allegorical or representational work, produced in the style that revivified English sculpture at the time. Important new buildings were noted as much for the designs of artists as for the architecture itself. Their contribution did not stop at external sculpture and relief. Murals and friezes occur internally, and artist craftsmen, often working for organisations such as the Bromsgrove Guild, which became a company in 1901, produced decorative plasterwork, wrought iron and carving. Items like light fittings and door furniture were often specially designed. Even the more mundane external decoration came from firms of

A workshop making plaster embellishments for the interiors of build-ings, to the designs of artists working in conjunction with architects. Stone-carving, brass-founding or woodworking could, alternatively, have been illustrated.

stone carvers skilled in producing high-quality, if standard, architectural detail. Whether there was too much, whether it was overdone, depended upon the taste of the architect and his client. The client's pocket, of course, also formed part of the equation, as major artists commanded high fees. This close collaboration, and the status of the visual arts in the public domain, was not satisfactorily re-established for the rest of the century.

The Edwardian scene

Around the turn of the century, Charles H. Reilly (1874-1948), soon to become well known for his role in the aca-demic world, decided to quit his father's dull office in the City

and obtain a position in a West End architectural practice. He and a friend '... discussed the relative values of Norman Shaw's, Ernest George's, Aston Webb's and John Belcher's offices ... endlessly and hopelessly'.[2] They finally decided upon Belcher's office, because of the fame of the Institute of Chartered Accountants building. Young architects, such as Reilly, who were to dominate the Edwardian scene, and in some respects the 1920s and 1930s, took their lead from Shaw, George, and Belcher, or, if ecclesiastically inclined, from G. F. Bodley, the most respected church architect of the time. Some sought employment or pupillage in their offices, others entered competitions, the assessments of which were in the hands of senior men. One gets the feeling of a fairly closely knit group centred on architects' offices in Bloomsbury, with articled pupils meeting at the Royal Academy Schools or the Architectural Association, in the Art Workers' Guild and at social events. All were curious to know what was happening in each others' offices, reading the architectural press and noting the latest developments. This was hardly a clique, then, but more a body of professionals, avidly interested in their discipline. As Reilly noted, 'we were in a new atmos-phere [Belcher's office] where architecture could be discussed all day long until it was displaced by gossip about Ernest George's office ... or about Aston Webb's ...'[3]

This description, of course, focuses on London, where by and large the most interesting and creative architects gravi-tated – especially the Scots, who formed a large proportion of London's leading practitioners. It would be unrepresentative, however, to leave out certain gifted individuals operating from regional centres, or those who made a significant contribution to other aspects of practice. In addition, the work of London-based architects was not confined to the capital, and, through both patronage and the large number of competitions that were held, their work was spread throughout the country.

Most of the Edwardian architects were born between around 1850 and 1880. At one extreme there are Aston Webb (1849-1930), almost old enough to be classed with the Belcher generation, and Edward S. Prior (1852-1932), and at the other Arthur Davis (1878-1951), Ralph Knott (1879-1929), designer of County Hall in London, and Sir Albert Richardson (1880-1965). Although some of these architects, such as Giles Gilbert Scott (1880-1960) and Charles Holden (1875-1960), were important in the inter-war period, much of their most famous work is Edwardian.

Belcher made as much of a contribution during the Edwardian period as he did during the 1880s and 1890s. This may have had something to do with the fact that during the first part of his practice he had Arthur Beresford Pite (1860-1949) as his chief assistant. Pite left his employment in 1897

Belcher's Institute of Chartered Accountants in Great Swan Alley,
Moorgate. A building which firmly established, in the 1890s, the
practice of incorporating the works of sculptors and other artists
within the architect's overall scheme.

Opposite
'Moorcrag', built about 1898, close to Windermere, by C. F. A. Voysey. This building, with its cottagey appearance, well exemplifies the architect's style, and demonstrates its use for substantial middle-class houses.

and went on to become an important practitioner in his own right – professor of architecture at the Royal College of Art and director of the Brixton School of Building. Belcher replaced him with the Scottish architect J. J. Joass (1868-1952), who had worked for Rowand Anderson in Scotland and Ernest George in London. Joass became Belcher's partner, and his idiosyncratic style became well known when it was applied to a variety of commercial buildings in the 1900s. Clearly, Belcher was not only an accomplished professional, but had the ability to choose associates who were able to stimulate a flow of ideas.

In order to pick a path through the great welter of Edwardian talent it may be easiest, at first, to divide the architectural world crudely into two: artist architects and those practitioners who worked for commercial and public clients. In the 1890s, artist architects designed mainly houses under private patronage. After the turn of the century these were often interspersed with commissions for other building types. Lutyens' career tends to follow this route, but he is not the most representative example with which to illustrate the world of the artist architect. A consideration of the contrasting careers of two contemporaries, in middle age and well established by the turn of the century, may illuminate the subject.

Voysey and Blomfield

Charles F. A. Voysey (1857-1941) and Reginald Blomfield were both sons of clergymen, although Voysey's background was radical and Blomfield's conservative. After an unsettled childhood, with a poor record of academic achievement, Voysey was articled to J. P. Seddon, a Gothic Revival architect, and then worked for Saxon Snell and George Devey before setting up his own practice. He developed his personal, rather idiosyncratic approach to architecture, drawing on his talent as a designer of both two- and three-dimensional work. Blomfield, on the other hand, possessed a strong intellect and studied classics at Oxford, leaving with a first-class degree and a record of sporting achievement before becoming articled to his uncle, Sir Arthur Blomfield, in 1881. Voysey adopted his preferred style early in his career. Influenced as he was by some of the tenets of the Gothic Revival and Arts and Crafts architecture, he sought qualities such as 'honesty' in construction and the influence of 'natural' form. His association with Devey also left its mark, as the older man was a first-rate country house architect, with an eclectic approach to the English vernacular. Having arrived at his own 'cottagey' style by the early 1890s, Voysey rarely deserted it, and the overwhelming majority of his buildings are domestic.

Voysey's distinctive style featured long, low buildings with roughcast walls and big Westmorland slate roofs. The eaves

John Belcher, portrayed around the middle of the first decade of the century, holding what appears to be a drawing of Electra House.

were bracketed out over the walls, which had buttresses that were sometimes battered – sloping inwards as they rose. The windows were often set in rows, emphasising the horizontality of the composition. Voysey's interiors are of modest height – establishing a ceiling about 8 feet (2.4 metres) above the floor. Internally everything had to speak for itself – plain surfaces, stained woodwork – 'simplicity, sincerity and repose', perhaps with a vase of flowers as the only frivolous, non-utilitarian item. He designed everything himself, from the simple latches and hinges on the doors through to the wallpaper. This comprehensiveness of design, the parts belonging to the whole, yet each individually considered, was typical of Arts and Crafts architecture.

Blomfield's work was completely different. He began, in his twenties, with 'Old English' and 'Queen Anne', but gradually developed a taste for the style of late-seventeenth-century England – facetiously known as the 'Wrenaissance'. This was not unprecedented, for the work of architects like J. M. Brydon

HOVSE TO BE BVILT AT GARTMEL FELL GILLHEAD BY WINDERMERE
FOR J·W·BVCKLEY·ESQ^RE   C·F·A·VOYSEY·ARCH^T

GROVND·PLAN

- DINING HALL 31'6" × 45'6" — 18'0"
- STVDY 15'0"
- PARLOVR 20'0" × 22
- SERVANTS BED RM 10'0" × 15'0"
- SCVLLERY 12'0" × 15'0"
- COALS
- LARDER
- ENTRANCE 7'0"
- LAV TO RY
- WINE 5'0"
- WC
- PANTRY
- KITCHEN 23'6" × 15'0"
- BOOTS & KNIVES
- PORCH

FIRST FL^OOR PLAN

- BED·ROOM N°1 18'0"×15'0"
- N°2
- N°3 20'0"
- N°4 10'0"
- N°5 12'0"
- N°7 18'0"×16'0"
- DRYING
- BATH ROOM
- WC
- HOVSEMAID CLOSET
- N°6 17'6"×15'0"

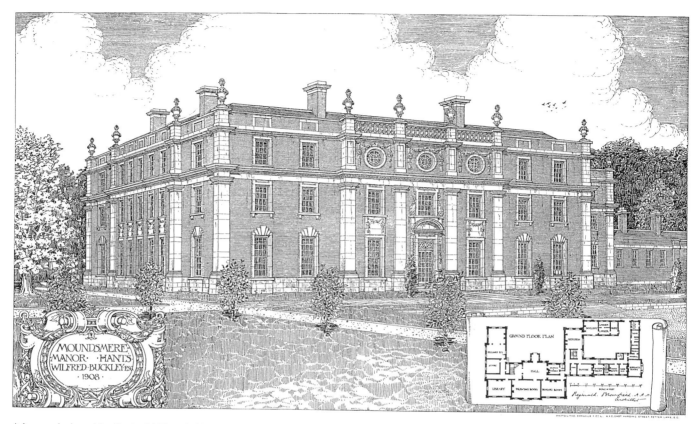

A house designed by Reginald Blomfield in his favoured 'Wrenaissance' style in rural Hampshire. Voysey's version of the vernacular
was less fashionable for bespoke houses by the time Blomfield's
'Moundsmere Manor' was built in 1908, but reappeared in innumer-
able suburban imitations.

(1840-1901), once an assistant of Norman Shaw, and even
that of Shaw himself, was moving towards a more consistent
and refined classical language. It appealed to Blomfield's romantic chauvinism, on the one hand, and to his sense of logic
and order on the other. His natural literary ability had been
harnessed early on in his career, and he wrote two books in
the 1890s that firmly stated his architectural interests and
helped to establish his practice. The first, *The Formal Garden in
England*, published in 1892, described Tudor and Jacobean
formal gardens and helped to crystallise a fashion for their re-
introduction. Blomfield's persuasive prose ensured that some
of the readership, who were amongst the gentry, were keen to
get him interested in their own projects, and this started his
career as a restorer and designer of country houses and their
gardens. Whereas Voysey's clients might have been radical
lawyers or even artistic celebrities, like H. G. Wells, for whom
he designed Spade House, Ramsgate, Blomfield's were often

baronets or minor aristocrats, or those who pretended to that
way of life.

Blomfield's second work, *A History of Renaissance Architecture
in England, 1500-1800*, was published in 1897, and although
Blomfield was an amateur by the standards of later professional art historians, his book was sufficiently scholarly and
well presented to be valuable and persuasive to those who
wished to know more. The English Renaissance was becoming very popular as a stylistic source by the turn of the century. Large civic and commercial buildings could use the
Baroque of Wren, Hawksmoor and Vanbrugh. In the country,
the quieter red brick and stone of the late seventeenth and
early eighteenth centuries was employed, a fashion which
transmuted itself into an even more restrained neo-Georgian
style as the Edwardian period progressed, and which continued to survive well into the century.

So, as Voysey perfected his cottagey style, Blomfield proceeded to encourage a return to classicism, as suitable for those liberated from late Victorian exuberance, who valued taste rather than originality. As more and more city centres were developed and new streets formed, the need for conformity and harmony of buildings became important. Blomfield's career took him on to design large public buildings, and he was responsible for completing the redevelopment of the Quadrant, Regent Street, left unfinished by Shaw, and other civic projects.

Blomfield also pursued a public career in architectural politics, rising to be President of the RIBA in 1912, and a member of the Royal Academy. Although he had resigned from the Institute at the time of the registration controversy in the 1890s, he was won back in 1904 by the machinations at the RIBA of Aston Webb, who was keen to enhance the status of the Institute. As the Edwardian period progressed, Blomfield became one of the most important figures on the architectural stage, whilst Voysey's influence and that of the Arts and Crafts movement declined considerably, and his work tended to revert to two-dimensional design, largely for wallpapers.

Despite these considerable differences, there were overwhelming similarities between the two men: each had a facility in draughtsmanship; each tried to produce 'reserved' architecture in his own very different way whilst encouraging a native tradition; each thought of architecture as an art before he thought of it as a profession. To both architects, personal artistic integrity was extremely important.

From the point of view of theory, some artist architects followed the Arts and Crafts beliefs which they had espoused in the 1880s and 1890s, though with increasing problems in how to apply their ideas in an urban context. Arts and Crafts philosophy could work very well when dealing with relatively small-scale buildings and an amenable client. Local materials could be used; the materials, crafts and techniques could speak for themselves; the architect could design throughout, controlling the process, and relying upon artist craftsmen and reliable contractors under close supervision; he could also indulge his own stylistic idiosyncrasies. This approach did not, however, succeed in towns and cities where office buildings, department stores and institutions of higher education, amongst other types, were being built. Roughcast was completely unsuitable for the centre of Manchester or London; Cheshire half-timbering may have been fine in a two-storey house, but was useless for a six-storey office block. In addition, the rise of new technologies and materials resulted in another quandary. Arts and Crafts architects were, as we have seen, wedded to 'honesty' in the use of materials, but behind this, unmistakably, was an aesthetic preference for the English

Even the manufacturers of mass-produced building products responded to the prevailing authority of the artist architect, as this advertisement for tiles shows.

and Scottish vernacular tradition of building – nationalism was rife in all European architecture at this time. The careful expression of the new rectilinear steel and concrete frames, although ideologically sound, was not quite what they had in mind. Some, such as W. R. Lethaby – who to many was the intellectual heir of Philip Webb – made a brave but rather unconvincing effort to come to terms with this problem, and built little after about 1902.

'It is absurd', he expostulated, 'that the writer should have been allowed to study cathedrals from Kirkwall to Rome and from Quimper to Constantinople; it would be far better to have the equivalent knowledge of steel and concrete construction.' He later went on, 'If I were again learning to be a modern architect I'd exchange taste and design and all that stuff and learn engineering, with plenty of mathematics and hard building experience. Hardness, facts, experiment, that should be architecture, not taste.'[4]

Lethaby did experiment with new materials to some extent, building the little church at Brockhampton in Herefordshire with thatch that conceals a concrete roof (1901), and being the driving force behind the celebrated competition entry for Liverpool Cathedral in 1902, which exploits the plastic nature of reinforced concrete.

Ironically, despite Lethaby's protestations, acceptance of the new technology did not come from Arts and Crafts architects, but from those who were very different in outlook.

Edwardian Baroque and the 'Wrenaissance'

Architects in the commercial world, and those gaining suc-

Norman Shaw's Alliance Assurance Offices in St James's Street, London. In the early years of the century, Shaw established his personal approach to urban Baroque, to be seen in this building, and followed it through in his scheme for the rebuilding of the Regent Street Quadrant and the Piccadilly Hotel.

cess in public competitions, had much less time for philosophical niceties, and they tended to follow in a stylistic tradition that several architects, including Norman Shaw, had been fostering since the 1890s: the 'Wrenaissance'. Essentially, this was a development of the visual and picturesque approach of the 1870s and 1880s, but with a narrower palette of stylistic motifs deriving from English Baroque architecture of the late seventeenth and early eighteenth centuries. Blom-field's writings on the English Renaissance, and those of J. Alfred Gotch and Belcher and Macartney, provided sufficient historical background and a consolidated series of examples from which to learn. This trend chimed in with the need for large-scale buildings in cities, for which the Wren-Hawksmoor-Vanbrugh Baroque palace style was appropriate, and with the desire to be English at this most jingoistic of all periods.

Colchester Town Hall. Belcher's flamboyant municipal Baroque was very influential in the early years of the century.

Large buildings, constructed around 1900, therefore, were usually 'Baroque', with an outer skin either of stone or of red brick with stone banding. Exceptions came from architects who were slow to throw off the styles of the 1890s, or who were hopelessly eclectic, like Aston Webb. Some retained a Tudorish, late Gothic style for use in the design of schools and colleges. A good example is provided by Henry T. Hare, a very successful architect of municipal buildings, in his work at

University College, Bangor, but even Blomfield adopted the approach, if without enthusiasm, at Sherborne School. Many churches also continued to be Gothic, often in a rather Arts and Crafts perpendicular style. A more powerful theme for ecclesiastical buildings was inspired by the new Westminster Cathedral, by J. F. Bentley, an architect whose fame rests on this *tour de force*, but who, sadly, died in 1902, before the fabric of the building was completed. Here a Byzantine style was developed, in part to distinguish the great Roman Catholic edifice from the Gothic style associated with Anglican buildings.

The path towards Edwardian Baroque, which was pioneered by Norman Shaw and encouraged by Brydon, had begun when Shaw moved more steadily towards a classical language with the design of country houses such as Chesters, Northumberland (1891-3), and Bryanston, Dorset (1889-94). This movement may also be seen in urban buildings such as two in Liverpool: the Royal Insurance Building (1897-1902), where Shaw acted as advisor to J. F. Doyle, a local practitioner, and Parr's Bank, designed in association with Willink and Thicknesse, the latter of whom had been a pupil. His Alliance Assurance Offices in St James's Street, London (1901), produced with the assistance of his ex-pupil and employee Ernest Newton, were compromised by restrictions placed upon them by the proximity of St James's Palace, and by height regulations. Nevertheless, the heavy rustication, ponderous ground-floor arches and erupting pediment are all symptomatic of the bold, wilful and energetic use of classical elements typical of the period. Although Shaw would still produce buildings in a complex and evocative stylistic mix, such as the extensions to Bradford Town Hall, designed first in 1902, his major Edwardian project, the rebuilding of Nash's Quadrant, Regent Street, was firmly in a heavy, vigorous and powerful Baroque. Of this scheme, only the Piccadilly Hotel was built (1905-8), with its major façade facing on to Piccadilly left incomplete owing to the intransigence of adjacent property owners.

Following in the wake of Shaw, and with the work of Belcher and Brydon before them, it is not surprising that architects favoured the 'Wrenaissance' for at least the first half-dozen years of the century. Belcher was particularly noted for the panache of his commercial style, to the extent that it was considered by some to be a distinct manner of design. He had pursued the English Baroque for many years, however, and his entry for the South Kensington Museums competition in 1891 is a bold early essay in the style on a very large scale. One of his most influential designs, though, made almost a decade after the Institute of Chartered Accountants, was the competition winner for Colchester Town Hall. Chosen by Shaw, who was the adjudicator, it was being built

Opposite
Belcher's Royal London House in Finsbury Square. This building is typical of the commercial palaces that brought the architect so much prestige. Extra storeys have subsequently been accommodated in a new roof, to the detriment of the building's massing.

as the century began. In some respects, it can be seen as heavy and ponderous, with rusticated ground floor and huge Ionic columns rising almost the entire height of the remainder of the building. These support, on the main elevation, no fewer than three separate pediments – one triangular, the other two segmental. In addition, the façade is tricked out with balustrades, statuary, a large cornice and a first-floor balcony supported on huge stone brackets. The composition breaks back and forth and is very heavily modelled, but as if this were not enough, the whole is surmounted by an enormous tower topped with a composition of stone elements created from the details of Wren and Hawksmoor churches. The overall effect, perhaps surprisingly, is not of mid-Victorian gloom; it is of vigour and richness. The design is positively joyous, providing a boisterous and appropriate Englishness, reminiscent of a none-too-serious or remote classicism, free from pedantry and appropriate to its setting: not Paris or Vienna, but Colchester.

Belcher's great London palaces for commerce, built a little after Colchester – such as Royal London House, Finsbury Square (1903), and Electra House, Moorgate (1900) – are more restrained and regular, perhaps strait-jacketed by repetitive accommodation and the structural necessity of repeating steel sections. Later commercial buildings, particularly Mappin House, Oxford Street (1906), and the Royal Insurance Building, St James's, Piccadilly (1907), display a strange, taut mannerism, which is usually ascribed to one of J. J. Joass's stylistic enthusiasms. The apogee of Belcher's Baroque, however, is really a building of no functional use, designed in 1900 and constructed a few years later. The Ashton Memorial, Williamson Park, Lancaster, built in remembrance of a local family of benefactors, consists of a large dome and lantern mounted on a drum guarded by corner turrets. The whole architectonic assemblage rises from a pavilion below, as though the centre chunk of a cathedral had been cut away, leaving nave and chancel behind. It is deposited high upon a hill above the diminutive city below.

Edward W. Mountford (1855-1908) and Alfred Brumwell Thomas (1868-1948) are, perhaps, less important as architects than Belcher, but both produced celebrated buildings in the 'Wrenaissance' style. Mountford's most famous work was the Old Bailey (1900) and Thomas's, Belfast City Hall, completed in 1906, which won a competition with Alfred Waterhouse as assessor. Both schemes were presided over by fine 'Wrenaissance' domes. Thomas's Plumstead Town Hall bears more than a passing resemblance to Belcher's earlier Colchester example.

Both Thomas and Mountford were successful competition entrants on several occasions, but one of the most outstand-ing 'competition men' was Henry T. Hare. Hare began by gaining commissions for municipal buildings in the 1890s, and by the first decade of the new century was well known as the foremost architect of public libraries. He changed his 'free renaissance' style to 'Wrenaissance' after about 1900. Although practitioners like Hare did much to further Edwardian Baroque, they were looked down upon by artist architects, and Shaw referred to them as 'swashbucklers'.

The manipulation of English Baroque elements – the juggling of pediments, domes, cartouches, cornices, columns,

The Ashton Memorial in Lancaster. This is a model of Belcher's proposal for a building that exemplifies his Baroque style at its most full blown, but is, ironically, functionally useless.

Opposite
Edwin Lutyens, known in the 1890s for his country house designs, adopted the 'Wrenaissance' style for one of his earliest urban buildings, the offices of *Country Life* magazine, in Tavistock Street, London.

The majority of architectural practices responded to changes in style and approach. The Royal Academy of Music, Marylebone Road, London, built about 1911, shows Sir Ernest George wholeheartedly espousing the 'Wrenaissance'.

friezes and decorative panels culled and adapted from the golden age of English architecture – was part and parcel of the movement. Essentially, like late-nineteenth-century architecture, it relied on the inventiveness and resource of the artist, rather than upon scholarly or intellectual activity to provide a foundation to design effort. The architecture that resulted was only as good as the individual, operating within what may be seen as a potentially anarchic aesthetic environment. Brilliant individuals had the opportunity to shine, untrammelled by constraints of dogma. One such was E. A. Rickards, a young and intuitive designer who was in partnership with James Stewart and H. V. Lanchester. This formidable partnership won the competition in 1897 for Cardiff Civic Centre, which was to comprise a city hall and law courts. Rickards was allowed to indulge his facility for sculptural Baroque invention both in this project, and in his design for the Wesleyan Central Hall, Westminster, won in 1905 after Stewart's death. It can also be seen in Deptford Town Hall and Hull School of

Art, both of which date from 1903, and which bear a marked resemblance to each other.

Mention has barely been made of perhaps the most successful Edwardian practitioner: Sir Aston Webb (1849-1930). The fact is that Webb had little impact on the progress of architecture as an art, even though he was a consummate professional who ran a successful practice with a large number of prestigious jobs. His talents were of particular note in the world of professional politics, and he had the ability to sail through projects apparently fraught with difficulties, without the problems that would have assailed many of his colleagues under similar circumstances. His design work was fundamentally rational and appropriate, but in some stylistic respects he belongs to what the architectural commentator H. S. Goodhart-Rendel called the 'bric à brac' generation of the 1880s. In some of his work it is difficult to identify the visual themes. This is the case in, perhaps, his most famous building – the main block of the Victoria and Albert Museum, in South

Kensington. It was designed in the 1890s, but was not completed until well into the Edwardian era. The Royal Naval College in Dartmouth (1899-1904) moves towards a more identifiable English Baroque, but Birmingham University, built at the same time, is largely Byzantine in inspiration. Webb clearly knew his business, but did not recognise constraints on the use of architectural language, a trait that probably derives from his start in practice over two decades before the period began. Nevertheless, he unnervingly followed trends, though not with much conviction, when he undertook arguably the most prestigious commission of his career – the processional route from Trafalgar Square to Buckingham Palace.

Practice

Aston Webb, as we have seen, is mentioned in C. H. Reilly's autobiographical notes dealing with his early aspirations. Gossip at John Belcher's, where he worked, was about Ernest George's practice 'or about Aston Webb's office with its fifty draughtsmen which we considered in our superior way a mere factory for government buildings'.[5] This appears to be no more than gossip, however, as it seems that Webb's place of work was very similar to those of other high-class architects of the time. It was not akin to American firms, nor did it resemble the large British practices of post-war years. One of Webb's former pupils, H. Bulkeley Creswell, has left an account of his practice in the 1890s. The principal was predominant in design and direction, and the number of permanent staff small. Webb's staff, Creswell notes, consisted of: 'a chief draughtsman aged about twenty-seven at a salary of £3 per week; a tracer and handyman at probably 30s [£1.50] per week; a secretarial clerk ditto; an office boy, say 7s [35p]; a newly employed ex-pupil £1, and five live pupils ...'[6] The premiums paid by pupils came to more than the salary outgoings. 'At times of pressure and of competition output, one or two seniors came into the office ...' Sir Reginald Blomfield, entering the office of his uncle, Sir Arthur Blomfield, a decade earlier, had found a similar state of affairs. 'I found myself in the company of a somewhat depressed managing clerk, two or three assistants and half-a-dozen cheerful young fellows who were serving the articles as pupils ...'[7]

The picture was little different in the Edwardian period, and office spaces were physically small. Blomfield, for instance, had his own chambers in New Court Temple, built as a place for lawyers and clerks, in contrast with the spacious architect's studio of today. In the lively practices, as described by Reilly, there was obviously a keen interest expressed in architectural issues amongst pupils, a number of whom became the leaders of the next generation. Principals gave words of

The Royal Naval College at Dartmouth. Here Aston Webb uses English Baroque in a wholehearted way, producing a more consistently successful result than some of his earlier designs.

encouragement to those in articles, usually advising them to attend classes – perhaps at the Architectural Association, as several foremost practitioners took an interest in this institution, or at the Royal Academy Schools. Little time was spent with them, despite the handsome premiums paid.

The copying of drawings was a task often given to pupils; it was useful, perhaps, to the principal, and possibly educational to those with enquiring minds. The system is now known as 'student-centred learning'. Even an architect with a keen interest in the educational agenda, such as Blomfield, was unable to devote much energy to his students, and Aston Webb 'concerned himself in no way with how his pupils were preparing themselves'.[8] Mr G. Berkeley Wills, articled to Blomfield, provides a concise picture: 'We really got little personal instruction from Blomfield. One picked up what one could about building design, how to run an office or how to deal with clients by observation, questioning the chief assistant and visiting the various jobs whenever we could. Blomfield used to dash into our room, see what we were doing, urge us to attend the Academy Schools, or perhaps raise Cain about

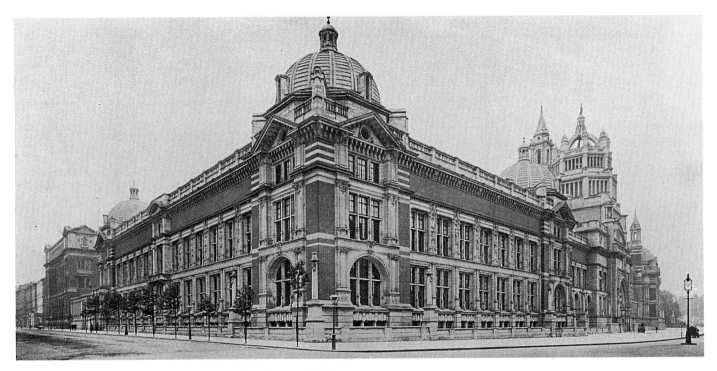

The Victoria and Albert Museum, as completed by Sir Aston Webb.
A curious mixture of styles, the design shows little commitment to a
controlling aesthetic. It is typical of Aston Webb, though, that he
could address this difficult problem and see it through to a successful
conclusion.

some mislaid drawings, depart like a whirlwind to meet a
client – peace would once more descend on the office.' [9]

Altogether, the process of pupillage seems dull, and can
have changed little for a hundred years up to the Edwardian
period. At least Blomfield's pupils visited sites. It seems that
no one in Aston Webb's office ever did, apart from the principal himself, and he did so only rarely. Paperwork was kept to a
minimum, and there can be no doubt that architects like
Webb actually spent productive time designing instead of
coping with bureaucracy, as is the rule today. Webb's clerks of
works attended the great man at his place of business to
present reports and receive orders, freeing him from the
necessity of tramping to some forlorn hut in the midst of a
muddy and remote site.

Some architects – especially those with special skills, such
as perspectivists – made a career out of helping temporarily in
small offices when a competition was under way. As a young
man, Stanley Adshead (1868 - 1919) was particularly notable
for this type of practice, and it is interesting to look back to
the early career of the person who was to become the first
professor of town planning in England. Apparently, out of the
six architects taking part in the limited competition for the
design of the Old Bailey, five presented perspective drawings
which were the work of Adshead. He was working here, of
course, quite legitimately as a presenter of someone else's
work. The process of 'ghosting', though, was common with
untalented but established architects, who employed shadowy
figures to design schemes for them, to be entered in competition or built under their own names.

The growth of a new kind of practice took place after about
1890. This was divorced from the vagaries of the competition
system, and not dependent on the good connections in private patronage that artist architects desperately needed. Architects had long been employed in public service, rather than as
private practitioners, but generally as 'surveyors' to boards or
corporations. With the growth of municipalities, salaried employment was now possible. The most significant example
was the founding of the London County Council. The LCC
assumed the role of existing bodies which had responsibilities
for construction, such as the Metropolitan Board of Works,

and established a department with major sections to deal with various categories of design, such as working-class housing. The formation of this section was stimulated by the Housing of the Working Classes Act, 1890, which empowered the LCC to remove existing slums and build new houses for rent. Those young architects with aspirations towards improving society could therefore design accommodation such as the Boundary Street and Millbank estates, whilst espousing the architectural ideals of Philip Webb. In addition, they could avoid gross self-expression and the necessity to toady to either big business or gilded aristocracy. Of course, this type of work was bound to give rise to a system of bureaucratic control, but the LCC was well served first by Thomas Blashill, who had been Architect to the Metropolitan Board of Works, and then, upon his retirement in 1899, by the appointment of the Yorkshireman W. E. Riley (1852 - 1937). Riley is usually credited with authorship of most LCC work in the Edwardian period, but, of course, this is with reference to his position as head of the department. He assembled a talented group of what would now be called 'job architects' to execute work. It was through his administrative skills that the department flourished and is deserving of mention. The responsibilities of his 'Chief Assistant, General Construction Section', Percy Ginham (1865 - 1947) give some idea of the range of projects undertaken. Ginham's task was to oversee all building work produced by the department, except for the Fire Brigade and Working Class Housing sections. Buildings included generating stations, park buildings, technical schools, homes for inebriates and schemes for the council's own offices.

Ginham had been Norman Shaw's chief clerk before joining the council. Shaw acted as informal adviser to the LCC on projects involving large-scale alterations to the urban fabric, and thus his influence was felt in the new organisation. Shaw's help was usually sought over competitions, and, despite the foundation of the council's own department, even its headquarters building was designed as a result of a two-stage competition in 1907. Riley and Shaw acted as assessors for the initial phases, and Aston Webb was elected as third assessor by the second-stage competitors. The competitors submitting the ninety-nine designs in the first stage were whittled down to eight for stage two. A strange mixture of competition stalwarts and artist architects were involved, many of them old pupils of Shaw. No doubt these gentlemen were attracted by the prestige of the building and the wonderful riverside site. In the event, the competition was won by a young architect from Aston Webb's office, Ralph Knott, who formed his own practice to design and supervise this very large and technically complex building.

Architects in day-to-day practice had to cope with a build-

ing process which, itself, was becoming more complicated. During the nineteenth century, the 'general contractor' had risen to prominence, and large building firms developed which employed various trades on a wage basis. Aston Webb, with his marvellous organisational abilities, may have been able to delegate responsibilities and keep his correspondence down to brief, hand-written notes; but the time was approaching when the whole process was to generate a large bureaucratic load. American influence and the demand for more rapid construction would push forward this movement; this is discussed in the next chapter.

London's County Hall was subject to a series of separate contracts: for the embankment wall; for raft foundations; for substructure; and for the superstructure. The latter went to Holland, Hannen and Cubitt, and was worth £968,211. Clearly, administration of these building processes required managerial and bureaucratic skills of a high order. In addition, methods adopted by contractors were becoming increasingly dependent upon technology, in terms of both site operations and manufacture. Joinery machinery, for instance, revolutionised the rapid production of timber sections and mouldings, and these processes took place in large shops, using electrical power. In the construction of Lanchester, Stewart and Rickards' Cardiff City Hall and Law Courts, the contractors, Messrs E. Turner and Sons, erected 'eight electric derrick cranes with 80' steel lattice jibs in addition to several other steam cranes and hoists'.[10] In this way, the huge stones, up to five tons in weight, could be assembled, enhancing the building's Baroque monumentality. Stoneworking, itself, was subject to mechanised processes, and 'a very extensive stoneworking plant had been laid down, including a large chain and saw, five horizontal frame saws, and eleven steam moulding machines'.[11] This contrasts starkly with contemporary efforts of Arts and Crafts architects to build from the spiritual and physical nature of the site. At Prior's 'Home Place', for instance, the architect kept a full-time clerk of the works to superintend the directly employed workmen as they literally built the house out of the site.

All was not rosy in the construction industry, however. It is hard to believe, today, but the industry was in recession from about 1901, after a boom in the 1890s. There were wage cuts, and many building workers found themselves unemployed. The Amalgamated Society of Carpenters and Joiners, for instance, had seventy thousand members at the beginning of the period, but had lost ten thousand by 1910. This depression was made worse by the introduction of factory processes and the advent of new products, such as building boards. In addition, the whole process of construction underwent a change (see Chapter 3), and rapid erection of steel-framed and excellent workmanship – is only smooth in retrospect. At the time there were bitter disputes, worries by both architects and operatives about new methods, professional rivalries, and pressures from clients that actually made the era one of unease for those involved. In the heart of the period, though, changes began to occur that would influence mainstream British architecture through much of the rest of the century. These form the subject of the next chapter.

1. Richard Norman Shaw and T. G. Jackson (ed), *Architecture: A Profession or an Art? Thirteen short Essays on the Qualification and Training of Architects*, London, 1892, pp.190-1
2. C. H. Reilly, *Scaffolding in the Sky: a semi-architectural Autobiography*, London, 1938, p.48
3. *ibid* p.40
4. W. R. Lethaby, quoted in Godfrey Rubens, 'William Lethaby's buildings' in Alastair Service (ed), *Edwardian Architecture and its Origins*, London, 1975, p.141
5. Reilly, *op.cit.* p.49
6. H. Bulkeley Creswell, 'Sir Aston Webb and his office', in Service, *op.cit.* p.331
7. Reginald Blomfield, *Memoirs of an Architect*, London, 1932, p.35
8. H. Bulkeley Creswell, *op.cit.* p.334
9. G. Berkeley Wills, obituary of Sir Reginald Blomfield, *Journal of the RIBA*, vol.97, 1943, pp.66-7
10. 'Cardiff City Hall and Law Courts', *Architectural Review*, vol.20, 1906, p.242
11. *ibid*

A portrait of Sir Aston Webb, commissioned by the *Illustrated London News* from the artist Cyrus Cuneo. Webb stands at his desk against a background of some of his buildings. Architects, it seems, enjoyed some popular celebrity in Edwardian times.

buildings and the use of reinforced concrete on a large scale instead of load-bearing masonry structures all assisted in causing job losses. There were many strikes during the Edwardian era. During the building of Cartwright Hall in Bradford between 1901 and 1904, for instance, there was a year-long masons' and joiners' strike (1901-2) and later, in 1903, a dispute involving plasterers. The unions themselves were involved in internecine warfare. In 1903, the plumbers were embroiled in long-standing quarrels with no fewer than five other craft organisations.

So the progress of Edwardian construction – fascinating and varied design, sumptuous materials of the first quality

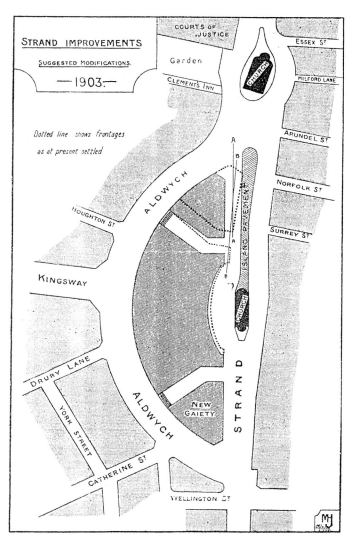

STRAND IMPROVEMENTS

SUGGESTED MODIFICATIONS.

— 1903 —

Dotted line shows frontages
as at present settled

A plan delineating the new Aldwych development in the Strand,
London. This drawing shows further suggested improvements.

produced a grand composition that was inspirational to the
population at large and to architects in particular. The landscape designer responsible was F. L. Omsted, but the chief
architect to the exhibition was Daniel H. Burnham. Noted as
a pioneer of skyscraper design, Burnham went on to advocate
Beaux Arts planning as a way of civilising American cities. He
made plans for Chicago in 1895 and Cleveland in 1903, and
in 1902 he was a member of a commission to rehabilitate the
major 'mall' feature of L'Enfant's original scheme for Washington. In 1904, he produced a plan for San Francisco, which
was given wide coverage in Britain.

As the decade wore on, this so-called 'City Beautiful' movement, with its broad boulevards, noble buildings and strict
geometrical control, must have loomed large in the minds of
British architects looking for classical certainty as an antidote
to eclecticism, which was obsessed with detail rather than
idea. Besides, it was felt that this should be the way to build at
the centre of Empire, particularly as the great new commercial
and civic buildings demanded an appropriately grand setting.
This was undoubtedly at the back of C. H. Reilly's mind,
when, as professor at the Liverpool University School of
Architecture, he visited the United States in 1909. Reilly,
whose benefactor was Lord Leverhulme, formerly W. H. Lever,
creator of Port Sunlight, was perturbed that the 1909 Town
Planning Act regulated urban development without reference
to design issues. He managed to persuade Leverhulme to endow a chair in town planning at the University. Stanley Adshead was appointed to the chair, with Patrick Abercrombie,
later to be his successor, as deputy. Money was also obtained
from Leverhulme for a journal, the *Town Planning Review*, and
for visits to Europe and America to see what was being done
there. Adshead went to Europe, and Reilly to the United
States, where he enjoyed himself for three months and chased
up Burnham, 'the architect mainly responsible for the new
plan for Chicago, which was the exciting thing at the moment'.[2] American influence was thus imported into Liverpool
through Reilly's enthusiasm. The notion of town planning as
an important and serious discipline also took root, and spread
to other academic institutions.

There was certainly a need for some kind of academic initiative, because although greater attempts had been made to
produce worthwhile urban design, it was usually ill-starred or
compromised. The decade started badly with the unfortunate
Aldwych competition. A new road was proposed, later known
as Kingsway, with a link to the Strand. This linking thoroughfare was to divide at its junction, avoiding an existing church,
and the new 'crescent' thus formed was to have unified
façades. A competition for the design was proposed in June
1900 by the LCC Improvements Committee between eight

taken hold, and how trifling it must have seemed at the time
compared to the French displays.

The Americans, in urban design as in many spheres of life,
were heavily influenced by French practice. It was, again, an
exhibition that helped to set the seal on the dominance of that
approach in the United States for many years to come. The
World's Columbian Exposition in Chicago in 1893, celebrating the four-hundredth anniversary of Columbus's 'discovery', was a demonstration of Beaux Arts principles on a
large scale. The great 'white city', built of classical buildings
and pavilions disposed around formal canals and axial routes,

A project by the young architects Richardson and Gill, for remodelling Trafalgar Square.

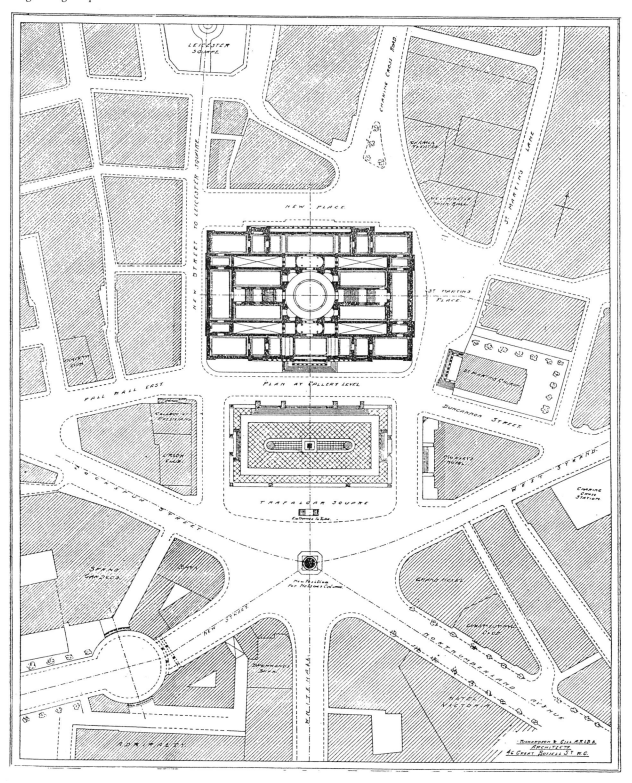

The Victoria Memorial, located on the central axis of Aston Webb's new façade to Buckingham Palace, which was the last item to be completed in the processional sequence. The sculpture around the pylon was by Sir Thomas Brock.

selected architects: a mixture of artist architects and competition men. H. T. Hare's scheme was thought to be the best; like most of the other competitors he used the 'Wrenaissance' style, and he bridged over intersecting streets in order to provide a continuous façade. Nothing came of the project, however, because the rules of the competition were badly conceived, and it proved impossible to select an overall winner. The street was eventually lined with a variety of designs.

Blomfield, a champion of the 'grand manner', following in Shaw's footsteps, had a chance to try his ideas here with 'a series of large arched openings in the ground storey ... interrupted at intervals by more solidly treated blocks ... being left almost plain'.[3] Although Blomfield relished this kind of opportunity – and a better one was to come his way – not only was he unsuccessful, but the manner in which the competition was handled did not endear the system to him.

At about the same time, projects were proposed for tackling the margins of the Thames, following on from the success of the Embankment built forty years earlier; but these were beset by problems. The spanning of the river, along with the seemingly perpetual problems of London's bridges, also came to

the forefront. Little was done during the Edwardian era to resolve these issues, and it was not until the 1920s and 1930s, with the building of Lambeth Bridge and the new Waterloo Bridge, that major progress was made. It must be admitted, however, that the new LCC Headquarters made a bold attempt to address itself to the river and to exemplify the broad and palatial scale which many felt should have been applied to the metropolis.

Meanwhile, a very grand scheme was under way. In 1901 Aston Webb had won the competition for the memorial to Queen Victoria to be erected near the main entrance of Buckingham Palace, at the top of the Mall. In its completed form, the Queen's statue sat against a stone pylon surmounted by a gilded figure of Victory. The sculpture was by Sir Thomas Brock, and the whole ensemble formed a *rond point*, a circular focal point, at the end of the vista along the Mall. Originally, it was to be surrounded by a semicircular colonnade, but this was omitted from the final scheme. The project was not completed until 1911, after Webb had extended the Mall as far as Trafalgar Square. Near the junction he erected Admiralty Arch, which formed a gateway to the triumphal route to

Webb's Admiralty Arch, which forms the entrance to the processional way leading from Trafalgar Square.

Buckingham Palace. Webb, with his usual political acumen, incorporated offices for their lordships into the arch, thereby satisfying the English desire for utility above conceptual gesture.

Webb's involvement did not end until 1913, when Buckingham Palace was rapidly refaced to his designs whilst the King was on holiday. Thus, one architect had some control over the whole urban sequence. The work is not quite as unified as one would expect, however, because during the twelve years of its progress Webb's style changed. The early work is in the fruity Baroque of the early Edwardian period, and the façade of the palace in the dry, eighteenth-century French style, which was more acceptable in 1912 when it was conceived.

Webb was fortunate in that his scheme had little effect upon existing properties. From the time of Wren this had been a stumbling-block to grand design. Such was the case in the rebuilding of the Regent Street Quadrant, where the problems of interested parties formed a difficult and trying background to the project. The Quadrant was part of Nash's great scheme of the 1820s, and aligned Regent Street to a 'hinge' at Piccadilly Circus, whence it ran down to what is

now Carlton House Terrace. By the late nineteenth century, the scale of operations demanded by shops was in excess of what could be provided by the existing structure, which, never strong or well built, was weakened by additions and alterations. It was decided to remove Nash's buildings, therefore, and to replace them with something new, on the same line of road, but on a much larger scale. Norman Shaw became involved with the new scheme, designing first the Piccadilly Hotel, completed in 1908, which also had a façade to Piccadilly. However, the front to the Quadrant established the pattern of what was intended. This was a heavy but vigorous Baroque design with rusticated stonework, arched openings for the shops at ground-floor level, paired Ionic columns rising through the subsequent storeys, and a large cornice surmounted by a steeply pitched roof with dormers and huge chimneys. The whole thing was a powerful architectural creation, though rather overworked and too large for the width of the street. Shaw ran into trouble with the shop owners, who thought that the architecture detracted from the goods on display, quite apart from the cost. In addition, there were other problems which delayed the scheme and caused Shaw a great deal of worry in the last years of his life. At his death in 1912, only the hotel had been built, and a series of committees was appointed to finish the scheme. Eventually, Blomfield, as chairman of one panel, took the bull by the horns and made his own proposals. These simplified Shaw's design, providing rectangular shop windows, whilst still following its main lines. Blomfield's drawings were produced during the war, and the scheme was not officially opened until 1927.

Thus the imperialisation of London proceeded fitfully. In the year 1911-12, however, two capital cities in the Empire were proposed: Canberra, the competition for which was won by an architect from Chicago, and New Delhi. Both of these were built on Beaux Arts lines, and it is not surprising that a practitioner from the home of the 'City Beautiful' should have taken the prize for the Australian scheme. The Indian capital, however, was the responsibility of Edwin Lutyens. Blomfield tells us that the government asked him, as President of the RIBA, to advise on a suitable architect, and he put forward Lutyens' name in the hope that Lutyens would choose him as associate, giving Blomfield a chance to try out the 'grand manner' which he did so much to promulgate. Unfortunately – and this was something that Lutyens was later to regret – he chose Herbert Baker, whom he had known as a fellow pupil in Ernest George's office. Despite the informal design background of its two creators, New Delhi was built in an axial, Beaux Arts manner. It would have been unusual to do otherwise by this date, and Lutyens could turn his hand to anything. Besides this, he had assistants of the calibre of A. G. Shoosmith, who had worked on the new LCC headquarters.

Apart from these distant capitals, the examples discussed have been in London. The reasons for this have been implied, yet it was not too long before some provincial cities began to demand grand new thoroughfares. These, though, were built in the inter-war years. Blomfield designed the general format for the Headrow in Leeds, and was assessor for Ferensway in Hull. Beaux Arts planning lived on until after the Second World War, and Lutyens had produced the Royal Academy plan for London's reconstruction by his death in 1944; Abercrombie the plan for Hull. Some schemes were built, but failed to deliver the promise of the 'grand manner'.

The Beaux Arts was not, in itself, a style, but a way of designing that had developed in France and was closely allied to that country's academic system. Its influence was to permeate Britain, and it was education that was to be the other main instrument for change in Edwardian architecture.

In order to fulfil the ever growing demands of the profession, it was obvious that the haphazard educational process then in existence needed reform. A great deal of debate was generated about the architect's education, setting in motion continuing controversy which has dogged the profession for the rest of the century.

Education

Little had happened during the nineteenth century to improve upon a pattern of education first established during the time of Sir William Chambers, who is generally credited with the foundation of architecture as a learned profession. In 1769, Chambers had established an architectural curriculum at the newly founded Royal Academy Schools. It was based to some extent on French precedent, in that students were expected to draw from the antique, had access to a library, and were able to submit drawings for competitions. All of this took place in the students' spare time, as during the day they would work in offices as articled pupils – the payment of the premium varying with the celebrity of the principal – and learn about practice and technical issues. Such part-time education persisted for at least the next 130 years or so. Architects such as Soane took their pupils' education seriously; others, the majority, were mainly concerned with the money to be earned from the premiums.

During the Victorian era a few schools were established to add to that already running at the Academy. These were at University College, King's College, and at the Architectural Association, all in London. The conscientious practitioner would recommend his pupils to enlist at the Academy Schools. They would complete a full day in the office, but attend school, typically, on three evenings a week from six to eight o'clock.

Meanwhile, the RIBA had instigated an examination which was, at first, voluntary. By the late 1880s, however, it became an obligation for candidates for Associateship of the Institute to pass the examination. There was no requirement for an architect to belong to the Institute, and no statutory regulation of the profession. Registration, to control entry, would depend upon standardisation of admission requirements. This, in turn, would make necessary an educational system which would advance students to the appropriate level. Debates about registration dragged on throughout the Edwardian period, but were not fully resolved until the 1930s. During the period, though, there was an upsurge in higher education which helped to promote change, and to encourage the idea that professional education was desirable.

In 1884 the Victoria University was established, with colleges at Manchester, Liverpool and Leeds. These were separated into three individual institutions in 1903; Mason College became Birmingham University in 1900; and in the same year London University reorganised itself into schools

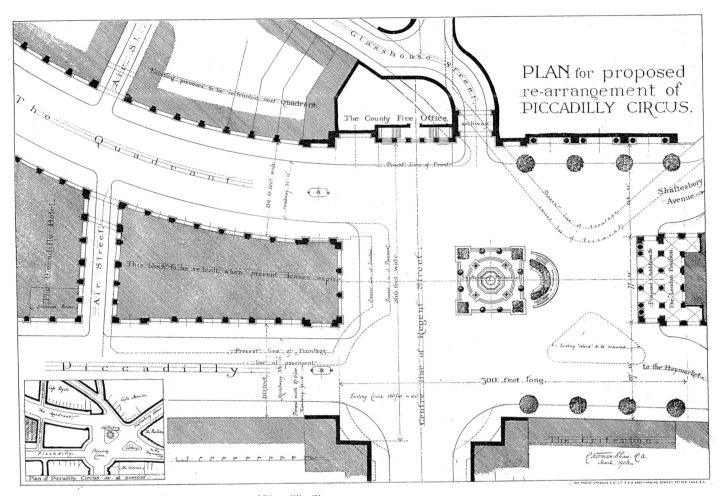

PLAN for proposed re-arrangement of PICCADILLY CIRCUS.

Norman Shaw's proposal for the rearrangement of Piccadilly Circus, which would tie in with his rebuilding of the Regent Street Quadrant after the removal of Nash's smaller-scale buildings.

on an up-to-date academic basis. Of these institutions, Liverpool Victoria had taken a lead in architectural education in the 1890s by opening a full-time course under Professor Frederick M. Simpson. He was succeeded by Charles H. Reilly in 1904, and moved on to the chair at University College, London. Meanwhile, Manchester had established an architecture course in 1903 through a joint operation by the council's Technical Instruction Committee, the local society of architects and Victoria University. Professor Capper was installed as head of school. The Architectural Association had already begun a daytime school in 1902.

Not many years before he gained his position at Liverpool, Charles Reilly himself had undertaken the RIBA final examination. The design component was based on a project for a town house (a favourite subject), and was supplemented with a construction paper and a viva. In order to sit this final examination, a candidate must previously have been through a preliminary one for Probationership of the RIBA, and the intermediate one for Studentship.

Liverpool School of Architecture achieved exemption from the intermediate examination of the RIBA for its three-year BA (Hons) course in 1902. One year's remission of articles was granted to students on gaining the BA. To give some idea of course content: the final examination on the Liverpool Honours course, in 1900, consisted of a review of design work carried out in the studio and special tasks in design and in the history of architecture.

The establishment of full-time day courses at provincial

Parisian sophistication was brought to a smart area of London with the construction of Mewès and Davis's Ritz Hotel.

and metropolitan institutions therefore gathered pace in the early years of the century. This upsurge in activity was crystallised in the return of the 'Profession or an Art' Memorialists to the RIBA fold, engineered by the wily Aston Webb, through the medium of the Board of Architectural Education. In 1903, Blomfield, Lethaby, Macartney and others presented a memorandum to the RIBA on architectural education, asking the Institute to reorganise the system. Blomfield says that 'it was felt that all men of goodwill whether in the Institute or out of it should unite for the purpose of a return of architec-

tural training'.[4] The upshot was that a Board of Architectural Education was formed in 1904, containing a balance of architect members and educational advisors, with Aston Webb in the chair. The Board was requested to submit a uniform scheme which could be applied to all the new and existing courses, and Blomfield presented a paper containing its deliberations to the RIBA council early in 1905. It is interesting to note that Blomfield stressed the importance of a mastery of constructional systems and a knowledge of new materials such as steel for the architect to exercise his art more effectively. He was probably also aware of the threat to architects posed by new building sciences and the fear of many of his colleagues that the engineer might take over.

Five major points were made concerning the educational system, including the desire that the course should be a minimum of four years in length, comprising two years' full-time education and two years' practical training, but with part-time school attendance during the practical years. A syllabus including studies of materials, construction, drawing, geometrical projection and design and architectural history was to be put in place. Drawing was to be used as a design tool rather than an end in itself. Blomfield expressed the hope that this course would simply form a foundation; 'It [the Board] cannot contemplate the full equipment of an architect as possible in a four years' course.'[5] Having thus laid down guidelines, the Board then set up a system of visitors who were allocated to various schools to approve their courses.

A mechanism for standardised architectural education was thereby achieved. Indeed, it was a platform from which to build, and from which Reilly could eventually introduce both B. Arch and M. Arch courses. However, what is more important from the point of view of architectural design is the theory behind much of the teaching. In some schools, such as that of the Architectural Association, an Arts and Crafts approach dominated, and Lethaby, as adviser to the LCC technical and art schools, promulgated theories developed from his Arts and Crafts ideals. This kind of teaching was to be found at Liverpool for some time, but with the advent of Reilly in 1904 it was swept away. He threw out plaster casts of Gothic details from which the students drew, and removed both the buildings and the staff which his predecessor had inherited as director of the applied art section. From now on, there were new enthusiasms that reflected advanced taste and established a pattern for architectural education for the next four decades. He bemoaned the fact that, 'A newly built fluted column, a sign of refinement in classical architecture, would have been hard to find in those days.'[6] He soon set about remedying this state of affairs.

Reilly's main competitor for the post at Liverpool had been, symptomatically, an American, and it was the joint influence of America and France that was to prevail from now on. In its current form, the Beaux Arts dated from J. N. L. Durand's establishment of the institution in 1823. It had devised and refined a method for teaching architectural design, something that was very necessary with the rise of full-time education. The articled pupillage/evening school system did not need to recognise this issue, as pupils picked up their principal's design methodology. Scholarship, knowledge of previous examples, systematisation of teaching and learning methods,

staging of outcomes, could all be applied to design teaching, by following the French and the Americans. What is more, this approach increased the authority and influence of the teaching profession. What was lost was the spontaneous, inventive style which we now think of as 'Edwardian'. True classicism, with a proper study of the 'orders' and Greek, Roman and Renaissance buildings, took over. The end products of such labour were beautifully rendered, measured drawings of buildings, or original designs based on a fairly limited range of subjects, appropriate to the level of the student. Such efforts could be seen at the same time in schools of architecture in France and America. Whilst the method lessened spontaneity, it served to enhance professionalism.

Reilly deprecated Waterhouse's terracotta buildings at Liverpool University as this style was now beyond the pale. He looked for 'good-mannered' examples of Georgian architecture – buildings with restraint, taste and sensibility. Exuberance might have been one of Reilly's personal characteristics, but he did not want it in architecture. However, in establishing his dominance at Liverpool, he set a pattern of work that was to endure throughout the century. Students worked in studios, except when they were in little partitioned *loges* to produce *esquisses en loge* – sketch designs undertaken by individuals in isolation, to avoid cribbing – a part of Beaux Arts methodology. In the studio, twenty or so students would receive design tuition over the drawing board, supported by a few hours of lectures. Design projects would culminate, as now, with frenetic 'all-nighters' and nail-biting, end-of-session viva examinations.

In that it established a way of teaching design that lasted for decades, stemming directly from the newest movements in Edwardian architecture, Reilly's method was extremely successful. The school of architecture system produced an education of the best possible kind, whilst providing steps up the vocational ladder at the same time.

French examples were widely studied now: Garnier's Opéra, the work of J.-L. Duc, Hittorff and Nenot. J.-L. Pascal, the Beaux Arts professor, became a figure to revere. In addition, books such as Blomfield's *The Mistress Art*, a compilation of his lectures delivered as professor of architecture at the Royal Academy, stressed the need for the 'grand manner', and his vast history of French architecture was also useful. Taste had begun to change, but so had design theory.

Reilly's visit to the United States in 1909 seemed to confirm the rectitude of his approach. The scope to improve education along the lines already started seemed endless. New empires appeared before his eyes, and the enthusiasm was reciprocated from other quarters. Reginald Blomfield was keen to start an *atelier* system, with pupils working for a patron in his studio whilst attending a central school for instruction, after the French pattern. He promoted the idea vigorously for some time, but although Arthur J. Davis – one half of the Mewès and Davis partnership, the bringers of true French architecture to Edwardian London – was head of the first, it failed and Blomfield's idea of a great final school of design at the Academy collapsed with it. At the same time new, younger men, like Albert Richardson, were ready to begin along the same lines. In 1914, he published *Monumental Classic Architecture in Great Britain and Ireland during the XVIII and XIXth Centuries*, and in 1919 he replaced F. M. Simpson as professor at the Bartlett School of Architecture.

Thus, for the very best of reasons, all the new young architects emerging from the up-to-date schools towards the end of the period were of a very different type from those of the preceding generation. They were imbued with a firm philosophy of design, a knowledge of how to execute it and a sound backing of scholarship.

Additionally, the rise of formal education had made it easier for women to become architects, and they had been admitted to classes at University College, London, on the same basis as men since the late 1880s. There was, however, still prejudice against women, and it was generally felt by the male-dominated profession – there were only seven female architects in England and Wales in 1901 – that despite gaining the same qualifications as men, they should confine their professional interest to domestic work. It has been maintained that it was the adoption of Beaux Arts teaching methods that gave women the confidence to enter the realm of large-scale public building design.

Books and publications

Books, magazines and journals are essential adjuncts to academic life, either as manuals or to reflect thought and scholarship. Albert Richardson noted that 'There was a surfeit of books.' Every architect had a library, '… and when one hadn't got books, we made our own.'[7] Blomfield's books were especially popular, and at Liverpool School of Architecture Reilly noted 'that its teaching at the beginning of the new century was based on Sir Reginald's. His books became text books for professors and students alike. It was due to his influence, more than to anyone else's, that the Orders, and all they implied in big scale and simple shapes, were once again thoroughly studied.'[8]

Blomfield had been one of the leading lights in the founding of the *Architectural Review*, with others of the Shaw circle, at the beginning of the period. It grew out of the Architectural Illustration Society, which had been set up to publicise the work of the Art Worker's Guild. Under Mervyn Macartney,

who took up the editorship a few years after its foundation, it moved forwards to champion the cause of Classicism. Eventually it began to print examples of measured drawings of seventeenth- and eighteenth-century buildings as 'practical examplars' to show architects what their aspirations should be. Other features that were introduced included 'Notes from Paris', regular reports on events in the United States, and a town planning section that seemed to occupy more and more space in the magazine as the new century progressed. The *Review* thus reflected, and even promoted, some of the changes that occurred.

Other journals and magazines were directed more towards professional and trade issues. Notable was H. H. Statham's *The Builder*, which was widely read, and fairly comprehensive in its coverage. C. H. Reilly became editor of one of its competitors, *Builder's Journal*, in the mid-1900s, rejecting editorship of *The Builder* itself, as it was too big a commitment. The *Journal* was owned by the Hastings family who also owned the *Architectural Review*. The magazine was retitled *Builders' and Architects' Journal* and then *Architects' Journal*. Albert Richardson eventually took over the editorship, and it became one of the major professional magazines of the century.

Thus a lively press, across a broad spectrum, was able to grow with educational and stylistic developments, reinforcing and interpreting changes and even, in some cases, leading them.

A more sophisticated manner

A review of changes in urban design and architectural education has served to show the increasing influence on British architecture of France and the United States. Lionel Budden, a successor of Reilly at Liverpool, has said that it was to France that Reilly looked for inspiration; but it was, in fact, to the United States that he looked for operative rather than philosophical ideas. This reliance on the solidity of a well-tried old European culture and the vigour of the 'new world' became widespread in many areas of endeavour during Edwardian times. It would form the background of the younger men and women whose ideas saw the close of the Edwardian era, and who would dominate the inter-war period. The respect for Continental theory and systematisation would provide the soil in which the work of the young architects of the modern movement would take root.

There are some key figures whose work during the period did much to promote the new approach. One of these, the Scot John James Burnet (1857-1938), was already well established in practice by the opening of the century. His father had been an architect in Glasgow, where there was a strong classical tradition. Burnet was sent to Paris to train, entering

The restrained Ionic colonnade of John Burnet's Edward VII Gallery
at the British Museum.

Changing taste is mirrored in this advertisement dating from 1904. Classical details, refinement and taste become more important than originality or 'honesty'.

the *atelier* of Jean-Louis Pascal, who was later to become a great influence on young British architects. Burnet's most influential building, for the younger generation, was the new Edward VII gallery extension, added to the British Museum and built between 1905 and 1914. In some respects the giant Ionic columns marching along the façade pay homage to Smirke's 'neo Grec' of more than eighty years before, yet its sense of control and abjuration of frivolity say much about the Beaux Arts and its suitability for grand projects.

Much younger, but of perhaps greater importance in making the French manner popular, was Arthur J. Davis. Davis was not born until 1878, but owing to his personal brilliance and an early start produced buildings which were inspirational to those of his own generation in the first decade of the new century. Davis, though a native of London, was brought up on the Continent, and in the 1890s enlisted at the École des Beaux Arts, finding himself in the Pascal *atelier*. Having completed the course quickly, and having gained medals on the way, he became associated with an established architect, Charles Mewès, who had also been Pascal's pupil. Mewès and Davis entered the competition for the 'Grand et Petit Palais' of the 1900 Paris Exposition which, it has been noted, was influential upon the British. Although they did not win, Davis was made Mewès's partner, responsible for the London office in a practice that had branches in France, Germany and England. Therefore, at an early age, Davis was involved with the design of the Ritz Hotel in Piccadilly, Inveresk House in the Aldwych and the RAC Club in Pall Mall, all of

which brought Parisian elegance to London. No doubt these sophisticated designs made the whimsical and ebullient 'Wrenaissance' architects like Hare and Mountford seem bucolic, provincial and crude. Young architects were certainly aware of this, Albert Richardson describing Davis's architecture as 'the real thing' when compared to Edwin Rickards' facile, though captivating, Baroque and Rococo detail.

American influence

Davis therefore led the way for many in terms of style, but his use of steel-framed construction also serves to emphasise the link between French and American practice, and the suitability of urbane classicism for incorporating new structural technology.

The influence of modern American building procedures was of paramount importance, and to the younger generation Daniel H. Burnham's Chicago work, though regarded as vulgar by some, made an impression, not least through the construction of Selfridge's store in Oxford Street. Another American, Charles F. McKim, of the great east coast practice McKim Mead and White, was also celebrated. A friend of Burnet – they had been contemporaries in Pascal's *atelier* in Paris – he came to England in 1903 to receive the Royal Gold Medal for architecture from the RIBA. Reilly went on to write a book about his practice.

America was free of many of the social and legal constraints that so entrammelled Europe. A directness of purpose and expression that would have been quite shocking in the old world permeated most aspects of life. This, allied with the great speed of growth and the presence of seemingly unlimited resources, allowed new techniques to be tried in all spheres. The development of tall office buildings in the reconstruction of Chicago after the great fire is a case in point. Yet the old world looked to the new not just for technical expertise, but also for commercial advice, and, in some respects, aesthetic ideas. The United States was able to offer examples of new methods that were initially regarded with suspicion, but which were eventually seized upon. In a way, the brute force of commercial reality and its physical effects mirrored what had happened in Britain a century before in the Industrial Revolution.

The 'skyscraper' most graphically represented transatlantic differences. Building high to maximise land values in expensive city sites in Chicago or New York strikingly demonstrated the capabilities of steel-framed structures. Frames, themselves, were designed using standardised sections produced in large quantities in rolling mills. For guidance, tables were used which listed the capabilities of various sectional sizes, but architects' offices also contained engineers who would be re-

The façade of Mewès and Davis's Royal Automobile Club in Pall Mall. The suave, French Beaux Arts style disguises the steel frame which supports the luxurious accommodation. The structure, services and capabilities of the building are of the twentieth century.

sponsible for structural, sanitary and mechanical engineering design. Everything was detailed thoroughly on drawings so that site operations ran as smoothly as possible. All dimensions were shown, whereas much British practice was vague in this respect. Consequently, components could be produced by specialist sub-contractors in their workshops, and the responsibility of the general contractor was to co-ordinate the supply and assembly of components on the site. Far from being a craft-based operation, the American building industry used methods not unlike factory production. This period, of

course, also saw the foundation of assembly-line motor manufacture and the institution of time and motion studies in the workplace.

Enormous buildings could thus be produced in a very short period of time. Financial pressure drove the necessity for speed and was related to producing a return on investment as quickly as possible and minimising loss of interest. In addition, the system of leasing was a potent force. Leases mostly ran from May each year, and a building completed after that month had to stand empty until the following May. If leases were promised, but not forthcoming, an action for damages might ensue.

The stark realities of speculative office building were unsentimentally noted by R. A. Denell, managing director of the Waring White Building Company, of which Sven Bylander, the pioneer in Europe of steel-frame design, was the chief engineer. In a paper given at the RIBA in 1905, Denell explained:

The basement and ground floor of this class of building bring in sufficient rental to pay all interest on the freehold or ground lease; the first floor covers all rates and depreciation; the next few stories … bring in interest on money invested to build and all maintenance expenses; the balance is profit; and all offices being occupied, this generally gives good returns.[9]

Denell's paper outlined many aspects of American practice, but met with a response from members of the RIBA that was stuffy and negative. There was, perhaps, concern at the range of responsibilities and competencies expected of American architects. English architects probably dreaded the heavy emphasis on engineering associated with new building technologies. Almost immediately, however, certain aspects of transatlantic construction practice began to find their way into new building projects in Britain. Denell's company and its successor were involved in the construction of the Ritz Hotel and Selfridge's department store, and Bylander went on to design the steel frame of Mewès and Davis's Royal Automobile Club. The Ritz was the first British building to be constructed with a regular and complete steel frame.

By the end of the first decade of the twentieth century, steel and concrete frames were the normal means of providing structure for large buildings. More and more, architects found themselves designing clothing for steel skeletons; eventually a new generation would cease to see virtue in rusticated stonework and baroque detail. For most Edwardians, however, it was a case of tradition and propriety. They were content to accept the benefits of new technology, providing the building was richly and decently clothed.

The younger generation, who were just instigating their own practices, or becoming partners in large firms, could stomach the stylistic and engineering implications, if not the starkness of commercial practice. Albert Richardson (1880-1965) was one of the band that was to carry the late Edwardian voice through to the Second World War and, in his case, beyond. Richardson had an innate personal interest in the eighteenth century, and from an early age admired the whole cultural background of the period. Indeed, he would frequently dress in eighteenth-century clothes, and he turned his house into a haven of eighteenth-century taste. As a young

The rapid growth of an American skyscraper depicted in a contemporary photograph. Such illustrations may have sowed the seeds of panic within British architecture.

man, Richardson worked for Frank T. Verity, an architect with a predilection for things Parisian, like his sovereign, for whom he carried out work at Buckingham Palace. This set the seal on Richardson's architectural tastes: either the urbane French style, or the modest, unassuming character of English Georgian. Although he promoted these vigorously, his taste was consistent with that of most of the more important of the younger generation of architects.

Richardson went on to become one of the great teachers of his time, as head of the Bartlett School from 1919 onwards, although he had begun lecturing before the war, at Regent Street Polytechnic. His book on monumental classical architecture helped to establish his lecturing career, and also

Richardson and Gill's New Theatre in Manchester, opened in 1912, illustrates the new severe Classicism promoted by the younger generation of Edwardian architects. The main elevation could have been produced in a Parisian Beaux Arts *atelier*.

indicates the kind of work that was admired at the time. Richardson, in fact, states that by 1910 a great classical revival seemed to be under way.

Other teachers preached a similar gospel, notably Robert Atkinson at the Architectural Association, who with his assistant, the American-born Howard Robertson, brought the influence of Charles McKim and other American architects into the school. He inculcated the spirit of the *atelier* system when he replaced the previous head of school, H. P. G. Maule, in 1912.

Some issues were common throughout Europe. The year 1906 saw the Seventh International Congress of Architects, held in London. It is instructive to note that such luminaries as Otto Wagner attended from Vienna, J. Guadet from the École des Beaux Arts, and Hermann Muthesius from Germany. The event seems to have been one enormous party, with five hundred foreign delegates attending; but the papers presented provide confirmation of the preoccupations of the time: 'official architecture', 'the planning and laying out of streets and open spaces', 'architects' registration', 'steel and reinforced concrete construction'. Although the congress can have had little direct result, it does represent the throwing open of Britain to ideas from overseas. Strangely, when taken together with Imperial confidence, there seems to have been an underlying feeling that some foreign nations may have possessed superior systems. The old British feelings of in-

Grown old: some of the most important figures in the younger generation of Edwardian architects photographed in 1947, proudly displaying RIBA Gold Medals awarded in the 1940s. Left to right, Sir Charles Reilly, W. Curtis Green, Sir Lancelot Keay, Sir Edward Maufe, Patrick Abercrombie and Sir Albert Richardson.

feriority in matters of taste certainly recurred and, as always, the intelligentsia looked longingly to France, not with entirely happy results. This gallicisation swept so far that even as early as 1906, Lethaby, most untypically, wrote to a friend, 'As to LCC [County Hall] I wish it were possible to get a Frenchman …'[10]

A younger generation of architects was now waiting to carry forward the new themes described in this chapter. Essentially they were late Edwardians, who were too old to take up the Modern movement when it came, but who were young enough to practise well into the middle of the twentieth century. Charles Holden (1875-1960) was perhaps the most outstanding, but there were also Giles Gilbert Scott (1880-1960), E. Vincent Harris (1879-1971), and William Curtis Green (1875-1960). All of these, even Scott, who had won the Liverpool Cathedral competition at the age of twenty-one with a Gothic Revival design, ended up producing monumental classicism, largely stripped of its detail. Much could be written about any of these architects, particularly Holden, who was a first-rate designer, able to combine an instinctive feel for the subject with an intellectual approach. Even established practitioners such as J. J. Joass, within Belcher's firm, be-

Even well established architects moved away from the lushness of the Edwardian Baroque towards a more self-conscious approach. Here in the Mappin and Webb shop in Oxford Street, London, Belcher and Joass have produced a tense mannerism, with the stone skin pulled taut over the steel frame.

came more austere as the Edwardian period wore on, cladding his office buildings in a taut, mannerist, stone skin over the steel frames. We have seen how the wildly eclectic Aston Webb tightened sufficiently to produce the *dix-huitième* French style for the façade of Buckingham Palace. Yet most British architects of the older generation never succeeded in mastering Pascal's abstract planning or the real nature of Beaux Arts work. They were still pictorial in approach: Lutyens could get on in any style; Blomfield tried to be French but without much success, despite his books. The 1930s stylistic chameleon Oliver Hill is the true heir of such architects as Lutyens.

The acceptance of 'stripped' classicism, the removal of decoration and intricate detail, the new primacy of structural systems and the teaching of rationalised Beaux Arts design, with form rather than context as the important issues, enabled future generations taught at schools like Liverpool to align themselves with the Modern movement when the time was right. After all, the Continental pioneers of the movement had been educated in a similar way.

Whatever the design approach, though, all architects had to come to terms with the rapid advances in structural, constructional, environmental and operational technology that had occurred during the Edwardian era, and to incorporate them into their design thinking. The interaction between technology and design forms the subject of the next chapter.

1. John Allwood, *The Great Exhibitions*, London, 1977, p.96
2. C. H. Reilly, *Scaffolding in the Sky: a semi-architectural Autobiography*, London, 1938, p.128
3. *The Builder*, 79, 3 Nov.1900, pp.379-81
4. Reginald Blomfield, *Memoirs of an Architect*, London, 1932, p.105
5. Reginald Blomfield, paper on education, *Journal of the RIBA*, vol.12, 1905, pp.237-45
6. Reilly, *op.cit.* pp.118-19
7. Nicholas Taylor, 'Sir Albert Richardson: a classic case of Edwardianism' in Alastair Service (ed), *Edwardian Architecture and its Origins*, London, 1975, p.455
8. C. H. Reilly, *Representative British Architects of the present Day*, London, 1931, p.61
9. R. A. Denell, *Journal of the RIBA*, ser.III, vol.13, no.2, 25 Nov.1905, p.39
10. Andrew Saint, *Richard Norman Shaw*, New Haven and London, 1976, p.351

Chapter 3
Technology, Form and Style

In Chapter 2 we saw the way in which design changed during the Edwardian period through the influence of intertwined factors. One vital aspect, though, requires greater attention: the rapid development of building technology.

Architecture is a practical art, and the mastery of structural and constructional techniques, together with the ability to control environmental conditions, are skills demanded of the architect. These are an integral part of design, and the means by which the aims of the designer are achieved in hard, physical reality. In certain periods of architectural history, technology had a strong influence over form; in others it provided the means by which abstract ideals could be realised. In the Edwardian era, new technologies came to fruition that had been in gestation since the Industrial Revolution began a hundred or so years before. As a result, the Edwardian architect was presented with new possibilities in terms of spatial organisation, planning flexibility and sheer size brought about by technological achievement. The interaction of style with these factors is one of the most fascinating characteristics of early twentieth-century architecture.

In order to gain a better understanding of the situation, it is necessary to look back a little to see how developments occurred, and how they form part of the overall context of the time. Change does not consist of a series of straightforward steps up a ladder, but is the result of a process of intertwined events and circumstances that permeate all spheres of existence. During the nineteenth century, patronage altered in a way that placed emphasis upon technological issues. The eighteenth-century gentleman may have wished to demonstrate his taste and knowledge by creating erudite works aiming for some idealised classical form, but Victorian clients were different. They were less likely to be from a narrow cultural élite, and more likely to be business or professional men, or even committees. They wanted performance, value and prestige from their buildings and, unlike British aristocrats who no doubt deemed it vulgar, began to demand comfort. Technology had to rise to these demands.

Victorian 'improvement'

In terms of structure, construction and environmental control, most new technologies stemmed from the building of the mills and warehouses necessary to maintain the thrust of the Industrial Revolution. There was innovative freedom, and cross-fertilisation between what are today completely different branches of engineering science, in inaugurating industrial building types. Such buildings, where scores of workers could congregate to produce goods in unprecedented quantities, may have been crude and austere as works of architecture, yet in conquering the practical problems associated with their construction, the foundations of many important techniques were laid.

A centralised power source – after about 1800 this was usually the steam engine – driving a range of machinery, and the need to accommodate as much as possible on site, led to the adoption of the multi-storey mill. Cast-iron columns were employed, which, because of their compressive strength, could be spaced in rows to hold up intermediate floors without using the large area required by load-bearing walls. The pressure to maximise capital investment, by keeping the mill running for as many hours as possible, resulted in the development of artificial lighting, using gas, although the external walls were punctured with a grid of large openings to let in as much daylight as practical. These openings were fitted with metal window frames produced by the burgeoning iron foundries. Many mills even had central heating installations, using steam from the engine, or a system of hot-air distribution from stoves.

When the mills burned down, as they frequently did, methods were tried for fireproofing floors. Timber beams were replaced by iron girders spanned by brick vaults.

The lessons learned from these new developments were not restricted to industrial buildings, however. As early as 1810, William Strutt, FRS, one of the great pioneers of textile mill construction, was able to apply innovative thinking to the technological design of Derbyshire General Infirmary that derived directly from industrial experience.

Distinguished architects soon made use of new methods. Soane, Nash and, notably, Sir Robert Smirke were all pragmatic enough to realise the opportunities which were provided, and their prestigious projects benefited as a result. The Duke of Wellington had central heating installed in his house, and George IV incorporated gas lighting into the Brighton Pavilion. By the 1850s, many such comforts were expected in a gentleman's house – as Mrs Proudie, the formidable wife of the new Bishop of Barchester, notes in Anthony Trollope's *Barchester Towers*. Whilst inspecting the bishop's palace, she complains that, 'there is no gas through the house, none whatever, but in the kitchen and passages. Surely the palace should have been fitted through with pipes for gas, and hot water too. There is no hot water laid on anywhere above the ground floor …'

Technological advance, therefore, was not confined solely to the efforts of the great Victorian engineers. Their works are well enough known, particularly in the field of innovatory building types. Brunel's station for the Great Western Railway at Paddington, built in the early 1850s, with the architect Matthew Digby Wyatt 'in the subordinate role', is a fine example, as is Barlow's St Pancras, begun ten years later. The

Opposite

A constructional section through part of the Wesleyan Hall in West-minster, designed by Lanchester and Rickards. Steel beams can be seen at appropriate places, which together with reinforced concrete enabled the explosion of Baroque space. The drawing, however, places more emphasis on the details of masonry construction.

Lister's Manningham Mill in Bradford (1871) exemplifies the bold and confident use of technology to produce a very large building meeting exacting functional requirements. Architecturally, it is more sophisticated than earlier buildings of this type.

remarkable gardener/entrepreneur Joseph Paxton, with his 'Crystal Palace' in Hyde Park, has been celebrated as a pioneer of modern building design. Inevitably, the split between the architect, obsessed with stylistic issues, and the engineer, the creator of exciting new forms, has been emphasised. This is an over-simplification, however, and most architects were happy to advance their art using the benefits of modern technology.

If one imagines a fairly large, typical building of the 1860s – say a provincial town hall – a good number of nineteenth-century innovations would be found that had rapidly become common. The foundations, to start with, would undoubtedly be of concrete, made with good-quality cement and mixed to a consistent specification. Smirke had used this material in

order to prevent the Millbank Penitentiary from sinking into the River Thames as early as 1817, though its modern use by engineers predates this by some decades. By the time the new Houses of Parliament were rising in the 1840s, raft or strip foundations were normal.

It is likely that the exterior walls of our example would be massive, load-bearing structures of good-quality brick or stone. Whatever the internal structure, local byelaws usually insisted on thick outer walls. Internally, intermediate floors may have been supported on cast-iron columns, or a mixture of walls and columns, with wrought-iron beams carrying fire-proof construction. A relatively lightweight roof of wrought-iron trusses may have been thrown over all, covered by Welsh slates fixed to battens on machine-sawn deal boards. This

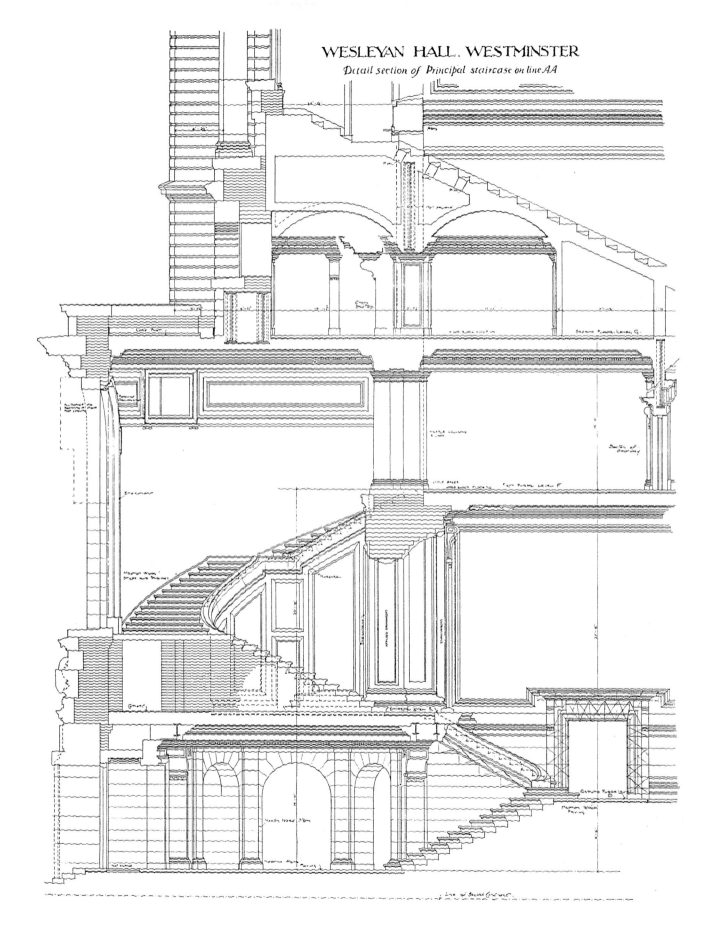

WESLEYAN HALL. WESTMINSTER

Detail section of Principal staircase on line AA

choice of material represents the erosion of regional differences during the mid-Victorian period. Local materials were undercut in price by large-scale operations made viable by the growth of transport networks.

A large building would require extensive environmental control. Ways of achieving satisfactory lighting, heating and ventilation were already well advanced, although there was still experiment, and considerable refinement was required before some of the methods could be safely adopted.

Gas lighting was first employed at the beginning of the nineteenth century, and some schemes for lighting mills date from the first decade. It remained, however, a dirty, hot and generally unsatisfactory method of illumination until the introduction of the mantle in the 1880s, by which time the incandescent electric lamp had appeared. At the time that our imaginary town hall was built, there had been improvements in the design of burners which enabled the gas flame to produce more light. One of the penalties paid for gas lighting, though, was the depletion of the atmosphere, with the consequent build-up of stuffiness inside the building. In addition, the Victorians were much concerned at the spread of disease, as they thought, through 'effluvia' and poisonous gases. Ventilation, therefore, became an important topic. In most buildings of size and complexity, a system of forced ventilation was introduced. A great deal of thought and experiment were expended on this issue, particularly in relation to the new Houses of Parliament. Sir Charles Barry, the designer of the building, was frequently in conflict with a Dr Reid, an 'expert' in heating and ventilation, who was employed to tackle the problems of moving air around inside the complex. The result was a whole maze of shafts, flues and ducts, interlaced between the various internal spaces and the building structure.

Barry had already had experience of a forced-air system when he began in earnest at Westminster. This was in his design for the Reform Club, Pall Mall, begun in the late 1830s. Here, a steam engine was employed to drive a fan which moved air to the principal rooms. The warm air was admitted at high level through inlets concealed within the decorative motifs of the upper walls and ceilings. Vitiated air was extracted at outlets above the light fittings, or gasoliers. With typical nineteenth-century ingenuity and economy, the engine was also made to pump water for domestic use from a well on site and to power hoists for raising coal (open fires were used as well as warm-air heating). Exhaust steam was condensed in heat exchangers, where incoming air was warmed.

The pragmatism described above is reflected in work from an unusual and unexpected source. Thomas Hardy, the great novelist and poet, was employed originally as an architect. He was articled first to a Dorchester practitioner, but from 1862 to 1867 he worked in London as an assistant to the well-known Gothic revivalist Sir Arthur Blomfield. During his years in practice he kept an architectural notebook in which he noted much on fireproof floors and the techniques of adequate ventilation. He specifically emphasised them in his description, taken from *Building News*, of St Thomas's Hospital in London, newly completed by the architect Henry Currey. Elsewhere, there is discussion of 'hollow' (cavity) walls, sanitation, and concrete floors and walls. Metallic construction is well represented with rules of thumb for sizing rolled-iron 'I' beams and descriptions of lightweight built-up roof trusses. One interesting specification encompasses the glazing of the ceiling to an iron roof using 'moulded zinc sash frames to receive the sheets of coloured glass laid loose on broad rebates and bedded on India rubber.'[1] Significantly, from the point of view of what is now known as 'technology transfer', Hardy also found time to note down a framing detail from a Great Western Railway carriage.

It is certain that Hardy was by no means exceptional in his eagerness to become familiar with techniques and methods in the Victorian 'high-tech' world. The popularity of architectural periodicals and their mixture of technical, professional and critical comment attests to this. The issues involved, by mid-century, were not merely seen as practical considerations. Theoretical thought was given to them by luminaries such as Pugin and Ruskin, who advocated honesty in construction and use of materials. Foremost Gothic Revival architects like William Butterfield followed these principals, but as far as practical building operations were concerned he believed fully in the modern practice of using large, well-organised firms of building contractors rather than local craftsmen. These large firms could afford to invest in the latest machinery, such as steam saws and winches, and to order materials from reputable national suppliers.

Whilst Butterfield was working with new methods within a theoretical framework that was essentially backward-looking, and confused by all kinds of moral and social issues, Eugène Emmanuel Viollet-le-Duc was expounding, in France, more radical opinions, though producing much less exciting buildings than Butterfield. Viollet's principal work consisted of a series of twenty lectures and articles written between 1856 and 1872 and published in two volumes as *Entretiens sur l'architecture*. These were translated into English, but were not published in Britain until the late 1870s. Viollet devoted much of his energy to attacking the neo-classicism of the dominant Beaux Arts approach in France. Iron architecture was widely used, but within formal Beaux Arts constraints. Viollet argued that to use ancient style was deceitful, and that raw technology, the direct result of man's triumph over the physical

A typical advertisement of the kind appearing in architectural magazines illustrating a proprietary fireproof floor system. Other systems used steel rods or bars embedded in concrete rather than rolled-steel joists.

laws of nature, provided the only true style. The steam locomotive is used as an example: 'The locomotive … has a special physiognomy which all can appreciate, and which renders it a distinct creation … The locomotive is almost a living being, and its external form is a simple expression of its strength. A locomotive therefore has style.'[2]

This kind of thinking is very familiar to present-day designers, but was no doubt radical at the time. It was extremely influential on those Continental architects at the turn of the century who attempted to revivify architecture by sweeping away the stylistic and social ambience of Victorian times. In Britain, architects were more conservative, on the whole, preferring to refer to past styles or to generate an aesthetic from the craft of building. Even the most conservative architects of our period, however, could employ a whole range of techniques to help them rise to the challenges to build bigger, more versatile and more comfortable buildings.

Architecture and technology in the Edwardian era

The arts do not stand still – architecture least of all … Fresh problems present themselves in planning, provision has to be made for an ever widening range of applied mechanical science, new methods of construction have to be considered, the practice of architecture becomes more difficult every year, and the modern architect has to deal with a range of subjects that would have paralysed his grandfather.[3]

These were the words with which Reginald Blomfield, the president of the RIBA, addressed the Institute at the opening of the 1913-14 session. They reflect the rapid expansion of technology and the fact that many of the experiments of the Victorian period had now been consolidated into well-proven systems, with which the architect was expected to respond to the increasing expectations of clients and the general public.

The majority of British architects saw this new technology as a means to an end. The architects of the Arts and Crafts movement, who may have been expected to promote its 'honest' expression in building form, had a genuine interest in traditional materials and techniques which was part of a romantic view of national heritage – rather like the folk-song revival in contemporary music. W. R. Lethaby, as we have seen, believed in exploring the use of modern materials, such as reinforced concrete, but somehow did not follow this through. He realised the implications for architecture, and so did his old master, Richard Norman Shaw. In his eightieth year, in a letter to Lethaby, Shaw discussed a seeming lack of direction in architectural design at the end of the first decade of the new century:

> I do not see at present any way out of our trouble. We know much about Leonardo and old Wren but the times are so different. Reinforced concrete ought to do a lot for us. What do you say to have a turn on those lines? I am sure we are doing no good at present; we have kicked the Gothic Revival out from below our feet, and we are doing the 'English Renaissance', which in turn we shall kick away too.[4]

Shaw's instincts were right, and reinforced concrete was already a widely discussed subject. During the 1900s it became more and more obvious that it would exercise a considerable amount of influence in building design, particularly as the pressure to build bigger and to increase performance grew.

Structures in reinforced concrete

In the history of its development, it is difficult to draw a line between the use of reinforced concrete as a fireproof floor technique, and the realisation of its potential as an exciting and versatile structural system. The idea of binding concrete with metal inserts had gained currency during the first half of the nineteenth century, but principles of reinforcement were not properly understood. An early example of true structural reinforcement was a house built in Newcastle-upon-Tyne in 1865, using Wilkinson's patent taken out in 1854. Here, the reinforcement was of flat bars and second-hand wire colliery rope. In France, François Coignet had built a concrete church in 1864 at Le Vesinet, and much subsequent development occurred in that country, especially in the formulation of a body of theoretical knowledge. Monier, Contamin, Hennebique and E. Coignet established principles of theory and design

The offices of Dronsfield Bros, Oldham, designed by J. H. Sellers. This bold statement seems to have set the pattern for subsequent work by Wood and Sellers.

that led to the patenting of various reinforced concrete systems, such as E. Coignet's in 1892. It was Hennebique's system, using plain, round, reinforcing rods with stirrups, forming trapezoidal beams, that was most influential in Great Britain. This was not necessarily due to the superiority of the system, however, for no small part in its success was played by the appointment of the engineer L. G. Mouchel as Hennebique's British agent in 1897. Mouchel took an active role in the promotion of reinforced concrete, and set up a network of regional engineers who could produce working drawings to architects' designs in accordance with the patent system. Contractors were licensed to use the system.

Mouchel was so successful that by 1905 'most reinforced concrete works and all framed buildings in Britain were in Hennebique's patented system.'[5]

This near-monopoly spurred a response, as it was felt that information about reinforced concrete should be made available to all. The RIBA Science Standing Committee had been interested in the issue since at least 1901, and both Mouchel and a British expert, William Dunn, had delivered papers on the subject in 1904. In 1905, however, a special committee on reinforced concrete was set up by the RIBA under the chair-

manship of Sir Henry Tanner, chief architect to the Office of Works. Among the main participants in the founding of this committee were Dunn and Charles F. Marsh, who had published a textbook on reinforced concrete in 1904. By the third edition (1907) it was prophesied that 'the book will take rank as the standard British work' and 'reinforced concrete is bound to obtain a large share of our future building.'[6]

Mention must here be made of Edwin Otto Sachs (1870-1919), another highly influential figure in the history of British building technology. Sachs, whose involvement in concrete technology stemmed from his concern for the improvement of fire precautions, in 1906 founded the magazine *Concrete and Construction Engineering* to document the interest in the new material. He then went on, with typical energy and initiative, to become in 1908 one of the founders of the Concrete Institute. This body subsequently became the Institute of Structural Engineers. Further details of Sachs and his work appear later in this chapter.

In the 1890s, before this growth of interest, buildings constructed completely in reinforced concrete tended to be of an industrial nature. Weaver and Company's provender mill, North Dock, Swansea, 1897, has claim to be the first large

Elm Street School, Middleton, Lancashire, designed by Wood and Sellers, making use of the flat, reinforced concrete roof to enable the curving plan shape of the lower block.

British building in the material, and one which exploited the structural potential of concrete. This, and other functional and austere structures, would not have been regarded as providing architectural evidence for the usefulness of the material. However, it was soon employed in the work of well-established architects, at first in a pragmatic way, but then as a true interactive design component. An illustration of this progression can be provided by a brief examination of some of the work of the well-known Manchester architects Edgar Wood and J. Henry Sellers.

Edgar Wood (1860-1935) was already acknowledged as a leading northern exponent of the Arts and Crafts movement when he was joined in a loose collaborative association by Sellers (1861-1954) in about 1904. Sellers had already used reinforced concrete in the roof of a house extension in Oldham in 1903. He claimed that this was for purely practical reasons – the need for a flat roof in order to maintain the view from a nearby property – but perhaps this was an excuse to try out something new. By 1906, Wood had designed a small, flat-roofed house in Middleton, Manchester, and Sellers an office building for Dronsfield Brothers in Oldham. In this instance, the reinforced concrete flat roof is an integral part of

the architectural language of the building. The same may be said about the two schools in Middleton designed by Wood and Sellers two years later. Indeed, the plan of the school in Elm Street, with its concave façade, would have produced architectural and constructional difficulties if reinforced concrete had not been available for the roof. The form, in other words, was a product of architectural desire and concrete technology.

Wood's celebrated house, 'Upmeads', in Stafford, was built at about the same time as the schools. Seen by some as a quirky forerunner of modernism, its appearance at this juncture is wholly understandable in terms of the firm's contemporary output.

The designs mentioned above are minor contributions in the history of concrete's acceptance as a potent building material, when compared to a contemporary project which must rank as the most important landmark in the use of the material in the first decade of the century. This was the construction of new General Post Office buildings in the City of London. These buildings comprised a public office and a sorting office on a site, bounded by King Edward Street and Newgate Street, formerly occupied by Christ's Hospital. The

The new General Post Office building in King Edward Street,
London, a stone skin cladding a reinforced concrete carcase.

total enclosed volume was in the region of 28,000 cubic metres. This figure had already been surpassed by certain industrial and commercial buildings (dock warehouses at Manchester and the North Eastern Railway Company's goods station at Newcastle), but the significance of the post office was that it was a major public building of architectural pretension on an important metropolitan site. What is more, it was commissioned and paid for by central government rather than by private capital, setting the seal on the use of reinforced concrete as a reliable and acceptable material given the most stringent requirements of a government department.

The building was designed under the direction of Sir Henry Tanner, chief architect to the Office of Works, who, it has been noted, was heavily involved in discussions about reinforced concrete as chairman of the RIBA committee on the material. The Hennebique system of 'ferro concrete' was chosen, and L. G. Mouchel and Partners were the consulting engineers. This may seem surprising in the light of concern expressed over the extent of Mouchel's control, but it must signify that most confidence lay in the tried and tested Hennebique system. Work began on excavating the site in late 1906, and by the spring of 1909 the main structural work was substantially complete.

The public office fronting on to King Edward Street rose to five storeys above ground level, and was separated from the sorting office by a covered loading yard. Both sections of the building were built above two-storey basements. Essentially, the structure comprised a framework of reinforced concrete columns and beams with monolithic joints and a thin floor slab running over, forming a 'continuous' system which provided an economical yet strong structure. In some cases, the columns were cast to incorporate ventilation ducts and parcel chutes.

There were a number of features about the building which indicated an adventurous use of the material. The basement itself acted as a major integrated structural element, enabling the whole enormous weight of the building – 800 tons per column at basement level – to be transferred efficiently to the earth, even though the floor was only five inches (127mm) thick, and the walls eight inches (203mm). Further exploitation of its advantages was to be seen in the roof of the boiler house, which was located below ground level, beneath the yard in which vehicles manoeuvred. Open-web beams of 15.2 metre span were constructed with a depth of three metres in order to support the yard above. Similar structural gymnastics were to be found in a footbridge connecting the public and sorting offices at second-floor level. The whole structure of the bridge was a concrete box girder with open-web sides which allowed light in. At one end, the bridge

An advertisement by building contractors indicating their expertise in dealing with this new structural type. The concrete carcase can be seen, top left, before cladding.

rested on beams cantilevered out from the main body of the sorting office by nearly four metres. There was another cantilever system on the west side of the building, where the upper storeys projected over a loading platform to provide shelter.

The structural design of the post office, therefore, was not a timid attempt to exploit reinforced concrete, but a demonstration of the enormous potential of the material. In extolling the virtues of this project, The Builder noted that it was a 'demonstration of the fact the new system of construction need no longer be regarded as an experiment'; and went on to say that it hoped that the successful application of reinforced concrete in this project would result in the abandonment of 'the vexatious restrictions hitherto placed on the employment of the same material by the Local Government Board.'[7]

Tanner had enabled the demonstration of reinforced con-

Opposite
Cross-section and basement plan of the RAC building, indicating the large amount of concrete work below ground-floor level.

Chicago comes to London: Selfridge's department store in Oxford Street. A grand American scale is presented via the medium of Beaux Arts Classicism. Glazed, bronze-framed panels form the wall between the columns.

British architects had not only to deal with innate conservatism, but also with restrictive legislation and professional lethargy. Building acts, for the best of reasons, were formulated to ensure structural stability and other aspects of health and safety. The advantages of steel frames – smaller structural members, increased size in wall openings, and the provision of larger open spaces internally – were negated by the restrictions of, for instance, the London Building Acts of 1894 and 1905. Many architects, brought up in an age of Victorian solidity, probably disliked the lightweight appearance of steel-framed buildings, on both aesthetic and intuitive grounds. It has also been suggested that 'architects resisted the use of steel in building construction because they dreaded the necessary study, or were reluctant to collaborate closely with engineers.'[11]

This conservative attitude was, however, overtaken by events, and in the years between about 1905 and 1910 there was a complete revolution in the way in which the steel frame was regarded. The catalyst for this seems to have been the presence in London of Sven Bylander, a Swedish engineer with American experience, who designed steel frames for important buildings in what, at first glance, appear to be radi-

cally different circumstances. His first well-known scheme was for the Ritz Hotel in Piccadilly, with the architects Mewès and Davis. Charles Mewès had already carried out work for César Ritz in Paris, and produced designs together with his young English partner, Arthur J. Davis, when commissioned in 1903 to build the London Ritz. As discussed in Chapter 2, the architects were noted for their sophisticated Parisian Beaux Arts projects, but although the building was designed in the style of the French *dixhuitième*, with elegant stone façades, this outer skin merely covered Bylander's steel frame, which supported the 'fireproof' concrete floors and the roof. The London Building Acts, however, which were based on load-bearing construction, required that the walls were almost one metre thick at ground-floor level because of the overall height of the building.

Trouble with the Acts also occurred when Bylander worked on Selfridge's department store in Oxford Street, yet in many ways it was the construction of this building that helped to change the situation. Selfridge was an American from Chicago who decided that transatlantic methods of selling could benefit the British consumer. Initially, his architect was the famous steel-frame pioneer Daniel H. Burnham. He was replaced after a time by R. Frank Atkinson who, incidentally, had worked for Doyle in Liverpool at the time of the construction of the Royal Insurance Building. The whole spirit of the new store militated against the Building Acts, in particular the need for huge display windows, and the desire to provide continuous internal space, instead of splitting the interior into fireproof compartments. Various waivers were obtained, allowing some of the provisions of the legislation to be ignored, and in 1908 the London County Council bowed to the inevitability of commercial evolution exerted by both this and other projects, and passed an Act allowing for greater con-

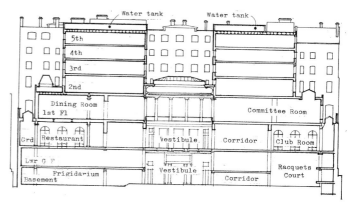

Diagrammatic longitudinal section of the RAC building. The heavy steelwork supporting the large water tanks at roof level can be seen.

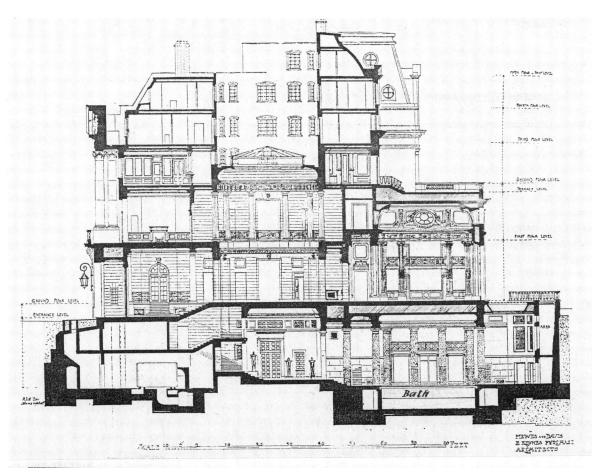

MEWES and DAVIS
E KEYNES PATERAST
ARCHITECTS

SCALE 10 5 0 10 20 30 40 50 60 70 80 FEET

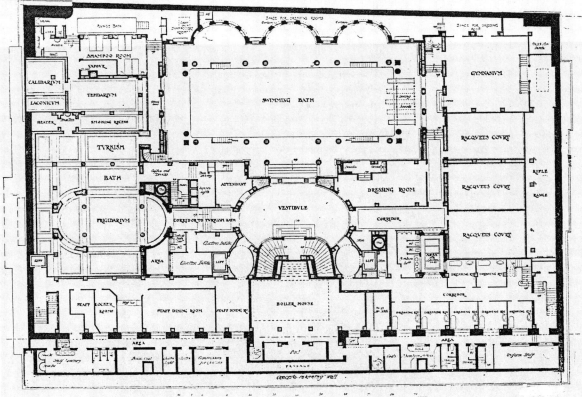

SCALE FEET

A general view of the façade of the RAC building from Pall Mall.

View of the basement swimming bath in the RAC building.

tinuous internal volume. In addition, the Council passed another Act in 1909 which recognised the notion of framed construction as a legitimate way of supporting buildings.

During the construction of the Ritz (1904 - 6) and Self-ridges (1907-9), much interest was shown by the professional press. It was perfectly clear that steel framing was such an advantageous method of construction that it would have to be recognised. John Belcher, president of the RIBA in 1905, had somewhat reluctantly pleaded the cause of the steel frame at his inaugural address, and its very practicality must have commended it to all architects involved with commercial work. Speed of construction was one outstanding factor. Already, in the USA, multi-storey office buildings could be constructed in a matter of months, and the structure of Selfridges was completed in under a year. Everything was clearly organised

beforehand, and much effort was put into ensuring the use of standardised sections and joints. American experience was useful here, as working practices and machinery had been developed to ensure smooth operation.

Bylander worked again with Mewès and Davis on the design of the Royal Automobile Club, Pall Mall (1908 - 11). This large, luxurious building – thought by the old guard to be rather vulgar – used 1600 tons of steel, with built-up stanchions and girders, the stanchions being at 12 feet 3 inches (3.7 metres) centres 'where the architectural treatment rendered this possible.' [12] The stanchions terminated in foundations made up of two layers of rolled-steel joists embedded in concrete. Reinforced concrete was used for intermediate floors in the building, as was the case in both the Ritz and Selfridges. The basement was constructed in concrete, forming a tank-like retaining wall round the perimeter of the building.

Many examples using similar structures followed. Thus American influence was brought to bear on the acceptance of steel-framed buildings in Britain. In certain cases this represented not only the arrival of a new building type, but also an appropriate technology with which to build it.

In the development of reinforced concrete and steel framing as building techniques, the period 1905-10 seems crucial in Britain. Before this time the methods were known, but only tentatively applied. After 1910, both became commonplace for important public and commercial buildings. This was certainly a quiet revolution in British architecture. It was not accompanied by extreme stylistic changes or radical design theories, but over the period of a few years new methodologies were adopted which established the basis of twentieth-century practice.

Environment and services

The rapid advances in structure and construction were mirrored by far-reaching improvements in environmental control and services installations. Healthy, comfortable and efficient conditions were needed, no matter how well constructed buildings may have been, and the larger scale made possible by new techniques demanded a more sophisticated response than had previously been necessary. Artificial lighting, heating and forced ventilation were desirable in most buildings of any size, and especially where there were deep plans, with long distances between internal spaces and external walls. Tall structures, or those with goods stored in high places, required efficient lifts for both passengers and goods, and new building types such as department stores and underground railway stations, where large numbers of people were constantly moving, needed escalators. In addition, problems of communication within big buildings led to the installation of electric bells, speaking-tubes and telephones.

Little of the technology needed for these advances was new. Experiment and theory had been undertaken in the previous century, by the end of which methods were well developed and proprietary products were available which made installation and running much easier. Some public utilities were well established. Gas, for instance, was supplied throughout urban areas, many local gas services dating from the 1820s, and some from before. The Leeds Gas Light Company was established in 1818, and parts of London had been supplied even before then. The concept of gas supply was so universal by the last quarter of the nineteenth century that the Public Health Act of 1875 gave local authorities the right to set up gas works if none were in existence. Although gas was initially

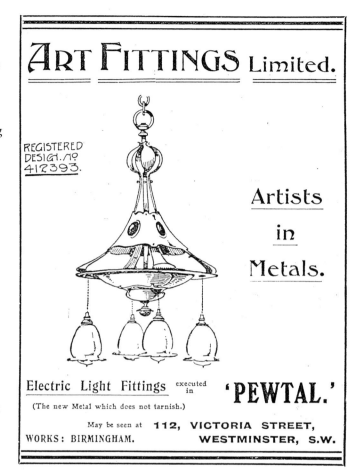

Electric light fittings in new buildings may have been specifically designed and manufactured, or purchased from a number of firms who produced stock items likely to attract the architect's attention.

empoyed as a source of light, gas cookers and heaters were in use by the mid-nineteenth century. It was also used as a fuel for mechanical power, and the provision of gas-fuelled internal combustion engines, which were much cleaner and easier to operate than steam engines, had become very common by 1900, especially for the generation of electricity.

Electricity, as a practical force, had been understood in principle from the days of Faraday early in the nineteenth century, when some of its most important applications had been revealed. However, it was not until the late years of the century that these became practicable or commercially viable. The work of Joseph Swan in Great Britain and T. A. Edison in the United States succeeded in producing incandescent electric lamps in glass bulbs by about 1880. The demand for the supply of electric power was as a result of these developments, and received a quick response from the authorities and private capital. The Surrey town of Godalming is credited with the first, if short-lived, public supply in England, using Siemens generators, but the first publicly owned electricity undertaking was established in Bradford some eight years later, in 1889.

Hydraulic power was also popular, and in London an extensive distribution system existed. The London Hydraulic Power Company had no less than 300 kilometres of water pipes beneath the streets of the Metropolis, customers using the supply to drive industrial machines and elevators.

Water supply for drinking and sanitary applications was readily available in urban areas by this time, having received an initial boost from the great sanitary reformer Edwin Chadwick earlier in the century, after his struggle to impress upon the authorities the necessity for a clean and reliable source of drinking-water, and a comprehensive system of sewers to remove waste. Only in this way were outbreaks of cholera and typhoid fever avoided amongst the new urban populations which were growing so rapidly at the time. Comprehensive water supply and sewage systems were provided by the burgeoning metropolitan authorities in the last quarter of the century, although London had to wait until 1903 for the establishment of the Metropolitan Water Board.

The need for artificial lighting in the workplace, evident from the onset of industrialisation, became even more vital with the advent of large office buildings in late Victorian times. Gas was inefficient, and it was only in the closing years of Victoria's reign that the incandescent mantle was perfected and brought into general use. By this time, electric light was becoming common, though it was not particularly cheap. Swan's early light bulbs were installed by Sir William Armstrong in his house, 'Cragside', at Rothbury in Northumberland as early as 1880, the power being provided from water-driven turbines; and Richard d'Oyly Carte electrically lit his new Savoy Theatre in London, opened during the first run of *Patience* in 1881, steam engines clattering away outside the theatre to drive the dynamos.

Electricity companies developed to respond to the need, and it is not surprising, therefore, that by 1893 *The Builder* was able to claim that most large buildings were fitted up for electricity. Electra House, a company headquarters building in the City of London designed by Belcher and begun in 1900, had no fewer than 1000 lights and seventeen and a half miles of wiring. Pickenham Hall in Norfolk, modernised by R.Weir Schultz in 1902, had an electric light installation powered by a generating plant in the stable buildings consisting of 'two $13\frac{1}{2}$ hp oil engines driving multipolar dynamos. Current is supplied to 364 lights in houses, stables, etc, and also to a motor driving a pump which supplies water for domestic purposes in the house …'[13] This early lighting was often harsh, and complaints were made about both its quality and the position of fittings. A lady at a dinner party noted that 'the light was focused into the eyes and face of everyone sitting at the table … showing up every wrinkle and line in the face. No one over the age of 18 should be asked to sit beneath such a light.'[14]

Nevertheless, many architects designed special fittings for electric lamps which exploited the aesthetic qualities of the luminous globes of light. Early bulbs were short-lived and inefficent, but during the Edwardian period gas-filled metallic filament lamps became available, and from 1910 the tungsten filament bulb gave a much more intense light. This, together with lowering supply costs and innate convenience, led to the dominance of electricity over gas as a lighting medium. Large buildings with deep-plan areas remote from windows could be used efficiently day and night all the year round, and even the householder of modest means could enjoy a well-illuminated residence.

The convenient supply of electricity also enabled the technology of integrated heating and ventilating systems to reach maturity. The development of principles throughout the nineteenth century has been noted, but systems were not standardised, and the machinery needed to operate and control them was cumbersome, to say the least. By the turn of the century, many manufacturers were offering powerful electric fans for sale to drive forced air installations. These required little maintenance or attention and could be switched on and off remotely. The use of steam engines, or of systems relying on the convectional stack effect to provide circulation of air, was therefore superseded. To some extent, the Victorian obsession with plentiful ventilation remained. Although the miasmatic theory of infection had been discounted, and a full understanding of bacteriological infection was on the way, people were still wary of scourges such as tuberculosis which were rife amongst all classes. Vitiated air had to be removed very efficiently and replaced by warmed fresh air.

The concept of central heating – burning fuel in one place and transferring the heat by a medium such as water or air throughout the building – was well advanced by the turn of the century. In many instances fireplaces were still provided, despite the problems of coping with the delivery of coal in large buildings and the complexities of flues for removing smoke. This may have been for psychological reasons – the comfort and good cheer of the blazing fire – or because the reliability or efficiency of the central heating system was in question. The smoke flue and open fireplace did, after all, provide heating and ventilation combined in a crude way.

New, large buildings, including those afloat, relied upon electric powered circulation systems.

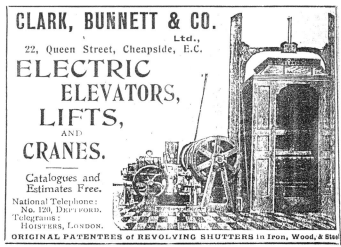

The advent of electric fans meant that forced ventilation became practicable. There was much debate in the earlier years of the period as to the relative merits of the plenum system.

A more modest advertisement for a lift manufacturer, whose product does little to inspire confidence in the modern observer.

More sophisticated versions had been tried, such as in Henry Currey's St Thomas's Hospital, noted by Hardy, where each ward was provided with three open fireplaces. A fifteen-inch smoke tube was provided to the fireplaces, which was surrounded by a cast-iron outer case. Vitiated air was drawn out through the gap between the tubes, which connected with a horizontal duct running above the ceiling, and was exhausted via a vertical shaft. This was heated by the smoke flue from the boiler and subsidiary hot-water coils, in order to rarefy the air and speed up its movement. Fresh air was drawn in through fine tubes laid within the floor construction after it had been passed over hot-water coils in the basement.

That this combination of central heating, open fires and forced ventilation continued into the Edwardian period is testified to by numerous examples. St Paul's Girls' School in Hammersmith, for instance, by one of Norman Shaw's ex-pupils, Gerald Horsley, was heated throughout by a low-pressure hot-water central heating system, but the majority of rooms had open fireplaces as well. Vitiated air was extracted from the rooms occupied by the young ladies via ducts opening into the roof space, whence two powerful 'Blackman' electric fans exhausted it to the exterior. In a large schools complex in Rotten Park, Edgbaston, Birmingham, a similar pattern was followed, except that the heating was by means of atmospheric steam and the 'Nuvacuumette' system. Ventilation was effected by:

St Paul's Girls' School, Brook Green, London, designed by Gerald Horsley. The 'Wrenaissance' exterior gives little hint of the up-to-date electric-powered ventilation system inside.

… two large centrifugal fans, driven by electricity [which] draw the foul air through underground ducts from the various rooms to the fan chamber, and discharge it up the tower into the outer air. Outlets in the rooms are provided in the riser of a step at the back of each room. Fresh air is admitted … by ventilating gratings at the back of the radiators and by opening windows.[15]

The fume cupboards from the chemistry laboratory were exhausted by a separate fan and motor located in the laboratory roof.

An interesting feature of this school was that, despite the use of electricity to drive fan motors, all of the artificial lighting was provided by high-pressure incandescent gas fittings, the gas being compressed by electric power.

Walter Brierley's North Yorkshire County Hall at North-allerton, which was opened in 1906, used fans to force warm air into the council chamber through a plenum system, providing at least six air changes every hour, rather than using fans to extract stale air. The relative merits of the plenum, as opposed to other heating and ventilating systems, had been under discussion for some time. It was cheaper to run than extract systems, and was considered to be particularly useful for buildings such as hospitals. Indeed, it was the use of the notion in the Royal Victoria Hospital in Belfast, designed by Henman and Cooper, completed in 1903, that gave rise to the presentation of papers at the RIBA in 1903 and 1904 and some lively debate. It was especially significant in this case, because the adoption of the method allowed the use of a building form that signalled the end of the pavilion-plan hospital type with cross-ventilation that had been originally recommended by Florence Nightingale.

The influence of services technology over built form is also seen in the case of the lift, as tall buildings became practicable only when high-speed vertical transport was introduced. Lifts had become familiar in Britain from the 1860s in buildings such as hotels, department stores and office blocks. By Edwardian times, they were commonplace. Initially powered by steam engines or, in London, by hydraulic machinery, they were expensive both to install and to run, and accidents were common. Electrically operated lifts, powered from the mains, were provided in buildings in the 1890s and into the Edwardian period, even though their task was to rise through only a few floors – a fraction of what was required of their American counterparts. The Alliance Assurance Building in St James's, London, completed in 1905 by Norman Shaw and Ernest Newton, had offices on the lower floors with flats above. The electric lift machinery was located in a sub-basement, together with the heating apparatus. One of the Otis lift cars rose approximately 18 metres at a rate of 61 metres per minute, could carry half a tonne and was operated from inside the car. Although installed in what was a prestige building, this example does give an idea of the performance possible, and the potential for moving large numbers of workers in city office buildings.

Edwardian buildings, therefore, had ceased to be merely examples of the constructor's art. They incorporated mechanical and power systems, the prime aim of which was to control environmental conditions and communication. It was as though a nervous system was at last integrated into the body of the building.

In discussing these technological advances, it is important to remember the contribution of individuals who devoted their professional lives to the advocacy and improvement of new methods.

John Slater, for instance, had taken a very early interest in the use of electric lighting in buildings, and other architects pursued the integration of modern services systems, particularly in cases where sophisticated methods were desirable, such as hospitals. As reinforced concrete developed and became a material that would inevitably find its way into common usage, so architects like William Dunn, Robert Watson and Charles F. Marsh involved themselves in its testing and application. Dunn translated European documents on the subject, conducted his own experiments with the help of the contractors, Messrs Cubitt, and was author of the RIBA re-

port on reinforced concrete produced in 1907. Others, such as William Bell, chief architect of the North Eastern Railway Company, helped in a pioneering and practical way. Bell used the material in testing circumstances – the large railway goods terminal at Newcastle – and opened up the results for inspection by his fellow professionals.

Of all these useful, worthy, and it must be admitted, rather unglamorous figures, one – Edwin Otto Sachs – stands out as a tireless advocate of new methods. Sachs studied at University College in London, but also at Berlin University. He began to practise in 1892, and quickly developed a special interest in opera houses and theatres. He was joint author of a book on the subject published in 1896, and was consulting architect to the Royal Opera House, Covent Garden. Sachs was interested in the safety aspects of theatre buildings, and was motivated after the Paris Charity Bazaar fire of 1897, in which many lives were lost, to form the British Fire Prevention Committee. He was chairman from its inception, and remained so up to his early death in 1919. The committee set up a testing station which was designed and largely financed by Sachs. Here, experiments into fire-resisting materials were carried out in a pioneering scientific manner. The station was a model for others, some overseas, and Sachs represented England on the International Fire Service Council. He was also a member of a small group who advised the LCC on theatre safety regulations.

This work was in addition to his practice, but is only part of the picture. His research into fire prevention had led him to take an interest in experiments with reinforced concrete, and he promoted the material for architectural purposes. In 1906 he founded the magazine *Concrete and Construction Engineering*, a forum for issues connected with the new technology, and one that reported objectively on its successes and failures. In some respects it aimed to open up the subject in opposition to the near monopoly of specialist patentees like Mouchel.

Following this initiative, the Concrete Institute was formed in 1908. It was largely Sachs' creation, and it existed in order to advance the knowledge of the material and to raise discussion between all those involved in the construction industry.

With all these initiatives, it is surprising that Sachs found time to conduct his practice. Yet he did so, and produced some quite diverse buildings. As might be expected, safety and modern technology were to the forefront in his designs. The three-storey Shannon factory at Dalston, in London, was built in 1902 to house an up-to-the-minute furniture and joinery plant, using American and European practice. The plant was run by electric power, which was provided by dynamos located in an on-site power house. Fire protection was effected by the use of fire-resisting floors installed by the

Columbia Fireproof Flooring Company, and structural columns were surrounded by two inches of concrete cladding. Sprinklers were used throughout. The welfare of the staff was also thoroughly considered, with dust removal, ventilation and heating all worked from machinery in the central boiler house. The basement was devoted entirely to staff mess and changing rooms. In addition, the factory had architectural pretensions, following on from the example set by Aston Webb in his Thames-side silos.

In contrast, Sachs had reorganised and rebuilt Walmer Lodge, in Kent, at about the same time for Mr Albert Ochs. In typical Sachs fashion, electric light was installed throughout, and there were speaking-tubes, telephones and central heating. Fire hydrants were also provided. The building was surmounted by an observation tower some eighty-five feet high, the finial of which was equipped with an electric light and weather vane. Inside the tower was a large gong activated by electricity, to summon those in this remote region to dinner below.

Sachs was obviously a man of energy, commitment and foresight, and his contribution to Edwardian architecture was as great in its own way as that of the acknowledged leaders of the profession.

The development of technology in order to expand the capabilities of built form, and the social and stylistic changes that occurred concurrently are all part of one picture. A more specific investigation of the demand for buildings in Edwardian Britain in the following chapter will set the scene for the second part of the book, where the presentation of a number of examples will provide the opportunity to explore the themes that have been discussed in Part One in a more detailed context.

1. From *The Architectural Notebook of Thomas Hardy*, with an introduction by C. P. J. Beatty, Dorchester, 1966
2. E. E. Viollet-le-Duc, *Entretiens sur l'architecture*, quoted in N. Pevsner, *Some architectural Writers of the nineteenth Century*, Oxford, 1972, p.210
3. Reginald Blomfield, presidential address to the RIBA, 1913
4. W. R. Lethaby, *Philip Webb and his Work*, Oxford, 1935, reissued London, 1979, p.77. This was a letter from Shaw to Lethaby, although the latter seems to have mixed up his dates
5. Patricia Cusack, 'Architects and the reinforced concrete specialist in Britain, 1905-1908', *Journal of the Society of Architectural Historians of Great Britain*, vol.29, 1986, p.183
6. Book review (anon), *Architectural Review*, vol.21, 1907, p.71
7. 'The General Post Office extension', *The Builder*, vol.96, 3 Apr.1909, p.394
8. Cusack, *op.cit.* p.185
9. 'Design for a club façade in ferro concrete', *The Builder*, vol.96, 2 Jan. 1909, p.xx
10. 'Queen Alexandra Sanatorium, Davos, Switzerland', *The Builder*, vol.97, 2 Oct.1909, p.364
11. Jeanne Catherine Lawrence, 'Steel frame architecture versus the London Building Regulations, Selfridges, the Ritz, and American technology', *Construction History*, vol.6, 1990, p.29
12. 'The Royal Automobile Club', *The Builder*, vol.100, Jan.-June 1911, p.511 *et seq*; p.538 *et seq*
13. 'Pickenham Hall', *Architectural Review*, vol.21, Jan.-June 1907, p.102
14. Mrs J. E. H. Gordon, quoted by Janet Marinelli, 'Home lighting 1880-1930: a history of early electrical fixtures', *Old House Journal*, Jan.-Feb. 1989, p.36
15. *Architectural Review*, vol.21, 1907, p.114

Chapter 4
New Buildings
in Edwardian Britain

William Young's War Office in Whitehall helped to establish the use of the English Baroque language for large public buildings around the turn of the century.

Much of architectural history is concerned with religious buildings and with the palaces of the powerful. During the nineteenth century, there was a considerable growth in the types of building which were considered worthy of architectural treatment, and by Edwardian times once humdrum structures were subject to as much design and craft skill as had been reserved for the grandest of edifices in the past. It was the period when the public building, the office block and the medium-sized 'artistic' house increased in significance reflecting the fact that local government, big business and the middle class were where power and wealth now resided.

These circumstances gave rise to a diversity of buildings which still form the background to our everyday lives. Many continue to operate as a testament to their functional and constructional capabilities and to their success as social symbols.

The variety of individuals, companies and public organisations requiring high-quality accommodation around the turn of the century must have been unprecedented. At the time, buildings symbolised permanence, and also gave a public face to otherwise anonymous bodies. It was important that they communicated effectively. In public and commercial buildings

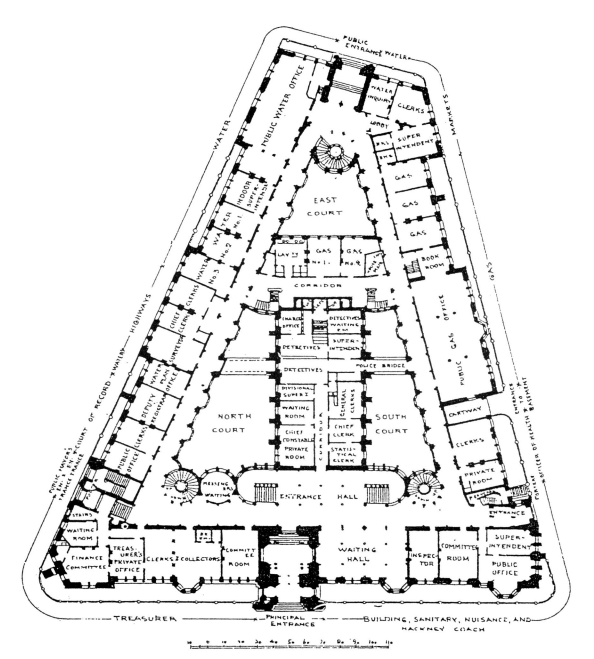

The ground-floor plan of Manchester Town Hall. The central section holds a police station, whilst the surrounding ranges contain offices for public services provided by the corporation, including gas, water, highways and markets, and rooms for council officials.

the message given was one of confidence, sometimes of links with the past, sometimes of taste and elegance, but usually bold and forthright. Indeed, criticisms have been made that Edwardian buildings, particularly at the beginning of the period, were too strident – the architectural equivalent of a radio blaring at full volume.

Although the period opened with the construction of two very important buildings allied to central government – new offices in Great George Street, Westminster, by J. M. Brydon, and William Young's War Office in Whitehall, both of which had been designed before the turn of the century – it was

work initiated by local government that provided some of the widest ranging opportunities for architects. Sometimes this work was funded out of rates; in other cases local authorities provided sponsorship, but funding was received from philanthropic bequests. As a result, a large number of public buildings were constructed for many different purposes.

Much of this municipal enterprise had begun in the last half of the nineteenth century. In Joseph Chamberlain's well-known reforms in Birmingham in the 1870s, the local authority paved and lit the city, opened public parks and provided water and gas services. This was not an isolated example; it

London's County Hall, won in competition by Ralph Knott in 1908. An example of the 'grand manner' in Edwardian architecture, it displays an imposing symmetrical palace façade to the Thames.

reflected efforts that, in some cases, had started even earlier elsewhere. A look at Manchester Town Hall, for instance, won in competition by Alfred Waterhouse in 1868, shows not only how he had to provide great suites of rooms for entertainment so that the burghers of the city could demonstrate their recently found wealth and power, but also a large number of offices for the functions assumed by the council. The building was at once an office block and a municipal palace, expensively carried out in the Gothic Revival style that Waterhouse favoured.

An Act of Parliament in 1888, reorganising local authorities, paved the way for more responsibilities to be assumed by these bodies. Together with the 1894 Local Government Act, which consolidated district boards and committees into rural district and parish councils, this implied that a system of control and administration had at last been resolved in order to cope with the very rapid growth in urban and suburban life that had occurred during the nineteenth century.

The result in terms of building commissions was twofold. First, there had to be proper provision to house the newly created bureaucracies. Many cities had built their town halls earlier, but in most cases the office space was inadequate, and either extensions were made, or completely new buildings were erected. This trend is pinpointed by the rapid growth in the number of clerical workers around 1900. Central government was the largest clerical employer, but there were no fewer than 321,000 persons employed in public administration by 1911. The buildings constructed to fulfil the needs of these administrators had to function as offices and to contain council chambers and suites of committee and entertaining rooms. Architecturally, they had to epitomise local pride and the status and importance that municipal bodies now had in the organisation and control of people's everyday lives. The most famous and spectacular example of this is the new headquarters for the London County Council, begun in 1908, and won in competition by a young architect, Ralph Knott. The LCC occupied a spectacular site on the River Thames, virtually opposite the seat of central government, and having started out with a palatial headquarters in the Baroque style, continued to expand both its responsibilities and the building

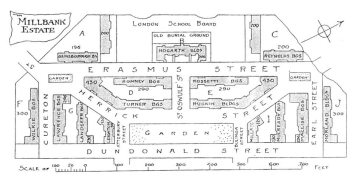

A plan of the Millbank Estate, and a view of one of the blocks showing the plain, brick, gabled style deemed appropriate for this 'housing of the working classes' development.

itself throughout the twentieth century, until its activities were rudely curtailed by higher authority.

County Halls and civic centres were the focus of administration and ceremony, but there was also the need to design buildings for expanded municipal activities. As has been noted, the LCC architects' department had sub-sections dealing with working-class housing, fire stations and general construction, including building types as diverse as technical

schools and electricity generating stations. Such efforts were not confined to the metropolis, however, and the effects of local authorities on architecture, if only in terms of regulations imposed, were soon felt throughout the country.

Local councils had long had powers to raise money from rates for building works. Libraries and museums could be established by utilising a halfpenny rate from 1850, for instance, although the sum was hardly adequate for the running of such facilities, let alone the provision of new buildings. It was not until the last decade of the nineteenth century and the first of the twentieth that a new breed of philanthropist came forward to provide money for capital expenditure. This, coinciding with powers to levy higher rates, ensured that there was an upsurge in the construction of public libraries, a type that is, perhaps, most often associated with building around 1900.

Schools in the provinces, on the other hand, became the responsibility of their local councils after the 1902 Balfour Education Act, which, apart from raising the leaving age, laid down physical conditions to be achieved. Schools were to be built on one level if possible, or two at the most if conditions did not permit. There were to be central halls, and the sexes were to be segregated. Despite this seeming rigidity, many Edwardian schools achieved stylistic and formal interest, and also used new structural and environmental technology to good effect, as in the case of the buildings designed by Edgar Wood and Henry Sellers at Middleton, near Manchester. The same may be said of technical colleges, which were run by local authorities after 1889. Many of these were based on technical schools, established somewhat earlier.

One particular responsibility caused the LCC to establish a completely separate architectural section. This was provision of housing for the poor, brought about by the Housing of the Working Classes Act of 1890. Despite an overall rise in the standard of living, poverty continued to be a critical issue during the Edwardian period, throughout the country. Rowntree's famous social survey of York in 1899 exposed the issue in a systematic way. The shock produced by the poor physical state of recruits for the Boer War did so in a more direct manner. The resulting Committee on the Physical Deterioration of the Nation was set up in 1904 and, once attention had been engaged, other measures followed. A system of health visitors was started, for instance, thanks to the initiatives of a doctor in Huddersfield. Nationally, there was high unemployment, which in cities such as Bradford, in the early years of the century, ran at as much as twenty-five per cent. The situation scarcely improved until 1910. An estimated thirty per cent of London's population lived in poverty.

Although decent housing for the poor had been a concern

ments, but the department store was relatively new. Early examples were operating twenty or thirty years before the turn of the century, and indeed, Harrods was rebuilt from 1900 on, but this scheme grew from an expansion on an existing site. The first purpose-designed department store of a kind that is now familiar in the United Kingdom was Selfridges. It was built by an American businessman who had previously worked for the Marshall Field Company in Chicago, and followed general United States practice in architectural design, management and sales techniques. The very large dimensions of such buildings, which required spacious display and sales areas, with ample room for customers to browse, and extensive storage and administrative areas, began to expand the scale of urban shopping streets. The structural implications of Selfridges have been discussed in Chapter 3.

These great new developments in business and commerce brought subsidiary activities in their wake. Industries rose to service commercial expansion, particularly those connected with communications and power. The telephone became an indispensable instrument in the world of business, and a new building type, the telephone exchange, came into being. Some distinguished examples were designed by Leonard Stokes, president of the RIBA from 1910 to 1912, who had married into a family with connections in the by now considerable telecommunications business. Architectural constraints were imposed by the need to provide a suitable civic presence, whilst accommodating operators and equipment.

Another new variety which exercised some thought, architecturally, was the electricity generating station. Large-scale examples were constructed to provide power to the general consumer, in most cases for lighting; others were built by transport undertakings for electric tramways, and, in the case of London, for underground railways. One architect in particular, C. Stanley Peach, became a specialist in the design of these buildings, and succeeded in making striking architectural statements out of what may be thought to be a prosaic and utilitarian building type. He even read a paper on the subject to the RIBA, reporting that by 1903 upwards of £64,000,000 had been invested in the electricity industry.

Outside the world of business, other changes were occurring in society, though some had to wait until after the transmutations wrought by the First World War before they could reach fruition. Charitable institutions and clubs flourished, particularly those connected with youth, such as the Young Men's Christian Association, the Boys' Brigade, and, later, the Boy Scout movement. Philanthropic gestures produced many interesting buildings, often located in poor areas and dedicated to uplifting the cultural and spiritual lot of the underprivileged. Institutes, art galleries and museums were built,

and the endowment of scores of public libraries by Andrew Carnegie and J. Passmore Edwards was one of the most notable ventures of the period, the background to which is sketched in Chapter 8.

On a grander scale, the National Gallery of British Art was founded in 1897, with money given by the sugar magnate Sir Henry Tate. Later to adopt its founder's name, it was located near the Thames, on the site of the old Millbank Penitentiary, and was to become the home of pictures purchased from the Chantrey Bequest, representing the work of contemporary British artists.

Another great national institution was undergoing expansion at the same time. The foundation stone for the new £800,000 extensions at the South Kensington Museum, designed by Aston Webb, was laid in 1899. Now known as the Victoria and Albert Museum, it was the culminating physical manifestation of the success of the projects set up to stimulate the arts and sciences in the aftermath of The Great Exhibition in 1851. Together with the Natural History Museum, built some years earlier by Waterhouse, and the Science Museum, it forms part of a huge cultural complex which had its origins in education rather than in entertainment.

Although the South Kensington Museums had educational objectives, the opening of so many libraries, galleries and museums on both local and national scales was indicative of the fact that many people had more leisure time than before. The Saturday half-holiday was well established, and between 1889 and 1897 over five hundred establishments had adopted the eight-hour working day, which had been advocated by the Trades Union Congress in the 1890s. Most workers, however, still worked fifty hours or more each week, and more women were now employed, many in the clerical and typewriting jobs created by expanding businesses.

Although wealth was very unevenly distributed, the reasonably well-paid lower-middle class and the skilled working class between them constituted fifty-four per cent of the population. Leisure activities began to flourish. In some parts of the country, such as West Yorkshire, there was a tradition of active music-making, but most pursuits for this sector of the population were passive. Professional football teams, for instance, had begun to appear in the 1880s, but early grounds were crude, with cinder bankings and few proper facilities. The first modern covered stands, with facilities for players and spectators, appeared in Edwardian times, and the name of the Glaswegian engineer-architect Archibald Leitch is associated with the development of the rather austere design using steel trusses that became archetypal. Leitch's early work was in Scotland: Ibrox, Parkhead and Hampden Park were completed by 1903.

A view of the Central Promenade area of Blackpool, 1905. Technical achievements provide a background to Edwardian fun. These include the pier itself, the Tower and the Ferris wheel. An electric tramway was already operating along the front.

The modern sports stadium established itself at the Olympic Games of 1908, which were held at the White City, in London. The stadium was built in conjunction with the Franco-British Exhibition, held the same year. There had been a similar international exhibition in Kelvingrove Park, in Glasgow, in 1901, and such large-scale events seem to have been popular at the time. Extravagant, ornate pavilions, set amongst lakes, were built from prefabricated plaster panels, stuccoed and painted white to resemble stone. They took their cue from the World's Columbian Exposition in Chicago in 1893, where the term 'white city' was coined.

The cinema was also beginning to attract audiences. Early picture houses, though crude by later standards, were recognisable as a type, as distinct from demountable fairground displays, public halls or variety theatres where very early showings of motion pictures took place. In line with the expanding market for this type of entertainment, cinema buildings were constructed not only in city centres, but also in the suburbs. In many respects, the designs of these buildings were derivative, and architectural progress with the new type was not made until the inter-war years.

To escape from the dreary suburbs and inner cities, however, was something that was becoming easier in Edwardian times, at least for a few days every year. Working-class seaside resorts, like Blackpool, were able to flourish, thriving on the carousing of mill workers from the Lancashire cotton towns. To attract the poorer sector of the population a resort had to be within reasonable proximity of the industrial conurbations, to enable the workers to take day trips – a longer stay would often be beyond the pocket. Seaside architecture followed the frivolous tradition begun in Victorian times, but some Edwardian buildings are more refined, and certain towns have a spaciousness and even elegance which seems to have come second- or third-hand from fashionable Continental watering places.

The countryside, too, was beginning to be thought about more generally as a leisure resource. Taking an occasional trip out from the city on the improved public transport networks was feasible for most town and city dwellers, many of whom might just travel to the terminus on the edge of the country to enjoy a walk. To the inhabitants of the Lancashire and Yorkshire mill towns, the Pennines were readily at hand; Birmingham had Clent and the Lickey Hills; things were rather more difficult for the Londoner, yet there was escape downriver. Undoubtedly, though, the advent of the safety bicycle was one of the major factors in promoting not only healthy, open-air country pursuits, but also social liberation, as it was acceptable for both men and women to cycle. Perhaps they would ride out to see some of the countryside saved from development or decay by the National Trust, which was newly established in 1895.

A nostalgic yearning for the countryside has long been part of the English character. Unfortunately, in Edwardian times, agriculture was suffering from a period of financial depression, and a large proportion of the rural population had been lost to towns and cities. However, the middle classes were keen to commune with nature, and a number of beautifully designed, smallish, comfortable houses in the country, in the suburbs of market towns, or just on the edges of cities, were built for wealthy professionals, sophisticated business folk and unostentatious gentry. Quite often they were quiet, reserved places, perhaps in a vernacular or cottagey style, built with local materials or techniques. Some were neo-Georgian: plain, red-brick houses with white sash windows and a leaded hood or portico over the front door. To one side there would be a courtyard hidden behind a wall with servants' quarters, stables, generator room and motor house grouped around it. Although the architecture may have given messages about a simple, pre-industrial existence, modern facilities were usually available, and comfort was high on the list of requirements for most clients of country-house architects.

The opportunity to enjoy the amenities of the countryside in daily life, however – the chance to see vegetation, the freedom to look out at a landscape not confined by narrow streets of mean houses, with nothing but the same beyond – must have seemed an increasingly remote prospect to most city-bound Edwardians. As towns and cities spread, so the

surrounding countryside was lost. Improvements in public transport and the success of the semi-detached suburb were making encroachments which in some places caused cities to expand until they joined with the suburbs of the next. In London, the extension of the 'tube' lines had encouraged outward growth. The 1900s saw the introduction and rationalisation of motor-bus services in the captial and the provinces. Electric trams were to be found in nearly all urban areas, and little towns grew at stages along some of the commuter rail lines into London. Better conditions were expected for all in Edwardian times, and so any development consumed more space. Furthermore, the middle classes who moved out to the fringes wanted spacious gardens and an illusion of openness, and so the edges of urban settlements were blurred.

Some philanthropic developers had attempted to achieve the housing of mixed populations at a reasonable density in juxtaposition with rurality. Both Lever and Cadbury had tried this in providing model villages – in Lever's case, at Port Sunlight, the houses were solely for his workers; Cadbury's houses at Bournville, in Birmingham, could be rented by anyone. Port Sunlight had been begun in the late 1880s, Bournville in the 1890s, and both underwent considerable development in the Edwardian period. Port Sunlight had more architectural pretensions than Bournville, as Lever was genuinely interested in architecture and town planning, and employed some first-rate designers on his Merseyside village. By and large, though, these two villages and New Earswick, built near York for the Rowntree family, were constructed in a rural, cottagey style with plenty of green space around. Lever felt very strongly that his employees should have access to gardens and allotments in order to provide gentle outdoor activity whilst supplementing the family larder.

Model villages were not a new idea, but the three which represent our period are more concerned with a nostalgic, village-like atmosphere than Victorian examples, such as Saltaire. This liking for a pre-industrial 'golden age' is part of the late-nineteenth-century idealistic view of the countryside fostered by writers and critics such as Ruskin and Morris.

Many of these aspirations were intended to be realised in the efforts of the Garden Cities movement, the chief inspiration for which was Ebenezer Howard, who had set out his ideas in a book, *Tomorrow*, published in 1898, and reprinted in 1902 as *Garden Cities of Tomorrow*. The first Garden City Company was set up in 1903, and land was acquired in Hertfordshire for the building of what is now Letchworth. Howard's ideas were diagrammatic, but proposed broad avenues, parkland and the zoning of activities. The industrial zone, for instance, was to be adjacent to the railway line on the periphery of the city. Most importantly, garden cities were to have

Cottages at Port Sunlight. These are in a Tudor-ish, half-timbered style, familiar to Cheshire folk. Many other designs were incorporated into the village over the years, and first-rate architects were employed.

inviolable areas of countryside surrounding them. Howard's diagram could not be translated directly into urban space, and a competition was held for a realistic plan for Letchworth, which was won by the architects Parker and Unwin, who had been involved in the design of Rowntree's New Earswick. The architects set a pattern of cottagey houses and village-like developments within the overall structure of their scheme, but it was unfortunately diluted and compromised as the town grew.

By 1911, Lawrence Weaver could say, 'There is a lot of very poor building at this first Garden City. The impression that anyone has been allowed to put anything anywhere is the first to be received.'[1] This was hardly Unwin's fault, however, and he was also responsible for the layout of Hampstead Garden Suburb, begun in 1907. The 'suburb' was to contain cottages for workers at cheap rents, but the aim was to accommodate a mixture of society, living as a community and surrounded by

nature. Social and leisure facilities were provided, together with residences for groups such as single women, all within a 'village' context.

Perhaps Letchworth and Hampstead Garden Suburb were idealistic projects that never stood much chance of complete success, yet like so much else that was done in the Edwardian era, in one way or another, their influence helped to shape developments later in the century.

It would be easy to oversimplify, and to discuss Edwardian architecture as two separate strands. On the one hand, there was the cottagey, cosy, vernacular style appropriate for the country or leafy suburbs, practised by architects working for clients whose ideas were philanthropic or 'progressive'. On the other hand, there was the architecture of burgeoning business and municipal authorities: big in scale, confident, expressing the ethics of new organisations, using a traditionalist language, often based on the English Baroque of the late seventeenth century. There are many variations on these themes, though, and a number of architects could produce convincing buildings in either style, depending upon circumstance.

Certainly, the Edwardian architect was extremely fortunate professionally, and the need for many new buildings in a variety of different types must have provided stimulating challenges. At the same time, the availability of new technology allowed for greater flexibility in the construction and servicing of buildings. A big scale was possible, where appropriate, as well as the opportunity to open up internal spaces, creating Baroque swagger both externally and internally.

In many cases, architects continued to make technology strictly subservient to stylistic intention. As the convenience of the steel frame became more obvious, however, the regularity of the structure tended to determine a rectilinear architecture of repeating bays. This, combined with the advent of Beaux Arts education, the fashion for things French and American and the futility of designing elaborate stone overcoats for steel and reinforced concrete structures, led to a simplifying of style and detail, and the increasing importance of outline and mass. The stripped Classicism of traditionalist architecture in the inter-war years had been born in Edwardian times. The Corbusian notion of 'great primary forms' and 'the masterly, correct and magnificent play of masses brought together in light' was close at hand.

The picture is fascinating and complex, and a review of some examples may help to give a better understanding of the whole.

1. Lawrence Weaver (ed), *Small Country Houses of Today*, London, 1911, p.56

Part Two
Introduction

The first part of this book explores the nature of Edwardian architecture. The second part goes on to illuminate some of the issues raised by the study of specific examples.

It seemed necessary to organise these examples into suitable sections, yet such categorisation can often lead to a dry, academic format which is of little interest to the general reader, and is not full enough for the academic. Division into building types might have been the easiest option, yet it would not have responded clearly to the ideas expressed in the first section. Division into stylistic categories would have been difficult because many Edwardian architects used a variety of styles – and, in any case, style does not provide a comprehensive clue to the fundamental nature of the buildings. A chronological treatment would have been unsuitable, for in the relatively brief Edwardian period there are no distinct divisions between one type of design and another.

It was therefore decided to discuss the buildings with reference to the themes arising out of the studies in the first part of the book, and generated by the examples themselves. Particular qualities which tend to mark out Edwardian buildings from those of other periods inform these themes, and the examples selected are types that seem especially representative: exuberant, palatial buildings constructed for civic and commercial enterprise, for instance, using expensive materials and involving the contributions of hosts of artists and craftsmen; municipal buildings associated with culture and care in the community, such as libraries, police and fire stations, public baths and institutions of further and higher education. These buildings are often identified by members of the public as the most significant features of their towns.

Two other themes are examined. The first concerns the ways in which increasingly complex functional programmes determined built form, generating some fascinating and unusual examples. The second theme takes the notion of the artistic house, symptomatic of the most widely known architectural occurrence around the turn of the century: the English domestic revival.

In deciding these themes, many important examples were neglected. Ecclesiastical buildings have been important in all periods, and would tend to occupy a large portion of a book dealing, say, with Victorian architecture. Yet, despite Bentley's Westminster Cathedral, and the young Giles Gilbert Scott's sensational late Gothic Revival Anglican Cathedral at Liverpool – two great Edwardian buildings – the emphasis has been placed elsewhere. Such is the richness and fecundity of Edwardian architectural invention that there are many other themes worthy of inclusion, but the amount of space available dictates the choice of those which are felt to be most representative.

Chapter 5
Civic Splendour

As has been noted in the first part of the book, major Edwardian civic buildings tend to exemplify the pride taken in themselves by the great municipalities. In the industrial areas of the country these towns and cities had grown rapidly during the nineteenth century, and their councils were now reaching maturity as providers of amenities and regulators of activity. New county boroughs had been created in conurbations, and these were joined by county councils which included rural areas. Much of the nation's power and wealth was under the control of these bodies. Councils had every right to be proud of their achievements, which included activity in the fields of culture, health and other forms of social welfare, education, safety, power, transport, sanitation and hygiene. They were also, of course, very large local employers.

This chapter looks at buildings which focus on the higher levels of civic life, and provide a background against which ceremonial can take place. The creation of an appropriate scale and display, and the presence of high-flown allegory to aid the pomp, are characteristics of these buildings. The benefits of the latest technology were necessary to create them without the expenditure of the large amounts of time and money that would have been required for the analogous eighteenth-century nobleman's palace, and to bring about the conditions of comfort expected by the occupants. Public meetings, banquets, recitals and receptions were all to be accommodated in rooms that were well ventilated, well lit and well heated.

The two buildings chosen as examples in this category are not ostensibly of the same type. Cardiff City Hall is part of a civic complex which grew in response to the city's new-found status and its position as the capital of the principality of Wales. It also fulfils a more mundane need as the hub of municipal administration. Although it provides offices for officials, it is also a perfect backdrop to those functions which help to form a sense of civic unity.

The Cartwright Hall in Bradford was originally intended to fulfil some of the same ceremonial functions as Cardiff City Hall, including receptions and the entertainment of important visitors, even though it functioned equally as a museum and art gallery. The scale, language and decoration of this comparatively small building all convey a message about pride in the city. In addition, the devotion of at least part of such a splendid building to the arts, dedicated to improving the aesthetic and spiritual wellbeing of the city's teeming inhabitants, illustrates the priorities of this burgeoning metropolis. Dedicated to a pioneer of the woollen industry on which the city's wealth was founded, and financed by a great mill owner, there could not be a more appropriate symbol of what the city stood for at the time.

The main façade of Cardiff City Hall. The dome in the centre of the composition rises over the council chamber. To the left, across King Edward VII Avenue, can be seen the Law Courts.

At eleven o'clock on Monday, 29 October 1906, Henry Lanchester presented the Marquess of Bute with a golden key, symbolising the opening of the city hall in Cardiff. This ceremony had been preceded by a long procession from the old town hall to the new building in Cathays Park. Taking part were practically any persons of note or position, officers of the council, the fire brigade, the police, the judiciary, a body of students from the university college and the people who had created the building: architects, engineers, quantity surveyors, contractors and artists. They marched to the accompaniment of a military band. This pomp and splendour may seem ridiculous to us, at the opposite end of the century, yet it marked a significant event for Cardiff, newly given the status of 'city'.

At the beginning of the nineteenth century, Cardiff was a modest town with a population of below 2000. Within a hundred years, this figure increased one hundredfold. It became the world's greatest coal-exporting port, the chief city of the principality of Wales, and one of the seats of the Marquesses of Bute, who stimulated much of the development. The third Marquess occupied Cardiff Castle, and indulged his medieval fantasies to an extravagant extent, employing William Burges as his architect over a period of sixteen years up to Burges's death in 1881. The fabric of the town was, therefore, essentially nineteenth century, and not notable for its urbane civic quality.

Cathays Park, a large area to the immediate north-west of the centre, belonged to Lord Bute, but was eyed enviously by the corporation during the 1890s as a site for expansion. There was a need to construct a new, large town hall, law courts, technical schools – up until then housed in the library – and accommodation for the university college.

This sweep of parkland would provide the ideal setting for buildings representative of Cardiff's new-found position and importance. Throughout the early years of the decade there were attempts to purchase the park, but the various parties wavered in their intentions. By 1897, however, a provisional agreement had been made and an architectural competition was launched to design both town hall and law courts. Lanchester, Stewart and Rickards won the first prize of £500, out of the fifty-six entries received. In late 1898, the fifty-nine acres of land finally passed into the corporation's possession. It proved to be an excellent purchase, for it eventually provided a setting not only for the buildings envisaged by the council, but also for Glamorgan County Hall and the National Museum of Wales. These large edifices of Portland stone, set amongst abundant greenery, give Cardiff the kind of grandeur – in some ways like a miniature Washington – which enhances its international position.

Lanchester, Stewart and Rickards succeeded in the competition with buildings which show a breadth of outlook in the 'grand manner'. They were able to establish a formal layout by responding to a requirement which stated that the city hall had to be positioned to the east side of what was to become King Edward VII Avenue, and the law courts to the west. This avenue, in fact, was constructed between lines of elm trees running north-west to south-east which had been planted by Lord Bute and which had to be preserved. This formed the basis for further development, and later another avenue was built to the east of the city hall, separating it from the Welsh National Museum. The south façade of the city hall therefore forms the centrepiece of a large composition.

Despite this grand concept, Lanchester complained of a restrictive approach by the council. There was a great deal of accommodation to be provided, and in order to allow this to function properly within the cost limits stated, the breadth of architectural treatment allowed in the United States or France was not possible. Nothing could be done simply for architectural effect, and every space had to fulfil a specific, prosaic purpose.

The architects were, however, equal to the task of rational, functional planning. The city hall contained spaces associated with civic ceremony and public activities. It also provided office accommodation for the many duties that the municipality had to perform. The court building housed magistrates' courts, assize courts and ancillary accommodation, as well as the 'A' Division police station.

Essentially, the city hall is symmetrical and consists of ranges of two-storey buildings surrounding a huge quadrangle, split into two by the assembly hall. The court to the south is sub-divided by the entrance hall. From the centre of the west range, a clock tower some fifty-nine metres high rises, forming a powerful landmark visible from afar. The ground floor is given over mainly to the prosaic business of council offices. Originally it accommodated the borough engineer's domain, and that of the medical officer of health. At the hub, beneath the assembly hall, was, appropriately, the rates office.

At first-floor level, the perimeter rooms are again largely council offices, but along the south front are located the Mayor's parlour, various committee rooms and, in the centre, the council chamber itself. On both floors, the perimeter ranges consist of single rooms on the outer face of the building, giving views to the city or to the other civic centre buildings, with a corridor running around, facing into the inner courtyards. It is a simple and convenient way of organising the building, particularly as a large-scale, palatial effect was required within the context of the park.

Credit has been given to Rickards for the design, yet the planning seems exactly the kind of rational exercise that Lanchester would have produced. In addition, Lanchester credited his late partner, James S. Stewart, 'who shared all the labour in the original design'.[1] There is certainly much of Rickards' Baroque swagger about the building, in outline and detail, but a scheme on this scale, containing so much design detail as well as strategic planning, must have been a combined effort.

Constructionally, expediency seems to have ruled the day. The external skin of the building is traditional ashlar Portland stone, with joints so fine they are almost impossible to see. The floors, however, are supported on steel stanchions, with steel joists spanning between, embedded in concrete. This heavyweight construction, designed to carry the high loadings generated by office accommodation and the assembly hall, also had the advantage that it was fire-resisting. The surrounding of rolled-steel joists by concrete was a fairly typical, if rather cumbersome, practice at the time, designed to reduce the effects of conflagration. Some of the roofs to the building, including that of the dome over the council chamber, were framed in timber. Where this occurred, steel and concrete 'fireproof' ceilings were positioned beneath.

The large span roofs over the major public spaces – the assembly room and the ante-hall – were of lighter-weight steel construction. Trusses fabricated from steel sections supported the roof covering these spaces, and hanging from them were angles to which was attached a surface of expanded metal.

Interior of the ante hall – now known as the 'marble hall' – the sumptuous space acting as the first-floor landing, which separates the assembly hall from the council chamber.

Bankart's rich ceilings, discussed later, were plastered on to this assemblage. This kind of disguise flies in the face of Pugin's doctrines of honesty in construction, and those of twentieth-century functionalists, also. However, the citizens of Cardiff have obviously found it more civilised to sit beneath a handsome curved ceiling, at numerous banquets held over many decades, than to worry about the constructional morality of doing so.

As in most buildings of this period – construction was started after 1900 – a full range of building services was provided, including electric cables for the supply of lighting fixtures, and telephone wires. Ducts were run under the main corridors to contain these as well as water and heating services, although their primary purpose was for input of warm air and extract of vitiated air, as part of an air-handling scheme. The plenum system, however, does not appear to have been used. Thus, circulation of services was combined with that of people, and incorporated into the sensible plan. A sunken boiler house to the inner side of the courtyard to the north range provided the steam and housed machinery necessary for these systems, and also served the law court building across the avenue.

The chief interest of this building, though, lies in its attempts to provide an appropriate symbol and setting, rather than in its up-to-date, if unexceptional, technical virtues. Externally, much sculpture is displayed, particularly on the south façade, facing the city centre. Needless to say, the work is largely allegorical. The corner pavilions which terminate the main façades support sculpture groups representing such

Interior of the assembly hall, showing Bankart's elaborate decoration of the curved ceiling, dividing it into three bays, each with its own enormous electrolier.

subjects as 'Welsh Unity and Patriotism', and 'Poetry and Music', by Henry Poole, Paul Montford and D. McGill. At the centre of the composition is the council chamber, with its large, arched window and dome above. Below is the entrance hall, and in front the heavily modelled porte cochere. On top of the dome is a ferocious Welsh dragon, cast in lead from the designs of H. C. Fehr, who also designed the figures on the angles of the clock tower representing the four winds and other features. Flanking a tablet above the council chamber window and in front of the drum of the dome are two sculpture groups by Montford and Poole representing the rivers associated with Cardiff.

Further modelling decorates parts of the façade, and this, combined with the sculpture and the rustication of stonework on the end and centre pavilions, gives a vigorous feel to what is, after all, an elevation consisting of a ribbon of stonework formed by a series of repetitive bays. This observation is fully brought home when examining the other three façades of the building.

The major ceremonial areas, internally, are also richly treated. Together, the council chamber, ante-hall and assembly hall form a sequence of related spaces which are sumptuously decorated. Progression from the ground floor is via a pair of staircases located to either side of a central axis. After turning through a right angle, they rise through a well to the ante-hall above. This is now known as the 'marble hall', and it is delineated by paired monolithic columns of orange-tinged sienna marble, set upon a marble floor. The columns have bronze bases and capitals. Door-cases are also marble. Guarding the stairwells are elaborate bronze balustrades, and the space is lit by tall, arched windows containing stained-glass coats of arms.

First-floor plan of the City Hall, showing the principal public and ceremonial spaces. On the ground floor, immediately below the assembly hall, at the hub of the composition, is, appropriately, the rates office.

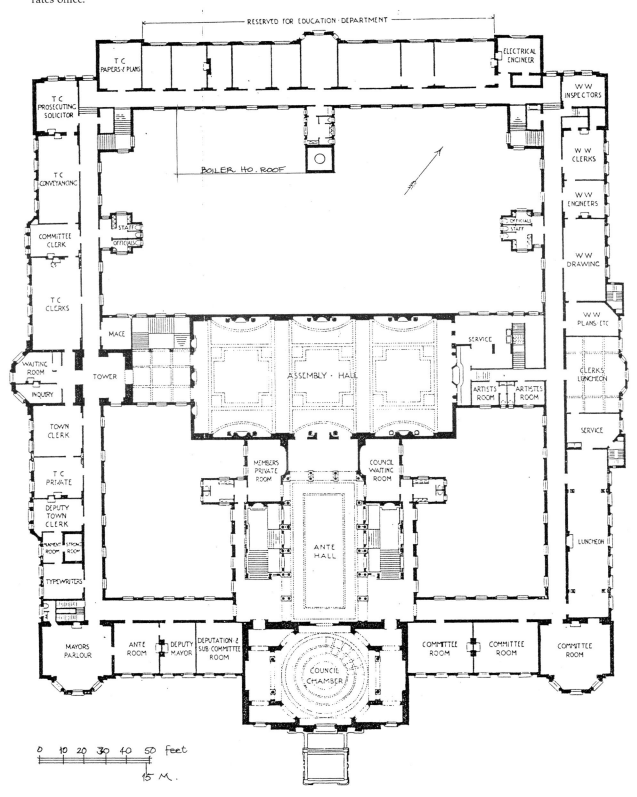

To the sides of sculpture niches over the stairs, and over the council chamber door, are scallop shells flanked by large, playful mermaids, modelled in plaster, whose tails curl down the walls. These delightful features lighten the mood and reduce any feeling of pomposity.

The marble hall gives access to the oak-panelled council chamber, lit from above by circular windows in the drum of the dome. The seating is laid out in a radial pattern, the mayor's chair being elevated and set between marble columns.

The opposite end of the marble hall leads to the assembly hall, capable of seating 800 for concerts, or of accommodating tables for ceremonial banquets. The axis of this room is at right angles to the marble hall. Its wall surfaces are arranged as three bays, each of which contains a pair of Ionic columns, canted at an angle to the wall, supporting a cornice and enclosing a niche. Above the cornice, a window is cut back into the vaulted ceiling, flanked by giant Mannerist scrolls. To mark out the bays, great bands of plasterwork rise across the vault of the ceiling, decorated by G. P. Bankart in a 'Wren-aissance' manner, and from the centre of each hangs a huge electrolier weighing over a ton. These can be lowered, as required, by a system of pulleys.

A full description of these interiors would consume many pages. Suffice it to say that they achieve richness without too much cloying detail, and alleviate oppressive grandeur with joyous invention and elaboration.

Throughout, the architects worked not only with sculptors but also with artists and craftsmen. Bankart's name has been mentioned, as has Poole's, who did interior wall decoration. Messrs J. W. Singer, staunch allies of Edwardian architects, cast the dragon on the dome and the intricate bronze balusters. They also manufactured the wrought-iron entrance gates and the bronzed wrought-iron electroliers in the assembly hall. Vietch and Fenn made the rest of the light fittings, and also a bronze crown which was to be suspended over the Mayor's chair.

Although Lanchester complained at the financial and planning constraints imposed on the building, allowance seems to have been made for these works of art and craft. Fortunately, Messrs E. Turner and Sons were first-rate general contractors, who, as we have seen in Chapter 1, brought a large amount of advanced electric and steam-powered equipment on to the site, and the architects' intentions were well realised. The contract figure accepted in September 1900 was £129,708 for the city hall, and £96,583 for the law courts. The electroliers in the assembly hall cost £200 each, and the bronze balustrades to the marble hall £960. Thus a high proportion of the cost was expended upon embellishments to the three main public areas, whilst elsewhere finishes were plain. Neverthe-

less, a luxurious affect was achieved, and it must be remembered that Manchester Town Hall, built two decades before, cost four times as much.

Cardiff was thus presented with a splendid, functional city hall. Even today, it is used in the way which was originally intended. It represents a particularly successful effort on behalf of the architects to combine a palatial scale and manner with constraints of cost and function. Questions may be asked about the suitability of the style adopted: would it look more at home on the Ringstrasse in Vienna? The architects certainly leaned towards a south German Baroque, which probably has to do with Rickards' preferences rather than any notions of contextual suitability. However, the city of Cardiff, itself, was not built in a homogeneous style, and the buildings were sited in extensive parkland.

It is strange to realise that Burges's Gothic Revival work was still continuing at Cardiff Castle only a few years before the competition was held. Here, in the city hall, is a complete change of mood. Doubtless the 'dishonesty' of much of the construction would have horrified Gothic Revivalists. No doubt Lanchester, Stewart and Rickards would have responded that architecture forms a setting for life rather than a demonstration of structural principles. However, what was acceptable stylistically began in turn, almost as soon as the building was completed, to change. Although Lanchester, Stewart and Rickards' work set the scene for a grand manner of large, urbane buildings, it very quickly began to look old fashioned and idiosyncratic itself. Thus, when in 1910, the competition for the new Welsh National Museum was judged, Lanchester and Rickards did not get the opportunity to build the third building in the sequence started by the law courts and city hall, and the prize went to Smith and Brewer. Glamorgan County Hall, also in the park, was designed by the rising star, E. Vincent Harris, and opened in 1912. In both cases, the contractor was Messrs E. Turner and Sons.

Lanchester, Stewart and Rickards

The way to success for any new architectural practice around the turn of the century was to win a major competition. This is exactly what happened when Henry V. Lanchester invited two ex-colleagues from the firm of George Sherrin to join him in 1896 in the business which he had been running for two years. Very soon they had carried off the first prize for the design of new civic buildings in Cardiff, in a competition judged by Alfred Waterhouse. Although it is known that due regard was given by the architects to Waterhouse's prejudices in terms of the spatial organisation of complex buildings, this can only have been for the best. The style and form of the building were certainly particular to the designers, though, displaying not a hint of the assessor's preference for red brick, terracotta and the Gothic Revival. In fact, the appearance of the building gave added stimulus to the development of Edwardian Baroque in general, and to the subsequent work of Lanchester and his partner, Edwin A. Rickards, in particular.

At first, there were three partners. James Stewart was involved in the design of the Cardiff buildings, but gave up practice in 1901 and died within a year or two, before the buildings were completed. Although he had won prestigious prizes as a student, Stewart is usually depicted as a canny Scot with his feet firmly planted on the rock of practicality. However lamentable his early death, it does not seem to have affected the quality of Lanchester and Rickards' output. In architectural terms, the two remaining partners were complementary, one devoted to the development of large ideas, a person of intellect and invention, the other an intuitive, creative artist of considerable ability.

Henry Lanchester (1863-1953) was the son of an architect. The family was talented, and at least two of his siblings achieved success, his sister as an artist and illustrator, and his brother, F. W. Lanchester, as a motor manufacturer. Lanchester cars were offered for sale from 1901, and were noteworthy for their radical engineering design. The first car has been called 'revolutionary' and 'from an engineering point of view … a masterpiece'.[2] This same spirit pervaded the work of the architect brother. Early in his career he designed a factory for Bovril Ltd (1896) with steel stanchions and reinforced concrete floors. In later years, he extended the factory by cutting through the stanchions, jacking up the concrete roof by three metres and inserting a new floor. The factory remained in production during the process.

Such ingenuity was also applied to the new trend in 'town planning' or urban design. Lanchester became an expert in this field, acting as first external examiner of the new Liverpool University planning course, preparing an independent report for the Government on the site of New Delhi, and producing development plans for many towns in India and the Far East. He helped to found the Town Planning Institute, and was, at one time, its president. In addition, he was professor of architecture at London University, and for a while editor of *The Builder*. After the First World War, he acquired new partners and was successful in competitions for large buildings, such as Leeds University.

It is certain that he chose his partners well. Edwin A. Rickards (1872-1920) was of lower-middle-class, south London origin. He was a brilliant draughtsman, with a natural flair for Baroque details and an intuitive approach to design. His zest for life and his urge to create was part of a fascinating personality, and his success was also aided by the fact that he was a very good conversationalist. So much so, that he rose from the obscurity of a draper's shop to become a friend of the clever and famous, particularly the novelist Arnold Bennett, who wrote Rickards into at least three of his books.

Lanchester and Rickards, then, were ideally suited. They established a kind of Edwardian Baroque that was not easily surpassed for swagger and sumptuousness in the early years of the century. By 1910, though, it was beginning to look rather dated. Rickards died after the Great War, and Lanchester took up with Lucas and Lodge to create big new schemes in the severe stripped Classicism of the inter-war years. He did not die until 1953.

1. 'Cardiff City Hall and Law Courts', *Architectural Review*, vol.20, 1906, p.242
2. D. Scott Moncrieff, *Veteran and Edwardian Motor Cars*, London, 1955, 1961 edn, p.42

the amount of architectural effort and, indeed, material put into it is illustrative of the Cartwright's civic symbolism, and is also a reminder of a time when architecture could command resources as a public art.

The building is symmetrical, with the porte cochere on the central axis of the south front, and an apse-like feature on the north side. This encloses a central sculpture court, rising through two levels. To either side, interconnecting spaces run to terminating pavilions. As originally conceived, the ground-floor galleries contained museum items, and the first floor had top-lit art galleries and reception rooms. The dramatic quality evinced by the exterior is demonstrated internally. The use of columns and arches to support openings, the two-storey sculpture court and the grand staircases all contribute to spatial freedom. There are continuous 'enfilades' – progressions of rooms – down the length of the building. The first floor was designed as much for civic receptions as for the art gallery function, and the panelled east gallery, currently in use for the display of paintings, was originally a banqueting hall. The building is a three-dimensional Baroque experience, not, as in some other cases, an applied façade upon an unrelated carcase.

Externally, a heavy rhythm is imposed by the use of coupled Ionic columns and pilasters which control the large areas of wall above the heavily rusticated basement. At entrance level, windows are grouped between pilasters, but the first floor consists of top-lit galleries and has no windows. The terminal pavilions are enhanced by decorative features above windows and segmental pediments at roof level.

The ceremonial entrance is almost a separate structure in its own right. Looking like parts of Blenheim Palace or Castle Howard that have escaped and fused themselves together, its features include very heavy rustication and huge, exaggerated voussoirs to the entrance arch. Coupled Ionic columns on either side of the arch carry a triangular pediment, broken by a Palladian opening framing the first-floor balcony. High above is a tower comprising a lantern with a cupola. Exuberance, not taste, is the order of the day.

Cartwright Hall was decorated with sculpture and carving, and appropriate allegorical figures were included in the design. Simpson was a member of the Art Workers' Guild, and had worked closely with George Frampton, one of the most important sculptors of Edwardian times, on the Glasgow Gallery. The Bradford sculptor, however, was Abraham M. Broadbent, a local man who had been one of Frampton's assistants. Frampton was particularly busy when Cartwright Hall was being built, and he was made a full member of the Royal Academy in 1902, as well as being Master of the Art Workers' Guild in that year. Moreover, during the period of

construction at Bradford he was producing very innovative work on Collcutt's Lloyd's Registry of Shipping and Belcher's Electra House in London. Broadbent was highly regarded, being employed by many first-rate Edwardian architects, including both Lutyens and Aston Webb.

Broadbent's contribution at Cartwright Hall included six allegorical figures representing the arts, seated next to the first-floor arches of the porte cochere, and four standing figures associated with industrial and commercial enterprise, at the base of the tower. In addition, apart from the usual decorative carving to be found on Baroque buildings, coats of arms of local families were added to the façade to reinforce the civic pedigree. Other artists were also involved with the design and many details such as electric light fittings, and the door plates and handles, were the result of special commissions.

The external impression of Cartwright Hall is one of a huge mass of local stone, in some places looking rough-hewn, in others carved into sophisticated sculpture and decoration. Indeed, in places the external walls reached a thickness of 7 feet 9 inches (2.36 metres).

Internally, expensive marble and hardwoods provided finishes to floors and walls. Steel was used to enable the internal spans and to provide the load-bearing structural qualities needed to open up the interior space. Fabricated steel roof trusses were used over the galleries. The floors themselves were of 'fireproof' construction, with concrete covering and filling between steel joists. Despite the use of steel and concrete, the building was not organised on a systematised and rational basis, as it might have been ten years later. The new materials, however, allowed the architect to enlarge and open out a plan that might have been impossible in traditional construction.

Heating and ventilation were provided in the building by the use of warm-air ducts built into the structure. Fresh air was drawn in from roof level and taken down to the sub-basement by means of a shaft running next to the main public staircase to the west of the sculpture court. Here it was drawn through a screen before being passed over banks of steam radiators supplied by two boilers. A fan then propelled it through horizontal ducting running to all parts of the sub-basement at this level and up vertical ducts to the galleries above. The ducts were built into the wall thickness, and air was admitted through surface-mounted grilles.

Although simple in concept, all of this labyrinthine system was executed in builders' work, the height reducing to little over a metre in places. The air-heating chamber was fitted with a door, as was an adjacent fresh-air by-pass. Thus either warm or cold air, or a mixture of the two, could be circulated

The first-floor balcony to the double-height central hall – or sculpture court – seen from the middle landing of the east staircase. A demonstration of spatial inter-penetration.

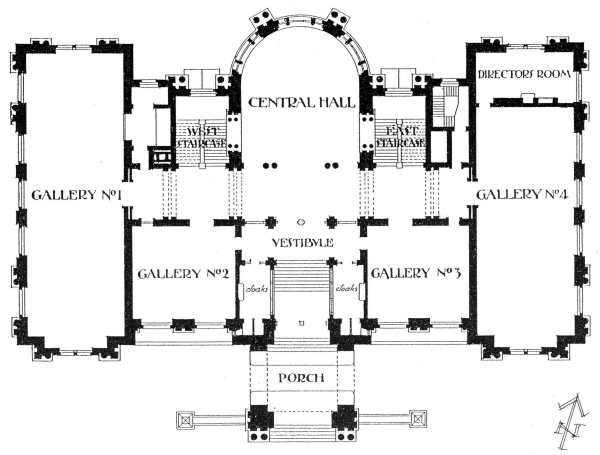

GALLERY Nº1

CENTRAL HALL

WEST STAIRCASE

EAST STAIRCASE

DIRECTORS ROOM

GALLERY Nº4

VESTIBVLE

GALLERY Nº2

cloaks

GALLERY Nº3

cloaks

PORCH

Ground-floor plan of Cartwright Hall, with original disposition of galleries.

by judicious opening and closing of the doors. The flue from the boilers ran up through the building on the opposite side of the sculpture court to the air inlet.

The building process was not without problems. A start was made in 1900, and it was hoped that all would be completed within two years. Unfortunately, it was not ready until the spring of 1904 at a cost of over £70,000 – £15,000 more than the estimate of 1900. First, there had been trouble with the site itself, formerly occupied by Lister's Manningham Hall, and the ground conditions required excavations for the foundations which were much deeper than originally expected. Then, following a severe storm, these extensive excavations were flooded. When, at last, the walls began to rise, there was irregularity in the supply of stone from the local quarries. As if this were not enough, a strike of masons and joiners began in March 1901 and lasted for a year.

Despite these upsets, it was decided to make an occasion of the opening of the hall, and an exhibition was organised, to be attended by the Prince and Princess of Wales. This included all the well-known ingredients of such events, such as displays of the arts and industry, but also popular entertainments and spectacles to ensure financial success. It ran for six months and well over two million people attended. As in the case of Glasgow, profits were used for providing additional exhibits and furnishing the hall.

Thus Cartwright Hall – memorial, civic symbol and public gallery – began its existence. Although modest in size and cost when compared to Glasgow Art Gallery, it was designed to equal the greatest public buildings in scale and pretension. There is no doubt that it has fulfilled its functions admirably in the ninety years since it was completed.

1. Quoted in Derek Linstrum, *West Yorkshire Architects and Architecture*, London, 1978, p.331
2. Giles Waterfield, *Palaces of Art: Art Galleries in Britain, 1790-1990*, London, 1991, p.83

Chapter 6
Palaces of Business

It is perhaps typical of the Edwardian period that the three headquarters buildings chosen to represent this section were constructed not for firms involved in the extractive or manufacturing industries, but for those involved in providing a service to others.

The North Eastern Railway Company grew rich on the goods traffic of Northumberland, Durham and Yorkshire. Its passenger services expanded, also, and it became one of the most profitable and efficient transport organisations in the country. This was at a time when railway companies were real powers in the land, having a virtual monopoly of internal transport and controlling many links by sea. Huge amounts of capital were tied up in railways, and they were amongst the largest employers in the country.

At the peak of its performance, around the turn of the century, the North Eastern Railway Company decided that more office space was required, and that existing accommodation should be rationalised. Its own architect, William Bell, was involved in the design of the new building, but Horace Field, a London practitioner, was brought in as 'consultant'. The resulting building is a highly successful product of this marriage.

The United Kingdom Provident Institution building, by Henry T. Hare, is included somewhat more briefly because, although it no longer exists, it represents the enormous lengths to which both companies and architects went to incorporate the works of artists into their buildings. This undoubtedly increased the prestige of the company, but it was also felt proper that a building of such importance should contain works of leading designers and craftsmen as part of the overall scheme, and not as mere additions and afterthoughts.

The final example comes from the end of the period. Just before the First World War, the Cunard Steam Ship Company commissioned a new building to provide extra office space and accommodation for passengers, and to equal the elegance of their great liners. It was to be sited overlooking the Mersey estuary in Liverpool, and was designed by a local partnership, Willink and Thicknesse, in association with the fashionable London practice of Mewès and Davis. This building summarises the changes that had occurred during the Edwardian period, in terms both of its style and of its technology. Its full reinforced concrete frame is clad with a stone overcoat, and it is severely Beaux Arts in appearance, with refined but rather dry detail.

The popular image of what a company headquarters should be was formed by buildings such as these. The three studies included here are sufficient to show similarities and differences, but also illustrate changes in design philosophy that occurred between the beginning and the end of the period.

The North Eastern Railway Company Headquarters, York

Railway businesses in Britain were just past their zenith during the Edwardian period. The first decade of the century represented the closing years of a period of consolidation and refinement, when the railways grew in confidence after the early years of experiment and wild expansion. After the First World War the importance of railway operations as a commercial activity, bringing good returns to private investors, was doomed to a steep decline.

It was a period when the companies still attracted great prestige, and held high importance in the community. Virtually all travel was controlled by them: the railway omnibus to the station; the branch line to the junction; and the main line train to the metropolis or port, from which the railway steamer would convey passengers to France or Ireland. Very large numbers of people worked for the railways, not only in 'railway towns' like Swindon and Crewe. Although the General Post Office was the largest single employer in the Edwardian era, it was followed by the London and North Western Railway Company, and then by many other railway companies. Competition was fierce in many instances, as was shown by the railway races to Scotland in the 1880s and 1890s, between the east and west coast routes.

As may be expected, visual presence – 'image' – was all-important. Trains themselves reached new levels of sophistication. Carriages with subtle liveries and high-quality fittings were pulled by gleaming and beautiful locomotives designed by a generation of artist-engineers such as Johnson, Drummond and Wainwright, who clearly believed that design refinement did not lie in the simple reflection of function. This kind of attention to visual issues permeated most of the railways' activities, and, of course, included buildings.

This is the context within which the new offices for the North Eastern Railway Company were built in York between 1904 and 1906.

The North Eastern Railway was a provincial company. It did not have a line to London, and passengers from York and the north-east of England usually travelled via the Great Northern to King's Cross. It did, however, cover a large and important area of the country, including the borders with Scotland; Newcastle and the industrial areas of the Tyne, Wear and Tees; the port of Hull and part of the West Riding, running as far as Leeds. Much of its traffic was founded upon goods transport, but it promoted and increased passenger traffic from the 1890s onwards.

The company was fortunate in that it had an enlightened general manager, George S. Gibb, at the time. Gibb scrutinised operating practices and company policy, making the NER the leader in railway reform at the turn of the century. Some American methods were introduced, and Gibb recruited

The North Eastern Railway Company Headquarters. The long range, running off to the left, turns the corner into Tanner Row. The staircase tower is surmounted by a gilded weather vane in the form of a North Eastern Railway locomotive.

young management trainees direct from the universities. The company became extremely profitable, and was able to pay a six per cent dividend at times during the first decade of the century. It was the fourth most profitable company in Britain. It also boasted 'the fastest train in the British Empire', which ran at a high average speed between Darlington and York. By 1910, it was noted as 'the most efficient and economically run railroad in England'.[1]

Despite this, the company was severely limited in terms of capital expenditure during the period, though this seems to

Opposite
The terminating block of the North Eastern Railway Company headquarters, facing on to Station Rise. Behind the bays on the first floor
are the board room and its ante-room.

have applied to railways in general. This restriction did not,
however, prevent the construction of the splendid new offices
which formed the headquarters of the operation. The reasons
for its commission were both practical and symbolic. Increased business, and the fact that much of the existing office
space was in temporary or unsuitable accommodation,
rendered the new headquarters practically necessary; company prestige and the need to demonstrate its commitment to
the region rendered it a symbolic necessity.

The company already had, as chief architect, William Bell,
FRIBA. He had worked for the NER for very many years and
had pioneered the use of reinforced concrete construction.
He opened up his goods station at Newcastle-upon-Tyne, for
instance, for reinforced concrete trials in 1905. He was later
mentioned by T. J. Gueritte, a former assistant of Mouchel, as
'one of the eminent British architects and engineers who "by
their open-mindedness" contributed to the spread of reinforced concrete in the first decade [of the century]'.[2]

The design of the new building is sometimes attributed to
Horace Field, yet railway history has it that 'the basic structural design was carried out by William Bell … A consultant,
Horace Field, FRIBA, was employed to design the exterior
embellishments and interior detail.'[3] This must be an over-
simplification. No doubt Bell was approached first, as no
competition was held for the design. He may well have
specified the general layout of the building and the disposition of spaces, and it is highly likely that he was involved in
the provision of ferro-concrete fireproof floors at each storey,
but Field surely did more than design embellishments and
details.

Horace Field (1861-1948) was already a successful architect
in his own right by the turn of the century. The son of an
architect, he was articled first to John Burnet, senior, in Glasgow, and then to Sir Robert Edis in London. Field was an
excellent architectural draughtsman, and contributed to published work, as well as writing his own book, with Michael
Bunney, on seventeenth- and eighteenth-century English
domestic architecture. He was also a member of the Art
Workers' Guild. Up to the time of the NER headquarters, he
had designed mainly houses and small-scale bank buildings.
He worked in the 'Wrenaissance' mode, developing his own
assured version of the style, and his work displays a love of
materials and crafts, so that whilst details have their own
special character, they form part of an overall scheme that is
rich but not vulgar. The details are bold and perhaps exaggerated, but are not riotous.

The precise nature of Field's co-operation with Bell is not
known, but the building has a delightful 'Fieldish' character
which may be seen in the architect's subsequent, though

smaller-scale work, including the London office of the North
Eastern Railway Company in Cowley Street, Westminster.

Essentially, the building in York consists of a long range of
offices with blocks at either end. The long range faces on to a
private road joining Station Rise and Tanner Row, and is
terminated by a block at right angles on Station Rise, and an
angled block at the other end, following the line of Tanner
Row. These offices are served by vaulted corridors behind,
with a staircase in the centre of the range, flanked by accommodation. There are five major office floors, some of which
are located within the roof zone, and a basement. The main
entrance is located halfway along the private road front, projecting slightly and being taken high above eaves level. It is
topped with a segmental pediment, the curved roof of which
runs back into the main pitch.

The block to Station Rise is the main public face of the
building. It has a substantial Norman Shaw-like gable at one
end, where it joins the long range, and one on the centre line
of its major façade. Below are three curved bays, behind which
important rooms, such as the board room, are located. The
Tanner Row block is not treated so directly, because it is at an
obtuse angle to the long range. Articulation is assisted here by
a splendid stair tower at the junction of the two elevations,
which would otherwise crash together in an unseemly
manner.

In total, more than one hundred thousand square feet
(9300 square metres) of space was provided. On the ground
floor were committee rooms and space for the stocks and
shares registrar's department. The board room was located on
the first floor, as were offices for the directors and the general
manager. Apart from these, the freight and passenger departments were accommodated in the building. Internal finishes
were of good quality without being extravagant. The floor to
the entrance hall was finished in Belgian marble, with terazzo
in the corridors and wood block in the offices. The corridors
had vaulted ceilings. Oak panelling in the board room and
elaborate hardwood doorcases, with gold leaf lettering
announcing the designation of the rooms, provided a high-
class but not over-elaborate interior. It is salutary to remember in today's meritocracy that many of the North Eastern
Railway's board members were noblemen, who would have
expected nothing less than the relative luxury evinced by the
first floor.

Environmentally, the building was fairly conventional. An
attempt to keep out the noise of trams rattling up and down
Station Rise was made by using double glazing to windows
facing on to the road. Heating was provided by a low-pressure
hot-water system, but coal-burning fireplaces were located in
all offices, some large spaces having back-to-back central

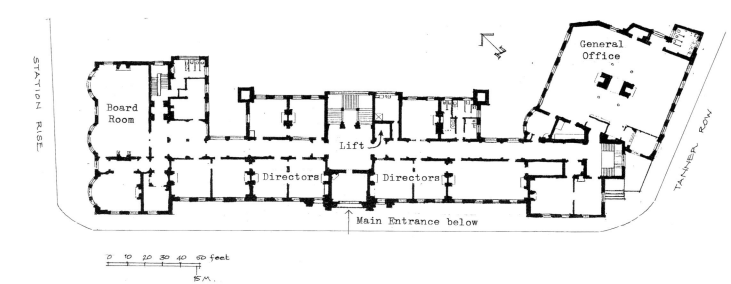

First-floor plan of the NER headquarters. The directors' rooms are served by a long, vaulted corridor, which terminates at the board room.

Below
The company's London branch office in Cowley Street, Westminster. A large scale is brought into a street of quiet terraced houses.

grates and flues. In order to service these, coal porters were employed until a new heating system was installed nearly fifty years after the building was completed. Even so, in winter, those sitting nearest the fires roasted, and those at the windows froze, despite wall-mounted radiators. There were also arguments amongst the clerks in the larger offices over the opening of windows for ventilation. Two pairs of rooms on either side of the central staircase, on the main floors, were ventilated by a forced-air system. To this end, electric fans were located in two towers, which expressed themselves architecturally even though they were located away from the major façades of the building. This system seems to have fallen out of use at some time during the first fifty years of the building's life. The heating and ventilation of the offices represents a somewhat half-hearted attempt at environmental control compared to what was achieved in some other contemporary buildings. Perhaps, as a railway company, the burning of coal was second nature and not something to be discarded lightly.

Externally the construction of the building, which took from 1902 to 1906, was largely of brick – the facings from Sudbury in Suffolk – with quoins, copings, window surrounds and other details in Ancaster and Portland stone under a Westmorland slate roof. Its style is 'Wrenaissance', and follows much of Norman Shaw's work. The use of brickwork with stone banding, and the glazed niches at the summits of the gables, reminiscent of the Classical aedicule, are also to be

found in New Scotland Yard and the White Star building in Liverpool. If anything, the gables most closely resemble that of one of Shaw's large urban houses – 180 Queen's Gate, Kensington, in London. The tall, banded chimneys on their stone plinths also have a Shavian character, and the dormers which run above the cornice in the long range, with their alternate triangular and segmental pediments, are typical 'Wrenaissance' domestic features.

The Baroque Portland stone heaviness of many comparable buildings is missing. Although lacking the tension and drama of Shaw's work, it possesses a rather relaxed, sunny disposition. Domestic details are 'writ large'. This is the key, perhaps, to Field's success. Despite the building's size and its serious commercial purpose, it has charm, and lovingly considered details, as though it were a much smaller, domestic property. Indeed, although Field affected the 'Wrenaissance' style for commercial buildings, he built himself a house at Hook Heath near Woking which, though very carefully designed, has the appearance of a thatched cottage.

Field's buildings are not in any way superficial, and quality and thoroughness of design and construction are evident throughout. Peripheral matters were not neglected either: the railings that were erected in 1907 to replace cast-iron bollards, installed to prevent the private road from becoming a public right of way, are furnished with a 'kissing gate' to let pedestrians through; a weather vane above the cupola to a stair tower was designed in the form of a North Eastern Railway 0-4-4 tank engine.

Field may not have been a great architect, but his work lifts the spirit. In his collaboration with William Bell – dare one say it – he produced one of the best buildings in York.

1. *The Statist*, quoted in R.J. Irving, *The North Eastern Railway Company, 1870-1914: an economic History*, Leicester, 1976, p.46
2. Patricia Cusack, 'Architects and the reinforced concrete specialist in Britain, 1905-1908', *Journal of the Society of Architectural Historians of Great Britain*, vol.29, 1986, p.185
3. Stuart Rankin, *A huge Palace of Business*, York, 1979, p.4

The apogee of lavish Baroque commercial palace architecture, which brought to a head the collaboration between architects and artists begun with Belcher's Institute of Chartered Accountants over fifteen years before, was reached with the United Kingdom Provident Institution headquarters in the Strand. We can view it now only through the medium of contemporary photographs, for it was destroyed in 1961.

Strangely enough, it was designed by Henry T. Hare, who was renowned for his municipal and collegiate buildings. It reflects Hare's fluent, almost facile, creativity. Without the financial constraints of public libraries or civic offices won in competition, it represents a case of not knowing when to stop; of having too much of a good thing. Erected 'to provide offices suitable to the standing of the Institution', as well as 'to meet the needs of its increased business',[1] it must have been one of the grandest of all Edwardian headquarters buildings. Certainly, the style in which it was built could not be taken much further forward, and change was inevitable. A shift in taste was to come, veering towards the austere, in reaction to buildings such as this. Hare's building was not the cause of such a reaction, but was merely symptomatic of the kind of work which must have led to it.

To the modern observer, brought up in an era when ornament was expunged from buildings and is only now, after over seventy years of absence, being timidly reconsidered, it is a phenomenon. Extensive works by fine artists and numerous craftsmen decorated and enhanced both inside and outside. Rich materials were used throughout, and scarcely a surface was devoid of decorative treatment. If it seems loud and vulgar to our eyes, it is because of an over-abundance of delights, not through the pretentious artfulness of the architect, but through his wholly admirable collaboration with artists.

Apart from some lettable space, the building housed a circular general business office fifty feet (15.2 metres) in diameter on the ground floor, with the board room and managing director's suite on the floor above. As the physical manifestations of an anonymous company, these major apartments were treated in a manner calculated to make the maximum impact on customers, shareholders or business rivals. The staircase joining them, together with the entrance hall and upper hall leading to the board room, was equally sumptuous – an ascent through spaces which could scarcely have been bettered in their richness by royal residences, or, indeed, the haunts of ancient Roman nobility. Instead of togas, black frock coats brushed against the *cipollino*-marble-clad walls, and bright, tight boots rather than sandals trod the *piastraccia* of the staircases.

This is a somewhat fanciful description. The architect and the artists working on the design intended the general office

A photograph of the United Kingdom Provident Institution head-
quarters, taken at around the time of its completion. Its scale and
Baroque vigour dominate the adjoining nineteenth-century buildings.
Much of the metropolis was rebuilt to this scale both during the
Edwardian period and in the 1920s.

and major circulation areas to be in the style of the French 'First Empire'. Notwithstanding this, the board room and managing director's room were in the Georgian style. Full-blooded Edwardians like Hare did not care about stylistic consistency or 'honesty'. Like a great ocean liner, the basic fabric of the building was fitted out with interior schemes to provide the appropriate ambience for each activity: a high-quality, durable material – marble – for public and circulation areas; oak panelling and modelled plaster, with painted ceilings, redolent of the English country house, for the directors.

Many different kinds of marble cladding were used for walls and floors, the scheme in the general office being green, purple and white. Ceilings and upper wall surfaces in some areas were covered with mosaic, and column capitals and bases, skirtings, doors and other decorative details were in gilt bronze. The mosaic and bronze works were designed by some of the artists who were employed in the building's decorative scheme.

Externally, the building was unexceptionally finished in Portland stone, two artists being used to elaborate upon Hare's already heavily modelled façade. Henry Poole provided three groups of allegorical figures over the pediments to the ground-floor openings, a sculpture above the first-floor angle window, and two figures on the angle tower. In addition, F. E. E. Schenck designed ten relief panels, occupying spaces between the second-floor windows and the huge, two-storey, attached Ionic columns dividing the façade. Schenck also worked internally, producing the heavy plaster modelling to the border of the board room ceiling.

Internally, J. Dudley Forsyth and Gerald Moira provided designs for the mosaic ceiling and tympanum in the entrance hall. Forsyth also designed a ten-light stained-glass window in the general office, and two windows on the principal staircase. Moira's expertise extended to stained-glass windows in the upper hall and the ceiling painting in the board room. The bronze work throughout was by F. Lynn Jenkins. Chiefly this comprised architectural enrichment of details such as the column capitals. He also designed large panels in the general office that acted as grilles to fresh-air inlets, and radiator frames. Jenkins's main work, however, was a figure frieze around the upper wall level in the general office, between the marble panelling and the 'dome'. It was five feet (1.5 metres) high and divided into seven bays, the eighth being occupied by Forsyth's stained glass.

To add to the richness, there was extensive work by firms of well-known craftsmen. William Aumonier and Son were responsible for the oak panelling and wood carving in the board room, and the Bromsgrove Guild supplied the light-fittings. Hare designed the furniture himself.

Interior of the general office, looking out towards the entrance hall. Some sections of the gilt-bronze allegorical frieze by F. Lynn Jenkins are visible. The fresh-air inlet grilles on the pilasters are also bronze.

Most of the artists' work was of an allegorical nature: figures representing what, one supposes, were the virtues of the United Kingdom Provident Institution, or at least the general ethos of the insurance industry – Prudence, Wisdom, Truth, Industry, and so on, though it is difficult to see where Chastity comes in. Jenkins's seven-bay frieze represented 'Life', not, of course, neglecting Providence – the paying-in and withdrawal of savings. Moira's board-room ceiling is perhaps most pretentious as a subject, if not bathetic –

The great corridor dividing the building at ground-floor level, looking south-east. The Cunard suite of offices is on the right, leading through to Pier Head.

with as much care and attention as they would be aboard ship.

Like contemporary liners, though, all this richness relied upon the latest technology to provide a framework within which it could work. The whole building was constructed around a reinforced concrete frame, built in the Kahn system by the Trussed Steel Concrete Company. Foundations for piers were sunk to the level of the underlying sandstone, requiring an excavation of thirty feet (9.1 metres) to the bottom of the old dock, which formed the site, followed by removal of the underlying boulder clay. The excavations were filled with mass concrete to basement level and the reinforced concrete columns built up from them. These rectangular columns were clad in marble in the ground floor offices. Between them were reinforced concrete beams of sixteen-foot (4.9 metre) span, with coffered concrete laid across. This allowed for floors of eight-inch (203 mm) thickness, giving a span to depth ratio of 1:24. Reinforced concrete was also used to frame up the cornice, which projected at least six feet (1.8 metres) from the face of the building, and which would have required the use of huge blocks of stone if built conventionally.

A sub-basement was located beneath the basement proper, between the mass concrete piers, which reached down to the foundations. To the river front, it had a thick retaining wall, but along the side adjacent to the Goree were stores, a com-

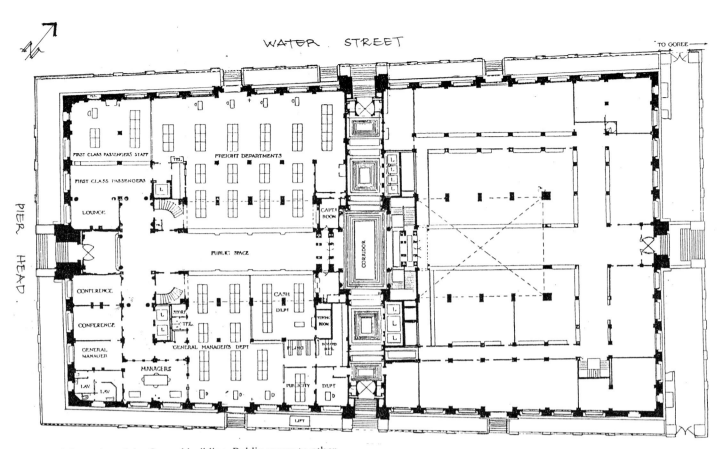

Ground-floor plan of the Cunard building. Public access to other parts of the building is from the central corridor; Cunard had its own lifts and staircases within its office suite.

Section through the building, showing the light wells above the ground-floor office spaces, and the great extent of underground works.

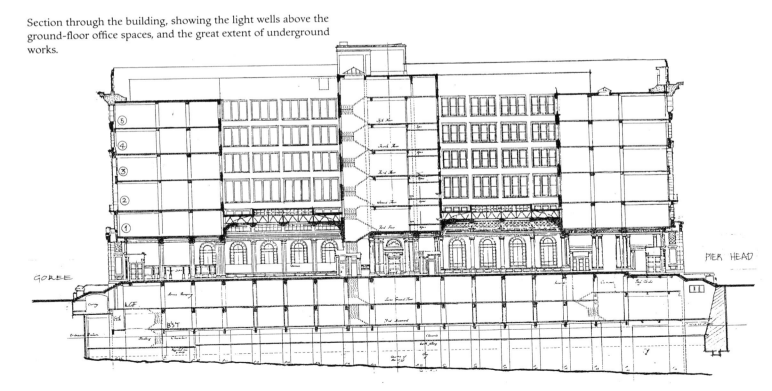

pressor room and, beyond, coke and coal bunkers. There was also a large heating chamber which was twenty feet (6 metres) high and rose through into the basement proper, above. Smoke and gases were carried away from it by a large central chimney, running the whole height of the building and located to one side of the central corridor. The sub-basement also contained sumps to catch flood water, whence it was pumped away.

Modern services were, of course, provided. Although conventional radiators were used for heating throughout most of the building, the major ground floor offices were provided with forced-air heating. Inlet was through grilles located in the frieze above the columns around the perimeter of the glazed roof. The air was admitted from below via the Ionic columns, which were, in fact, hollow vertical ducts decorated with a marble finish. They stand adjacent to the rectangular, structural piers. Fresh air was drawn into the building at basement level, and passed through a water spray filter before being heated and forced through ducts by an electric fan. Stale air was extracted by roof-mounted fans.

Where 'real' fireplaces were installed, smoke was taken by branch ducts to steel risers which were collected on the roof, and exhausted by fans.

Electric lifts were used for vertical circulation. Access to upper floors for the general public was provided by banks of lifts from the main hall. Lifts specifically for Cunard staff, linking to the fifth floor, were located in the general manager's department. In the basement areas, hydraulic goods lifts were used. The electric services in the building, run from a transformer chamber in the basement, used no less than fifteen miles (24 km) of cables, and in addition there was wiring for bells, telephones and clocks.

Construction of the building commenced in mid-1913, and appears to have taken three and a half years. Site record photographs show scaffolding being dismantled and hoardings ready for removal in the closing months of 1916. The building was opened in the following year. There was, of course, considerable excavation work initially, and much was involved in the construction of the basements. The building did not appear above pavement level until May 1914. Once this had been achieved, it grew rapidly, roof level being reached early the following year. The stone cladding was added as the building rose, but could not keep pace with the concrete structure, though even to modern eyes it seems to have progressed very rapidly.

The whole process of building appears to have been highly efficient, especially as much of it occurred during wartime.

Planning of operations took advantage of the form of the building, and the two great light wells illuminating the ground floor offices were occupied by large construction platforms with cranes which extended as work progressed. Its success reflects well on the general contractors, Holland, Hannen and Cubitt, the specialist reinforced concrete contractors, and the host of subcontractors. It demonstrates that by the end of the Edwardian era, those employed in the construction process were thoroughly competent in the production of a building containing elements to be found in most subsequent large-scale twentieth-century structures.

Thus, the Cunard building represents the culminating developments of the Edwardian period.

It is interesting to note the tone of an article in the *Architectural Review* which described the completed work. Published in 1917, it demonstrates many of the preoccupations of the time.

In the first place, it is written as a criticism in a pompous, dry, academic style. This was to be expected owing to the formalisation of architectural education and the need to generate academic credibility by using jargon and professional terminology. It is also mealy-mouthed: 'At certain points the exterior detail indicates a possibly over-generous latitude in control', and 'The projection of a cap, the modelling of a decoration, might have benefited with re-study and it might not'.[2]

One cannot imagine this kind of writing in the heyday of Edwardian exuberance. Indeed, the architecture of ten years before was all now rather *passé*. In praising the building, the author reminds us '… nor does it perpetuate the parochial mannerisms of our Edwardian Renaissance'.[3] Luckily, he notes, the building is on a par with American work, which is much to be admired, partly because American commerce is a patron of architecture on a large and imaginative scale, and partly because there is a body of 'Paris-trained' architects ready to avail themselves of these opportunities.

Our period ends, then, with a rejection of the spontaneity and exuberance that made Edwardian architecture, at least before about 1910, so attractive. In its place, good taste, formalism and academic correctness were to dominate, until replaced by the Modern movement which was, in any case, influenced by the Beaux Arts.

1. *The New Cunard Building*, commemorative programme for the opening, undated (1917?) p.53
2. 'The new Cunard building, Liverpool', *Architectural Review*, May 1917, p.96
3. *ibid* p.97

Chapter 7
Function and Form

Among the themes inherent in the Edwardian period, there is one that is very significant, and although it is not defined by use, it can apply to a number of cases. That is the building complex which is heavily influenced in its form by complicated functional programmes. Some of the issues behind the design of these buildings, and the problems which they had to address, have become associated with later twentieth-century developments, resolvable only through the ideas of the Modern movement. Here, at the beginning of the century, problems were confronted that were to become familiar in the 1950s and 1960s.

The King Edward VII Sanatorium at Midhurst, in Sussex, was a machine for the treatment of patients with consumption. Its operational system was multi-layered, and the type of accommodation required to fulfil different functions was varied. The University of Birmingham, similarly, had to provide a range of purpose-built spaces to respond to the teaching programmes and administration of one of the first 'modern' universities. In addition, in a situation where regular funding was uncertain, provision had to be made for future growth, and for the adequate operation of the complex without a full range of buildings.

How the architects coped with these problems is interesting. They certainly seemed to be able to provide solutions that worked as well as, if not better than, those that could have been produced by a later generation of functionalists. They did, however, find it necessary to incorporate design languages taken from the past in order to humanise their creations. It would have been inconceivable at the time not to do so, unless the buildings in question had come well down the social scale – such as warehouses.

Despite questions that may be raised about the applications of arbitrary styles, the complexes described have functioned adequately for nine decades, and have proved themselves durable and adaptable.

King Edward VII Sanatorium, Midhurst
Photograph from *Architectural Review* (1906), showing the long blocks of patients' rooms facing south across the countryside. The architectural language seems to be a mixture of neo-Tudor and the Arts and Crafts version of farmhouse vernacular. Above all, despite the building's sprawling nature, there is a sense of strong, three-dimensional manipulation, typical of Holden's work.

The King Edward VII Sanatorium, Midhurst

The design of hospital buildings has to respond to complex functional programmes, and these complexities are also to be found in the tuberculosis sanatorium. Here, though on a relatively small scale, they are overlaid by other considerations, some operational and some social, which result in an extremely taxing problem for the architect. On one hand, the form of the building is closely determined by the programme, yet on the other it has to communicate appropriate messages. Neither Edwardian architects nor the general public were prepared to allow a functional programme to speak for itself through architecture. Questions of propriety had to be addressed. Although sanatoria may have been 'machines for curing people', it was certainly not thought proper that they should nakedly represent this fact.

Tuberculosis – or consumption, as it was known when it attacked the lungs – was a scourge throughout the nineteenth century, and was still so in Edwardian times. Exacerbated by poor living conditions, it was, however, no respecter of social status. The disease causes lesions within the lungs which in some cases lead to the consumptive state. This may progress slowly over a long period of time, but is sometimes more active than at others. Advances in the understanding of bacterial infection in the late nineteenth century, particularly the discovery of the tuberculosis bacillus in 1882, gave impetus to tackling the problem through more refined methods of patient care. Tuberculosis could be caught, in the first instance, by ingesting infected food, particularly unpasteurised milk, but it was then transmittable by droplet infection through saliva. This fact informed the design of sanatoria, but as sufferers could be infectious during a latent phase, it weighed heavily on decisions to do with the design of the workplace – particularly the large offices which were becoming common.

As hospital buildings diversified and specialised institutions were set up during the nineteenth century, 'chest' hospitals were established. Ordinary hospitals excluded TB patients, largely because of the long-term nature of the illness. The Royal National Hospital for Consumption and Diseases of the Chest, established at Ventnor on the Isle of Wight in the late 1860s, was designed in a way that foreshadowed later sanatoria. There were ten three- or four-storey blocks containing individual bedrooms, connected by corridor, all disposed along a south-facing coastal site. Patients could enjoy maximum exposure to sea and sun, as well as the cheering nature of the countryside, as opposed to the gloom of an urban hospital.

By Edwardian times, hygiene, cheeriness, and exposure to fresh air and sun had become the keynotes of treatment. As Jeremy Taylor notes in his book on the development of hospital design, quoting E. T. Hall, a well-known hospital architect, the need for the sun's rays to 'permeate every room, cheering, and cleaning, and germ-destroying' was considered essential. 'To this were added the necessary balconies, sunrooms and south facing terraces that gave the [sanatorium] type its distinctive architectural features.'[1] Plans with long ranges of single-aspect rooms, often arranged in 'butterfly' fashion centred on a facilities block, were becoming more and more common as the architectural response to such a regime. Such progress seems to foreshadow modern attitudes to health and illness, and is certainly a step forward from the more grisly aspects of Victorian health care. However, it differs from later practice in a very significant way. Most sanatoria were built for the wealthy. Taylor points out that in a discussion at the Architectural Association a physician noted that the £200,000 spent on the Mount Vernon Consumption Hospital at Northwood, in Middlesex, housing 114 patients, would have been enough to build sanatoria for the whole of London. What was needed, said another speaker, was 'sheds rather than palaces'.[2]

The best-known and probably the most interesting of sanatorium designs was that of the King Edward VII Sanatorium at Midhurst, in Sussex. It was conceived as a direct result of the interest shown by the sovereign himself. Whilst visiting south Germany in 1901, he had examined a sanatorium at Falkenstein, and was impressed enough to promote the idea of constructing a building in Britain to provide facilities which would equal or surpass those in Germany. He gathered around himself an advisory committee of medical men, but also included personal friends like Willie James, from whose home, coincidentally, he opened the doors of the Royal Edward Institute for Tuberculosis at Montreal in 1909 by telegraph, 'completing by the magical aid of science a noble landmark of mercy'.[3]

A competition was announced in 1902 for an essay, with plans, by medical men 'on the construction and working of a sanatorium for 100 beds'.[4] The £500 first prize was awarded to Dr Arthur Latham, who had worked with an architect, William West. The well-known hospital architect H. Percy Adams (1865 - 1930) was then commissioned to design the building. Charles Holden was well established in Adams's practice by this time, having begun his employment in 1899, the year that work started on the Royal Victoria Infirmary at Newcastle. Although he was not made a partner until 1907, it is generally accepted that Holden had considerable influence in the design. Adams was, no doubt, a master of hospital planning, but the building bears the hallmarks of Holden's expertise in the manipulation of form. The stylistic language, also, was drawn from a kind of free Tudor which was evident in the output of the practice after Holden's employment.

A recent photograph of the range of patients' rooms, taken from the south-east.

The prestige of the project was in no doubt. The building was funded by a gift from Sir Ernest Cassell, the millionaire financier friend of King Edward. Willie James presented a billiard table for the medical staff common room, and Sir John Brickwood provided funds for the extraordinary open-air chapel, described later. The King opened the sanatorium on 13 June 1906.

A site of 150 acres (60 hectares) was chosen on the sheltered south-western side of a wooded hill near Midhurst. Located at a height of about 150 metres, and remote from settlement, the whole site was part of a peaceful and undisturbed rural scene. The common land surrounding it, and the woodland, removed even the sights and sounds of farming.

To some extent, activity was self-contained. The water supply, for instance, was obtained from a hygienic source to the north-east of the sanatorium, whence it was pumped to a service reservoir at the highest point of the site, with gravity feed to the buildings. Typical of Edwardian as opposed to Victorian practice, the pumping was effected by machinery connected to two 16 hp oil engines.

Essentially, there were two major blocks, one providing administrative and service accommodation, the other containing the rooms for patients. They were separated by squares of formal garden and linked by a broad, covered concourse, the administration block lying to the north, arranged in a shallow 'U' shape to form an entrance court. To the south, the patients' block comprised a three-storey central section, parallel to the administrative block, with long, two-storey wings, cranked to face south-south-east and south-south-west, on either side.

This 'machine for healing' greeted its guests in the manner of a country house. Holden used an 'Arts and Crafts' Tudor style, breaking what were quite substantial masses of building down into smaller units, and achieving a domestic scale wherever possible. Bracknell red bricks and Luton greys were used for the walls, texture and warmth without stridency being introduced by varying the brick courses and by the introduction of simple patterns. Bath stone dressings around window openings were employed, and at the principal entrance more extensive use was made of the stone, including a large, carved coat of arms over the doorway. Elsewhere, the scale was diminished by the stepping of wall areas, the expression of staircase towers and service areas and the liberal use of stone-mullioned bays. Over all, the great ridge-lines of the roof, though reading strongly, were broken by a variety of brick and tiled gables and dormers. A series of lofty chimney-stacks added vertical emphasis to balance the long horizontals.

As originally constructed, there is nothing in the entrance court to suggest that the prospective patient had not arrived for a house party at the retreat of a wealthy friend. Indeed, the drive of over a mile from the main road through woodland must have heightened the expectation. Nothing in the immediate expression of the architecture says 'institution'.

The impression was not false. This was no façade masking an unpleasantly functional interior, and the design intentions ran throughout the building. It is, however, only part of the picture. Beneath the stone and timber floors were a network of passageways and ducts linking several parts of the long ranges of building. Remote units, like the mortuary and the laundry/engine room, were connected to the main body of the building by subways running to the west and north. Beneath the administration block were basement corridors, and the porters, who had bedrooms and sitting rooms on the lower ground floor of the western side of the building, could gain access to many parts of the complex without having to pass through departments above. The kitchen, itself, had a basement with store rooms and an ice-making machine, and subterranean corridors connecting to the patients' zones. Beneath the patients' block and the connecting concourse were drying and linen rooms. Indeed, the 'country house' sits above a 'below-stairs' world on a grand scale.

Many of the passages were served not only by stairs, but also by electric lifts. The main central patients' building had, for instance, a lift of the latest type with push-button opera-

tion. The whole complex, in fact, made considerable use of electrical power. This was supplied from the laundry and engine room, and cables ran along the connecting subway, together with heating pipes from the boilers. Branches were taken into various zones of the building and were used not only to power lifts, but also to provide electric lighting, of which full use was made, to operate machinery and to enable communication. All patients had electric bells in their individual rooms so that they could summon a nurse. Where patients were confined to bed, a telephone attachment was provided, via the bell system, for talking to the nurse.

Internally, the buildings were a strange mixture between the domestic and the functional. Upon entering, visitors found themselves in a double-height entrance hall of no more than domestic scale, with a gallery running round at first-floor level, enclosed by timber columns and banisters, and lit through the leaded lights of stone-mullioned windows. Nurses, who could gain access to the gallery from their sitting room, could gaze down into the double-height dining hall, adjacent to the entrance. The walls of this space were hygienically lined with Doulton's 'Carrara' ware, although the floor was of York stone. Here, then, the country-house cosiness gave way to a strange hybrid: no panelling, tapestries or carpeted floors, but detail too sophisticated for a conventional institutional dining room. This kind of ambiguity was to be found throughout the building.

To some extent, then, style reflects the social aspirations of the building, but is overcome by hygienic priorities. However, social mores were responsible for basic planning decisions which distance this building from us now more fundamentally than any aspects of style. The patients' building was designed so that both sexual and class segregation was effected. The sexual division is what one might expect at this time, with men and women occupying separate wings to left and right of the centre block. Separate sitting rooms and other facilities were provided, thus duplicating accommodation. Even the chapel was provided with two naves, arranged in a 'V' shape with the point at the altar, women worshipping in one arm of the plan, men in the other. Clearly, it was felt that any preoccupation with the opposite sex diverted energy that was better devoted to getting well.

More surprising is the class distinction, which occurred across a very narrow social range. King Edward had originally intended that the sanatorium should accommodate patients from the impecunious lower-middle classes, such as clergymen, clerks and schoolteachers, who could not afford to go to the Alps to recover. However, his committee's actions seem to have produced a two-tier system, and it is clear that it served the middle and upper-middle classes, who had to pay to re-

The junction of the link block with the patients' block. Here the inflated Arts and Crafts domestic vernacular style is much in evidence. The door beneath the chequerboard panel gives access to the elevated walkway to the communal facilities block.

Ground-floor plan of the entire building. The two major blocks are separated by formal gardens, and joined by a link at basement, ground and first-floor levels.

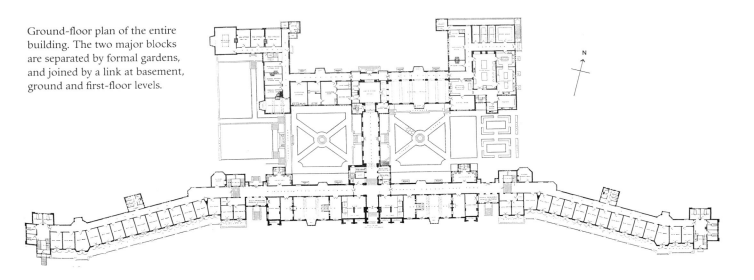

ceive treatment. Class A and Class B patients were provided for, 'the latter class paying higher fees and being rather more luxuriously fed and housed'.[5] However, the planning of the building was organised so that the wealthier patients did not have to recognise those with slightly less money: 'It will be seen that Class B have access to the grounds, the dining-hall, the consulting rooms, and the hydropathic rooms without passing any of the rooms used by Class A.'[6]

Such careful consideration of these criteria indicates the importance of the building as a social organism. Its prime purpose, however, was healing. As much care was put into this as possible, from detail right through to large-scale design. Throughout, the principles of cleanliness, hygiene, and maximum exposure to fresh air and sunshine were used to guide design.

The single-aspect rooms in the patients' block were about the size of a small hotel bedroom, but were made higher than proportional rules would suggest, in order to increase volume. A through-flow of ventilation was made possible by opening hopper windows in the façade, above the doors to the rooms, and the sashes in the corridors behind. Each room was fitted with French windows giving access to south-facing balconies. Canvas awnings were fitted, and shutters supplied, so that windows could be left open and air could flow into the room, even when shelter was required. Within the room, dust traps were eliminated as far as possible. Even the wardrobe had a rounded top, and the wallpaper was washable. Soiled linen and flasks of sputum could be removed and sent to the basement in a separate lift, where the sputum was destroyed by a special steam apparatus. Patients could visit the hydropathy rooms to be sprayed with hot and cold water, by taking either the stairs or the electric lift, secure in the knowledge that they would not run into anyone of a rather lower class, or of the opposite sex.

This careful thought was also extended to include recreation. The roof of the linking concourse between the administration and the patients' blocks could be used as a high-level promenade, overlooking the formal gardens. Even the grounds themselves were part of a healing and recreation process. Laid out and planted in consultation with Gertrude Jekyll, Lutyens' collaborator on some of his best-known country houses, a series of walks was created, 'not only picturesquely arranged and commanding fine views, but of

proper gradients to suit the treatment of patients, so that it will be possible for the medical superintendent to prescribe the right walk with the proper gradient for each degree of lung power.'[7]

Nor was spiritual wholeness neglected. A fine and unconventional chapel was provided. Its aim was to enable fresh air worship. As already noted, the plan consisted of two splayed naves, the 'V' shape opening up to the south, and focusing on an altar at the north end. The sides of the naves which faced onto the inner sides of the 'V' were open to the air, though each had a double row of columns forming a vaulted cloister. This cloister prevented all but rain driven horizontally from entering the building, but one cannot help imagining the misery of the poor consumptives on a dark autumn afternoon attending a chilly and seemingly interminable service.

The novelty inherent in the design of the chapel emphasises the fact that, throughout the scheme, Adams and Holden were willing to espouse functionalism in a way that would satisfy even the most severe and dogmatic of Modern movement architects. The building and its surroundings were truly a 'machine for healing', and the form of the building reflects the function very directly. Hospital designers, faced with the complexities of the operational programme, had, since mid-Victorian times, reflected function in form. The sanatorium, though, goes further than this. It espouses a domestic language, in some ways superimposed upon the basic form, but in other ways an integral part of it. This language, necessary for propriety in Edwardian architecture, makes the building welcoming and friendly. To modern eyes, Arts and Crafts gables and mullioned windows may seem absurd in a building of this type, but part of its function was to deal with the wellbeing of the patients and staff, and one can only assume that this would be enhanced rather than otherwise by signs of home.

1. Jeremy Taylor, *Hospital and Asylum Architecture in England 1840-1914: building for Health Care*, London, 1991, p.28
2. *ibid* p.36
3. Clive Aslet, *The Last Country Houses*, New Haven and London, 1982, p.26
4. 'The King Edward VII Sanatorium', *Architectural Review*, vol.19, Jan.-June 1906, p.278
5. *ibid* p.280
6. *ibid*
7. *ibid* p.278

The façade of the Great Hall and two of its flanking pavilions seen across the semicircular courtyard on the upper plateau level.

'They've swallowed the lot!'[1]

This, allegedly, was Aston Webb's triumphant cry on returning to the office after persuading those responsible for creating a new university for Birmingham to accept his scheme. Although it may sound as though Webb had just pulled off a confidence trick, this was not the case. In the first place, his proposal was unusually radical, particularly for a building type which normally adopted conventional architectural themes. Secondly, Webb, as we have seen, was an exceptional architectural politician and diplomat, a man whose negotiating skills were renowned, and his comment must be seen not only as a result of his pride in the architectural design, but also in the successful conclusion of a process of discussion and persuasion.

Although Webb's design, undertaken in conjunction with his partner Edward Ingress Bell, may have been difficult for traditionalists to swallow, it obviously chimed in with the needs and aspirations of the university. Like most other provincial institutions of higher education which grew during Victorian times, Birmingham did not achieve separate University status until the beginning of the new century. Its origins lay in a science college established by Sir Josiah Mason, an industrialist, who repaid the city of Birmingham for his own success by undertaking this philanthropic project in old age. Mason's College was functioning by 1880, occupying buildings in the city centre. Links were eventually made with the local medical school, which had been in existence since 1825, and together a strong foundation for higher education was laid. It was at first thought that Mason University College might join Liverpool, Manchester and Leeds as a component

Two of the pavilions built in the first phase and the Great Hall, seen from the lower level to the south.

of the Victoria University. Later, it was considered that it might be associated with Bristol and Nottingham in a Midlands Federal University. However, interest was shown by the redoubtable Sir Joseph Chamberlain, whose energy had contributed so much to Birmingham's success, and who was now Colonial Secretary. In 1898 he became president of the college, and seems to have vigorously pursued the notion that it should obtain its own charter and run as an independent institution.

Chamberlain used his influence to persuade the wealthy and famous to support his project. Amongst those contributing large sums to the university fund were Andrew Carnegie and Sir Charles Holcroft, the Black Country industrialist, who eventually provided the £25,000 needed for the construction of the clock tower. Lord Calthorpe gave twenty-five acres (10 hectares) of land at Bournbrook, Edgbaston, as the initial site for new buildings. Aside from these generous donations, a very large amount of money was required to establish and endow chairs, to employ staff and purchase equipment, and to provide specially designed accommodation. Nevertheless, the will to succeed was strong, and it was probably felt that the creation of a powerful identity for the new institution would be achieved by the erection of distinctive buildings. This physical act of faith would no doubt encourage further contributions to the university coffers and act as catalyst for further development.

A charter was granted in May 1900, and in that year work began at Edgbaston, modelling the contours of the sloping site and building a new access road. In 1902, Webb exhibited

drawings for the new buildings at the Royal Academy. Although a complete scheme was shown, it was always intended that the project should be phased, not built all at one time. Clearly, a completely new venture had to grow gradually, and finance had to be found for academic as well as constructional purposes. Webb displayed revised drawings at the Academy in 1907, by which time some of the buildings had been completed and in use for over a year. In 1909 the first phase was declared complete, and a ceremonial opening took place in July, attended by Edward VII and Queen Alexandra.

It was to be another eighteen years, however, before any more work was done to implement Webb's great scheme. Money was tight. Sir Oliver Lodge, the University's first principal, later noted, 'Under the influence of the Chancellor [Joseph Chamberlain] buildings on a great scale were here provided; but to maintain corresponding staff and equipment has been a great burden all through my time of office.' [2]

Before discussing Webb's design, it is interesting to note the type of accommodation desired. Birmingham University grew not from a medieval collegiate body, but from the requirements and priorities of nineteenth-century Britain. Furthermore, it was located in one of the most highly industrialised areas in the world, and its academic ethos reflects this fact. So what was required was 'all the departments necessary for the purpose of a modern university devoted to scientific instruction in many subjects and especially those which have a bearing on the several trades and manufacturers of the Midlands.' [3] Most of what was to be taught would, today, be thought of as technological, vocational and professional sub-

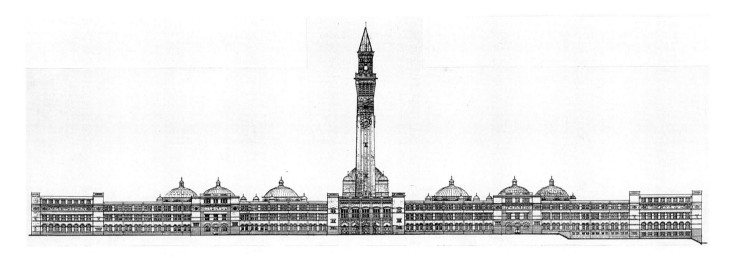

Intended elevation of the buildings, looking along University Road. The range of accommodation to the left of the central gateway, except for the end pavilion, was never built.

jects. These included, amongst others, various branches of engineering, mining, metallurgy, commercial subjects and useful activities such as brewing. There was also a faculty of arts, where more traditional disciplines were taught, but overall one receives a picture of an institution making a break from the conservative Oxbridge notions of higher education, and boldly setting a pattern for study in a modern industrial age. As if to emphasise this, the first principal appointed to run the University, Oliver Lodge, had been professor of physics at Liverpool. He specialised in electrical subjects, and was a pioneer of wireless telegraphy. Birmingham was, therefore, the first thoroughgoing 'red-brick' university, and it is generally maintained that the term itself derives from Webb's unremittingly roseate architecture.

The first thing to be said about the buildings is that they contained academic and administrative accommodation, not student dwellings. The whole was a kind of academic centre, with all the facilities students would need located in one great sweep of buildings. As a plan, in broad terms, this boldness almost verges on naivety.

Lord Calthorpe's twenty-five-acre site sloped fairly steeply from north to south. Interrupting the slope was a semicircular 'plateau', which was chosen as a topographical feature to help generate the plan. Many architects faced with a large, virgin site cast about desperately to find parameters or constraints to act as a clue at the beginning of the design process. Webb and Bell were obviously canny in their choice of the plateau, for from it they developed a semicircular building form related to the upper and lower levels of the landscape.

The architecture thus generated comprised a series of buildings radiating from a central point marked by a tower, with another range of buildings forming, more or less, the bottom chord of the semicircle. In itself, this meant that there was flexibility in phasing the building of accommodation – all the blocks were part of a whole, but could be built when desired. Unfortunately, however, such a shape is focused inwards on itself, and it becomes difficult, architecturally, to add anything which is not part of the original concept.

Preliminary site works established the plateau on two levels, and created University Road, running on the 'diameter' of the semicircular layout and forming the northern boundary to the scheme. To the south of the site, at a lower level, another road was constructed roughly parallel to University Road. This was to provide the main access route for everyday purposes. Students would arrive at the lower level of their teaching blocks and would be able to reach all parts of the complex via a distribution corridor. For ceremonial occasions, University Road was to be used, the centre line of the scheme intersecting the road at a point where a gateway gave access to the courtyard around which the teaching blocks were ranged.

The master plan provided for six blocks to radiate from both sides of a 'great hall'. This was to be given prominent architectural treatment and was to be used for special occasions, such as awards ceremonies and examinations. Proportionally, it was twice as long as it was wide, measuring 150 feet by 75 feet (45.7 × 22.9 metres), and beneath it were located dining rooms and common rooms for staff and students. Because of the fall of the land, it was possible to site

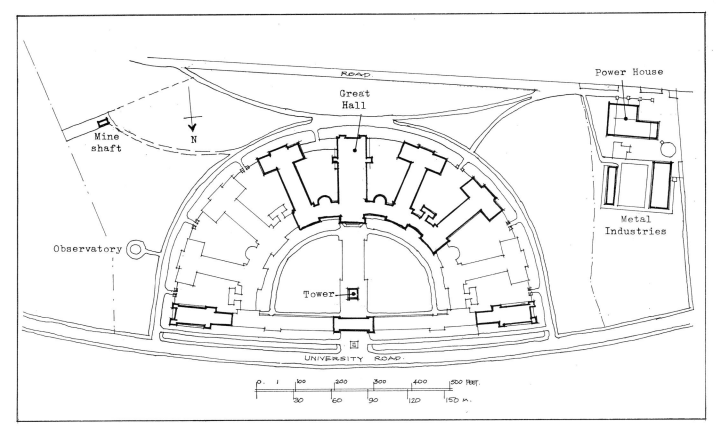

Block plan of Webb's intended development. The buildings with the bold outline were constructed during the first phase.

kitchens below all of this, at ground-floor level on the south side of the complex.

Three specialised teaching blocks were constructed in the first instance, to accommodate instruction in aspects of engineering and electrical science, mining and mineralogy.

These were pavilions, two storeys high, radiating from a central point, which contained laboratories for specialised experiments and demonstrations, areas for testing materials, classrooms, drawing offices, a technical library, research rooms and rooms for staff. At the junction with the semicircular buildings fronting the courtyard on the upper level of the plateau were large lecture rooms. A spacious, vaulted corridor running around on all three levels connecting the pavilions also gave access to secretarial rooms, research rooms and shared spaces, looking on to the courtyard. Above were museums and libraries.

The three-storey range fronting University Road, and linking the two arms of the semicircle, contained, at one end, facilities for the Department of Physics, and at the other, the Chemistry Department. In the middle, a five-arched gateway led into the central court, over which was the university library. Within the courtyard, and positioned at the focus of the axes of the radiating blocks, was a tower, some 327 feet (99.6 metres) high. The size of the whole proposal was enormous, each of the teaching blocks, for instance, running

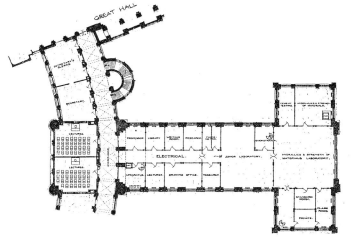

Plan of a typical pavilion. The vaulted corridor runs between pavilions, and also serves administration and lecture rooms facing on to the court. Semicircular staircase 'pods' link different levels.

back for 160 feet (48.8 metres), with a width of 50 feet (15.2 metres). Sadly, the original plan was only partly realised. Only the three blocks and great hall scheduled for the first phase, together with the tower, end pavilions and central gateway, were built to Webb's design. The chemistry block was linked with the gateway in 1927, but the range from the gate to the physics block was never built.

The boldness and confidence of the overall plan and the clarity of thinking which it represents is not really present,

View along the flank of the Great Hall, from the lower level, looking up towards the Chamberlain Tower. The change of level allows substantial accommodation to be incorporated below the hall.

however, in the architectural treatment of the buildings. Webb, as has been argued, was something of a stylistic chameleon, who adopted whatever was fashionable or specifically appropriate to his own ends. In some of his work, if there is a contextual framework, such as at Gonville and Caius College, Cambridge, the resulting design seems consistent and appropriate. Later work, such as the Buckingham Palace façade, may be lifeless, but one feels a controlling hand at work.

Most of Webb's architecture, however, is unsettling – almost anarchic. This is nowhere more apparent than in the Victoria and Albert Museum, where the lack of a convincing design philosophy is only too plain. It is difficult for the observer to fit the main façade into a mental framework, and, despite the vast mass of building, it is curiously unfulfilling, with few of the qualities that mark out first-rate design.

Birmingham University suffers from this, too, though perhaps not to the same extent. Ostensibly, the style is Byzantine, possibly following on from the contemporary success of J. F. Bentley's Westminster Cathedral. Byzantine architecture had also received attention in Lethaby's influential book *Architecture, Mysticism and Myth*, which looked at symbolism in building worldwide. Webb was probably right in thinking that the broad massing of the style fitted in with the morphology of his building. Whether there is a need for the plethora of domes and turrets is another matter. An astylar approach would probably have been quite successful in this building, where, because of the semicircular form, all views contain confusing overlays of shapes.

Having adopted 'Byzantine', Webb was not content to let it speak unaided, and the façade contains large traceried windows, small-paned, metal-framed casements, and areas of decoration which are part of a different architectural language. The clock tower, which is a major landmark, and the focal point of the composition, looks as though it might have been more at home on a Tuscan hilltop, and was based on the Mangia tower in Siena. Visually, however, because of the consistency of the materials – red brick, stone and lead – the disparate elements seem to unify themselves: Hampton Court 'Wrenaissance', Byzantine, Italian Romanesque, Gothic and Tudor, all knit together.

The scheme was executed in bright red facing brick with Darley Dale stone dressings. The steel-framed domes were covered with lead, and sloping roofs slated. Henry Pegram RA, who had previously worked with Collcutt and Blomfield, contributed nine life-size figures to the façade of the Great Hall, representing great artists, philosophers and scientists, of whom, perhaps not surprisingly, five were British. William Frith designed the carving and other decorative work, having been associated with Webb and Bell on the Birmingham Law Courts scheme. Robert Anning Bell, the brother of Webb's partner, added friezes to the first floors of the teaching pavilions, where they front on to the courtyard. These were executed in red and buff ceramic tiles, and show scenes from Midland industry in a stylised, almost Classical way.

Internally, with the exception of the Great Hall, the buildings are rather austere, with plaster finishes. Fairly elaborate oak fittings were allowed in the library, but these have been removed. The Great Hall itself has a vaulted ceiling, with plaster decoration by G. P. Bankart of the Bromsgrove Guild, the coats of arms of the City and the University alternating. The elaborate panelling and woodwork to the platform has been destroyed, but the stained-glass south window remains. Outside the Great Hall, much is made of the entrance hall, with marble floor and columns around the periphery. Above, at first-floor level, is a circular gallery, mirroring the shape of the dome above.

Webb was not particularly interested in the technical means by which he gained his ends, but the buildings do have steel-framed domes and fireproof floors of composite construction using rolled-steel joists and concrete infill. What is, perhaps, more significant is the use to which some of the elements of the scheme were put.

In producing this 'model of a modern university', everything was considered a potential source of instruction. The tower, regarded as a memorial to Chamberlain, was built under a separate contract let to the Waring White Company, whose activities have been noted in Chapters 2 and 3. It rose from a huge concrete foundation ten feet (3 metres) thick, and was surmounted by a belfry. Below was a clock, but beneath this about a hundred feet (30.5 metres) of its height was allowed for materials testing. It was not long, either, before Lodge and his staff had attached a wireless aerial between the tower's pinnacle and one of the teaching pavilions.

Within the pavilions, expensive equipment was located, such as plant for the treatment of ores in the laboratories of the mining and mineralogy department. The power station, to the west of the buildings, with boilers to produce steam for heating and for driving electrical lighting generators, was viewed as a teaching tool, and provision was made for incorporating student facilities. Next to the power station were a gas-producing plant, foundry, smithy and Siemens steel smelting furnace. A six-foot-high subway, ten feet (3 metres) below ground, carried mains services from the power station to the main buildings.

In addition to these elements of practical instruction, a model coal mine was built to the east of the main block. Covering about an acre (0.4 hectare) of the site, it had over a mile (1.6 km) of galleries, allowing for instruction in underground surveying and principles of ventilation and safety.

The splendid provisions of the university, so enthusiastically thought out at the beginning of its life, were increased and improved, though there appear to have been years of financial vicissitude. Little more was added to Webb's scheme after the first phase was completed in 1909. By the time the university was ready to build again in earnest it was profoundly unfashionable. Nevertheless, a post-war expansion scheme shows new buildings in a formal layout planned around the great central axis of Webb's design. The new library responded to this. However, in the brave new world of the 1960s, a step was taken, as bold as Webb's original, to ignore the dominating formality and, in fact, to destroy it. It may have been a wise choice in terms of the new climate in education and the fact that Webb's scheme was inward-looking. What has resulted, however, is a menagerie of cubist buildings using a vast variety of materials. Beside them, Webb's scheme looks humane, controlled and unified, and not the least bit anarchic or pompous. It is a pity that his whole design was not completed.

1. Quoted in H. Bulkeley Creswell, 'Sir Aston Webb and his office', in Alastair Service, *Edwardian Architecture and its Origins*, London, 1975, p.331
2. Maurice Cheesewright, *Mirror to a Mermaid*, Birmingham, 1975
3. *The Builder*, vol.82, Jan.-June 1902, p.448

Chapter 8
Local Landmarks

Some buildings occupy a very important place in our local communities. They are landmarks in towns and cities, important public buildings that help the citizen to define what comprises the urban centre, and are the sort of buildings chosen when giving directions to strangers. Apart from their physical presence they symbolise the facilities that a town has to offer, and it is their presence that gives character and substance to the town.

Many buildings of this type were built in the Edwardian period. The growth in the number of public libraries, for instance, has been noted, and also the provision for higher education. Sir John Summerson has said that by the turn of the century, 'Swimming baths had become almost a municipal necessity.'[1] Few townsfolk would not have used the facilities provided by at least one of these building types. None of them was essential to maintain life and safety; they were of a secondary category that arose only when civilisation was established. Many towns which had grown almost uncontrollably in the nineteenth century were keen to demonstrate how civilised they were by its end.

Wolverhampton Central Library is a good example of a turn-of-the-century public building in a town getting to grips with the problems wrought by unprecedented industrial expansion. It was designed by the doyen of library design, Henry T. Hare, and is thus representative of the work of this significant architect.

The college of art in Hull, as will be seen, was built following the resolution of an unsettled situation in the provision of further and higher education in the city. This relatively modest building was designed by one of the foremost practices in the first decade of the century, Lanchester, Stewart and Rickards, architects of Cardiff City Hall.

The public baths in Chelsea followed a practice begun in Victorian times of providing slipper baths of two classes in the interests of public cleanliness, in addition to male and female swimming pools. The building has a façade in the 'Wrenaissance' style, making it a fit neighbour for the adjacent town hall, and was won in competition by Wills and Anderson, architects noted for their expertise in the design of municipal buildings.

Although cost was an important consideration in all these buildings, an effort was made to give them an acceptable public face. The latest technology was used in their construction, but it was clear that propriety and civic pride demanded an exterior, or at least a façade, in keeping with the aspirations of their instigators.

1. Sir J. Summerson, *The Turn of the Century: Architecture in Britain around 1900*, Glasgow, 1976, p.4

Hull School of Art

Leeds School of Art, built at about the same time as Hull, but occupying a very different site, and much more utilitarian in character.

Wolverhampton Public Library

The history of the public library is long. Chetham's Library in Manchester, for instance, was made accessible to the inhabitants of the city under the terms of Sir Humphrey Chetham's will in 1653, and there are many examples of town and parochial collections of books in Great Britain and America dating from the seventeenth century. In the eighteenth and early nineteenth centuries, subscription libraries became popular, and the growth of Mechanics' Institutes also encouraged the development of publicly available collections. So-called 'free' libraries, however, specifically promoted and administered by local councils, were first introduced in the mid-nineteenth century, and increased rapidly in number in late Victorian and Edwardian times.

William Ewart MP, the nineteenth-century social reformer, was the prime mover behind the Public Libraries Act of 1850, which enabled the collection of a halfpenny rate to finance such projects. However, it was not until this and subsequent Acts were consolidated in 1892, and the amount of money that could be raised was increased, that many councils were persuaded to create adequate facilities.

There was, in addition, a great deal of enthusiasm for the promotion of cultural activities in the latter half of the century. Concerned at the rapid expansion of urban life and the unprecedented problems that had resulted, city fathers, paternalist employers, clergymen and philanthropists all gave voice. To provide uplifting entertainment for workers in place of the 'pub' was seen as an important concern, if only to alleviate the social evils associated with drink. In opening Hammersmith Library in 1895, J. Passmore Edwards stated that what was wanted was 'fewer Public Houses and more Public Libraries'.[1] Despite this pragmatism, however, there can be little doubt that there was a genuine desire on behalf of those involved with library promotion to encourage and spread learning for its own sake and to open a world of education to the underprivileged.

At first it was suggested that the top priority in the establishment of a public library was the provision of a building to house the books. It was hoped that reading matter would be supplied by donations. Even so, the rate revenue was often inadequate to accomplish this, and conversions of existing redundant buildings were undertaken so that money would be saved. Between 1890 and 1909, however, there was a terrific upsurge in building activity. No fewer than 369 local authorities adopted the Libraries Act, whereas only 153 had done so in the forty years between the passing of the original Act and 1890. A major underlying reason was the pressure to provide libraries for a society becoming more literate, following the 1870 Education Act, which formalised elementary education for everyone.

More than any other factor, though, it was the advent of large-scale philanthropy that encouraged the construction of new libraries. Despite generous individual bequests, two men stood out as prominent 'mass benefactors'. One, John Passmore Edwards (1823-1911), was the son of a Cornish tradesman who rose to become the proprietor of magazines and newspapers. Edwards was a progressive social reformer with many interests, and libraries formed only one part of his endeavour. Nevertheless, he provided money for over twenty buildings in London and the West Country.

Andrew Carnegie (1835-1919) made a contribution on an altogether grander scale. Carnegie had emigrated to the United States with his parents from Scotland in 1848. He succeeded, first as a railroad official and then with business interests in the iron industry, eventually becoming a multi-millionaire. He made specific gifts at first, but by 1897 an office had been set up to deal with his library donations to both sides of the Atlantic. The size of the operation is shown by the fact that of the 514 towns in Great Britain with public libraries, no fewer than 263 received grant aid from Carnegie.

The libraries that were built during this outburst of construction varied considerably in size and style. Some central libraries incorporated a museum or art gallery, and in many cases lecture rooms were provided, science and art classes being held in the buildings. The public library could therefore be seen as a powerhouse for local culture and education.

Major functions specific to libraries were threefold: a lending facility where books could be borrowed for reading at home; a reference library where books such as technical works and commercial directories could be consulted; and a reading room for the perusal of newspapers and periodicals. In this period, access to lending facilities were usually 'closed' rather than 'open'. In other words, the borrower had to state his or her choice of book to the library attendant, who would then collect it from a stack and pass it over the counter. The concept of 'open browsing' was not usual, but an indicator board was provided to show whether the desired book was available. Consequently, library buildings dating from the period were originally provided with a large counter area and a public space, behind which was book shelving accessible to library staff only. The most heavily used area, the reading room, was located nearest the main entrance.

Environmental issues were of great importance, particularly the provision of artificial lighting, as libraries stayed open until nine or ten o'clock at night. Electric light was preferred, even though it was considered cheaper in some cases to generate power on site with a gas engine and dynamo, rather than pay the high rates demanded by the electricity companies.

Ventilation was a topic which also received careful con-

The main entrance of the Wolverhampton Public Library addresses an important junction, with flanking wings running along Garrick Street and Cleveland Road.

sideration. The newsrooms of under-ventilated buildings had a poor reputation because of the stink of 'malodorous idlers'. It was recommended that ceilings should be at least fourteen feet (4.3 metres) high in large reading rooms and in addition there should be three or four air changes per hour. 'Natural' ventilation through windows led to draughts and was not feasible in many plan types, so a system of extract ducts with remote high-level fans was favoured, input air being drawn over radiators. These technical issues, and more, were tackled in some detail in articles and books written at the time. The public library was, therefore, a building type which received much attention in late Victorian and Edwardian times.

Wolverhampton Public Library was built at the peak of this interest by, arguably, the foremost specialist architect, Henry T. Hare. Up to the construction of Hare's building, the borough library, founded in 1869, was housed first in the Old Athenaeum, the former Mechanics' Institute, and then in a building in Garrick Street that had been a police station,

barracks and magistrates' court. Here, evening classes were held, a museum was opened, and a series of popular lectures started. Sometimes concerts took place. By 1899, some 1200 students were attending sixty-five classes in science, technical and commercial subjects. At about the same time, the work of the library itself had expanded to the extent that 1100 people each day visited the reading rooms and 330 volumes were lent for home reading, out of a total of nearly 28,000 in the lending library's book stacks. Selection of books was made simple by the provision of special indicator boards designed and marketed by the chief librarian, John Elliot.

By the 1890s, then, Wolverhampton Library was far more than a repository for books. It was a centre for self-improvement and entertainment. Now, on the verge of a new century, it was time for a purpose-built library of which the town could be proud. Funds were to be provided by the committee set up in 1897 to celebrate Victoria's Diamond Jubilee, and a competition was announced by the committee, inviting architects to 'supply Plans, Designs and Estimates for a New Free Library'.[2]

Prior to the publication of the competition conditions, the committee had already acquired a site for the project at the corner of Garrick Street and Cleveland Road, a prominent position in Snow Hill, and not far removed from the existing library buildings. The old Theatre Royal, which then occupied the site, was acquired for £2500, and demolished to make way for the new building. Altogether, the committee had raised nearly £11,000 by public subscription, and this was enhanced by bank interest and the sale of materials from the demolished theatre.

The schedule of accommodation which was detailed in the conditions confined itself purely to library functions. Accommodation connected to more specific educational tasks was omitted. It seems that a decision must have been taken to separate these activities, probably because of growth in both operations. The science and technical school libraries were to remain in the old building. The borough surveyor, who was responsible for drafting the competition document, zoned the accommodation into two floors: on the ground floor were to be a newsroom and a magazine room, with certain ancillary accommodation; and the first floor was to contain the reference library, lending library, and committee and librarians' rooms. All of this was to be achieved within a £10,000 limit.

There were scarcely any further practical stipulations, except that it was desired that the materials for the shell of the building should be bricks and terracotta.

The competition was restricted to twelve selected architects, but in the event only nine took part. The professional assessor was the ubiquitous Alfred Waterhouse. Those submitting designs included three nationally known architects, J. M. Brydon, Maurice B. Adams and Henry T. Hare; a Birmingham architect of distinction, W. H. Bidlake; and a number of other provincials, including two from Wolverhampton itself. Hare won the competition because of his undoubted mastery of the situation. As Adams said somewhat later, 'The Wolverhampton plan shown by Mr Hare was considered the most capable and admirable one they could possibly have on such an extremely awkward site.'[3]

His plan was simple but effective: the major spaces were organised into two-storey wings running parallel with Garrick Street and Cleveland Road. The 'web' formed by the meeting of the wings at an obtuse angle was occupied by the entrance hall, stairs and staff accommodation. Apart from the porter's lobby on the ground floor, there were no internal corridors, and major rooms received natural light from both sides.

The ground-floor provision, the magazine room in the long wing and the newsroom in the short, was divided into structural bays which coincided with spatial usage. The magazine room, for instance, was six bays long, each bay being delineated by columns which divided the room into a broad central section and two narrower side sections. Each bay also had its own window, lighting the table layout which coincided with the spacing of the grid. Despite the provision of two large windows in the gable end, the plan was too deep to have been lit completely by natural light, and artificial lighting was included in the plans from the start.

These ground-floor spaces were designed for a high level of occupancy, but with frequent changes of user. They were not very interesting architecturally, and the main effort was reserved for the rooms on the first floor. Here, in the lending library, the bays were the same as on the ground floor. The ceiling of the central section was, however, taken up to form a large glazed vault, through which light permeated into the centre of the space. The side bays were provided with galleries which ran down the lengths of the wings at either side. Each was individually lit – the lower level by small, two-light pedimented windows, the upper level by bull's-eye windows. This now provides an exceedingly pleasant reference section, but when it was originally designed most of it accommodated book stacks and was used only by library staff. The public were held at bay in a square space off the central lobby, surrounded on three sides by a substantial wooden counter, on top of which were positioned several of Mr Elliot's indicators, forming a high screen around the space.

The original reference library was given a glazed, domed ceiling, supported on corner columns with vaulted niches to each side. On the centre line of this dome and the counter beyond was an oriel window, helping to reinforce the idea of a squarer plan form, in opposition to the repetitive bays in the other major spaces. There was also a glazed 'dome' over the lobby and principal staircase, illuminating the treads of polished Hopton Wood stone.

Externally, the main façades of the building were treated in a way that reflected internal organization and at the same time produced a major contribution to the urban fabric. Hare made much of the corner entrance façade, raising an enormous gable with an aedicule, following the Norman Shaw manner, above the band of mullioned windows to the first floor and the arcading of the entrance porch below. The first-floor windows, lighting the librarian's room, and more bathetically the repairing room, have a pediment, and a richly decorated apron beneath, with a coat of arms below the central section.

The way in which Hare effected the stepping-back of this façade allowed for an amount of drama at little expense. The main, central, gabled portion projected by perhaps no more

Ground- and first-floor plans, showing the original designation of rooms. The enormous magazine room to the left of the entrance on the ground floor is now the lending library.

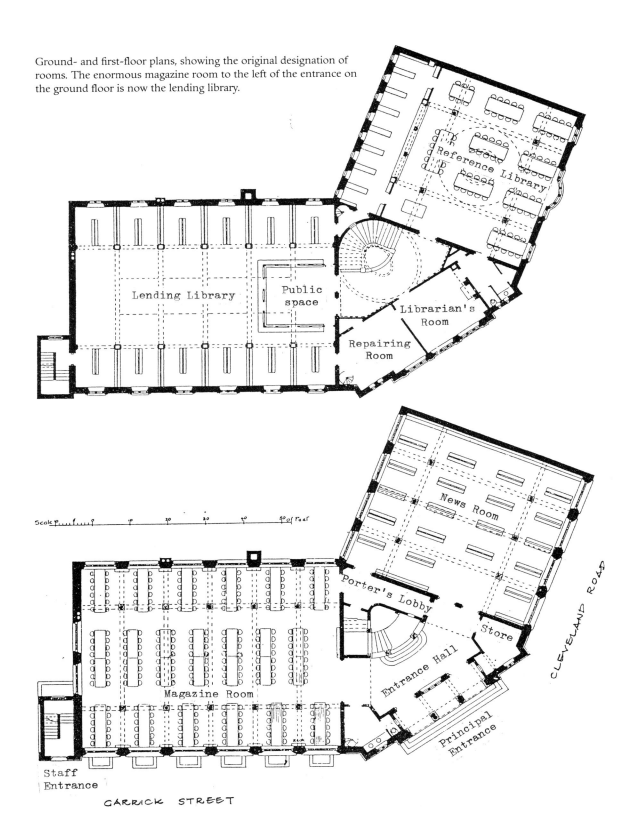

than the thickness of the wall. At either side the wall surfaces returned at right angles, thus providing a planar break between themselves and the wings. This enabled them to be taken up and expressed as 'towers' flanking the gable. The feeling of 'towerishness' was heightened by the use of small, paired windows at first-floor level. Above them were miniature balconies and then the 'turrets' themselves, terminating in highly attenuated finials. The towers were fascinatingly redolent of their period – a mixture of Baroque, Arts and Crafts and Art Nouveau influences. The tall, slender spire above the gable continued this vertical emphasis. It balanced the horizontality of the windows and banding, and the weight of the arches below.

The long wing to Garrick Street was terminated by another pseudo-tower. At ground-floor level, piers, horizontal banding and arched fenestration all added to a feeling of weight and solidity. The long plane of the wall above was punctuated by the small-scale windows lighting the lending library. The terracotta banding, running along the top sections of these windows, was inscribed with the names of British literary worthies.

The richness and variety of the façades was achieved with the use of good-quality red brick and yellowish terracotta. They formed the outer, load-bearing shell of the building. Structurally, like many of its contemporaries, this building was a hybrid. A grid of steel columns and beams internally supported the floors and the roof, but it was the perimeter walls that took the loads at the edges. The roof was fabricated from relatively lightweight steel sections, with a curved bottom member supporting the glazed barrel-vaulted ceiling to the lending library. The 'domes' to the stairwell and reference library were framed-up internal features, and the glazing simply appeared as a flat 'laylight' on the ordinary pitched roof outside.

The floor slabs were of 'fire resisting' reinforced concrete construction, typical enough of its time, filling between steel joists. It is interesting to note that although the general contractors were a local firm, the steelwork and reinforced concrete were carried out by W. H. Lindsay and Company, of London.

Up-to-date methods were also used to provide suitable environmental conditions. Central heating was run from a basement boiler, steam being initially used as the heat transfer medium. It seems that fresh air was admitted through wall grilles over the radiators or pipes. Although there was a degree of natural ventilation, an electric fan was housed in the spire which drew stale air out of the building through ceiling grilles and wooden ducts located in the roof space.

From a technological viewpoint, therefore, the building used the most convenient and appropriate modern methods without being in any way exceptional. It would have been difficult to make the chosen plan form work well without metal construction and electrically powered lighting and ventilation. At the same time, none of this technology was gratuitously expressed – it merely played its part in the overall scheme of things.

Once commenced, construction was not a lengthy process. The Duke of York laid the foundation stone in July 1900, and the library was open and functioning during 1902, allowing the Annual Report of the Free Library Committee to state in a self-congratulatory way that the public was 'delighted with the change', and that the work of the institution was not suspended for a single day during the removal. In the years that have passed since then changes have occurred, such as the conversion to open access and the addition of an extension to the Garrick Street wing in 1936. The reading rooms are now lending libraries for adults and children, and the fine first-floor spaces are occupied by reference and audio-visual libraries. Although heavily used, the fabric and finishes appear to be bearing up well. Externally, the terracotta has proved its worth and the building looks clean and fresh.

Henry Hare and the library design

Henry Hare became one of the most successful architects of his generation, and the history of his association with the Wolverhampton Library is representative of his ability in dealing with this type of project. The reason for his not now generally being included in the first rank of architects is also worthy of consideration.

Henry Thomas Hare (1861-1921) was born, educated and served his articles in Yorkshire. He then spent some months in a Paris *atelier*, joining the Architectural Association on his return to England. Despite a false start, by 1891 he had begun his own practice, and set the pattern for the rest of his career by winning the competition for the design of the county offices in Stafford in 1892. From this time on, most of his work involved the production of public or educational buildings often won, like Wolverhampton, through competition. His career outside practice was also notable, and he was president of the Architectural Association in 1902 and of the RIBA from 1917 to 1919.

The Wolverhampton building is a skilful piece of design, especially when it is realised that expectations were high and cost constraints were unrealistic. Hare himself was only too well aware of this type of problem. He had to cut down substantially on his initial design. The overall area was reduced, but careful replanning meant that space was recovered by, for instance, the introduction of galleries into the lending library.

Interior of the original lending library, photographed soon after completion. The indicator boards can be seen, and only library staff occupied the space beyond the screen. Today this is a reference library, and the balconies to either side contain study tables.

The roof structure was also simplified, becoming an asymmetric double pitch, replacing the costlier, though architecturally more satisfying, method originally intended. Even so, the construction cost was £13,954 and fitting out another £3000.

Hare judged that the building was of great significance within the physical and social fabric of the town, particularly with respect to its prominent position. He made as much as he could of the main façades, using relatively inexpensive materials to great effect, though he did, for instance, employ William Aumonier, the prominent London craftsman, to execute the carving for the terracotta mouldings. Unfortunately, though, despite the care lavished upon it, the design is a prime example of Edwin Lutyens' famous witticism: 'Queen Anne front and Mary Ann back'. Hare wisely spent money on the major façades, but the rear of the building could be the meanest mill ever built.

It seems evident from a review of Hare's work that he had a special facility for clarity of spatial organisation and the design of effective and appropriate exteriors. There is an interest in variations of scale, and an ability to manipulate a number of architectural elements so that, even if disparate, they combine to form a successful façade. Hare's work is never dull, and there is an obvious sense of enjoyment in his own creative ability. His buildings have civic dignity, but they are also light-hearted.

This strength is also the weakness. 'Facility' is too easily related to 'facile'. Even though there is no doubt that Hare

Hull School of Art

worked hard at his vocation, it could be that architectural design came easily and that he never thought much about principle; that he was successful in business not only because he was a consummate professional but also because he was willing to compromise. He could adopt the façadism of the Beaux Arts without taking on board its theoretical constraints. Similarly, he would use Arts and Crafts motifs without really being an Arts and Crafts man, or carrying the moral and spiritual weight that was implied. This may explain the comment that Hare was 'essentially practical, and his art may have suffered a little in consequence'.[4]

Certainly the lack of *gravitas* and his ability to satisfy everyone, apart from the theorists in the architectural profession, did not stand him in good stead. Hare was of his time. A few years after his death, Charles Reilly used him as an example of the 'bad old days':

The entanglements of detail, how well we know them even today! But in what was called the 'free classic' of a quarter of a century ago the building was never free from them. Oxford Town Hall by H. T. Hare, occurs to me as an example of the kind of work, effective enough on paper when presented by a skilled draughtsman, and attractive to the amateur, which was sweeping the country, until Sir Reginald (Blomfield) called us all back to bigger and simpler things.[5]

From the 1920s up to recent times, architecture has been po-faced, and there has been no room for the work of the man who gazes down so jovially from his portrait at the RIBA, like a character from a play by Priestley; but one could only wish that some of his virtues were shared by modern practitioners.

1. Quoted in John Minto, *A History of the Public Library Movement in Great Britain and Ireland*, London, 1932, p.23
2. *Proposed new free Library, Conditions for Competition*, County Borough of Wolverhampton, 1897.
3. Debate, 'Public libraries', *Journal of the RIBA*, vol.11, 23 Mar.1907
4. Obituary of H. T. Hare in *The Builder*, vol.120, 14 Jan.1921, p.59
5. C. H. Reilly, *Representative British Architects of the present Day*, London, 1931, p.58

Hull School of Art was designed by Lanchester, Stewart and Rickards, whose practice is discussed in the section on Cardiff Town Hall. They were awarded the commission as the result of a competition held in 1902, which was one of a series of such successes for the firm, starting with the Cardiff scheme and culminating in the Wesleyan Central Hall, Westminster. At about the same time, the architects were designing Deptford Town Hall, and the two projects bear a marked similarity in external form, although the Hull building is smaller and less lavish in detail. Essentially, in both schemes, there is a parapeted two-storey façade on the main elevation, its top being emphasised by a strong cornice line. At the centre of the façade, a pitched roof over a third storey, with its ridge on the axis of the building, is brought forward, its gable forming a pediment. The centre of the composition is also emphasised by a first-floor bay, semicircular on plan, enriched with sculpture and carved detail. This theme is, perhaps, more related to English precedent than much of Lanchester and Rickards' other work, which has a Continental flavour. In the case of Deptford, A. S. Grey has pointed out the relationship to custom house design, and also to the carved poops of ships. Nevertheless, the Hull building, although unified in its own right, has detail and form which demonstrates a variety of influences and makes a trite categorisation of style difficult.

There is no doubt that the school of art is one of the most distinguished buildings in Hull. It has few regional references, however, and could have been sited in any large provincial town. In Hull, it marks the successful conclusion of a rather convoluted attempt to provide art teaching, within the patchy general history of higher education in the area. A school of art had been opened in 1861 in the Public Rooms, 'to teach applied art and industrial design in aid of local manufactures'.[1] Funds for this came from the Department of Science and Art as part of the government initiative for improving the standard of design in the kingdom. Object drawing, modelling and graphic technique were all important in this type of education. Eventually, the school became affiliated to the Hull 'Royal Institution', which provided science teaching for adults. It was hoped that this combination might form the basis for a college, similar to those in Birmingham and Manchester, from which a university would grow. Unfortunately, a public subscription set up to assist the transformation yielded little result and it was decided, instead, to begin a technical school. Here, again, little was subscribed and the scheme fell through. Despite its importance as a port, perhaps Hull lacked the stratum of really wealthy citizens to be found in Birmingham, Manchester and Liverpool who could make these ideas into realities.

Eventually, the Technical Instruction Act of 1889 allowed

The Anlaby Road façade of the Hull School of Art, showing the mosaic in the gable/pediment, executed by the Bromsgrove Guild, the stone belvedere atop the boiler flue, and Fehr's mermaids supporting the balcony cornice over the headmaster's French window.

the council to provide finance, and a municipal technical school was begun, of which the school of art was part. This was further consolidated when an Education Committee was established following the 1902 Balfour Act. It had been clear for several years before this date that adequate premises for the school of art were necessary, especially following the collapse of plans to build a combined central library, public hall and technical school. There was much debate over the choice of a site, and the wrangling went on for some time, public attention being drawn to the prevarication and inaction of the bodies involved. The decision to build near the city centre in Anlaby Road, and to hold a competition, in 1902, was perhaps due to the impetus provided by the newly founded Education Committee.

The foundation stone of the new building was laid in April 1903. At the time, mention was made of the success of students, who numbered about two hundred on average, and the inadequacy of the existing premises in Albion Street. Altruistic motives were tinged with more practical issues when the Mayor, speaking on behalf of the council, said that they 'trusted that the work of the school would be one which would not only lift the tastes of the people but increase their usefulness and make the city more than ever a prosperous commercial centre.'[2]

The new Municipal School of Art, opened in October 1905, provided extensive, purpose-built accommodation, and by 1911 it housed 189 full-time and 251 part-time students, supervised by six members of staff. There was a range of five large studios, with various specific functions including modelling and carving; antique studies and painting, and architecture. In addition, a lecture room, life room and exhibition room were incorporated, the latter being near the entrance on the ground floor.

The plan is virtually square, and the main rooms are disposed around a central staircase and light well. Access is gained to the entrance hall at ground-floor level by passing up a flight of stairs from the pavement in Anlaby Road, between two plain Doric columns supporting the bay above, and in through a lobby between the secretarial office and the assistant master's room. Facing the entrance are two columns which support the landing. Steps down to a substantial basement area lie between them. To the east side of the entrance hall and staircase, the section of the building is disrupted by a series of mezzanine floors designed to respond to the minor spaces which have to be accommodated. These include lavatories, and the caretaker's suite of rooms, which is served by a separate staircase.

The first floor occupies much the same area as the ground floor, but the second floor, beneath the pitched roof, takes up roughly the central third of the plan, and glazed lights in the roofs to either side illuminate the studios below. The second floor is arranged on two levels, and the north side is raised to allow a high ceiling in the painting room beneath. Most of the teaching accommodation on this floor was devoted to life study. One particularly delightful feature was a conservatory, entered from the second-floor landing, and sometimes used as a retreat for senior members of staff, but originally intended to allow the cultivation of plants used for drawn and painted studies. Another unusual item, originally proposed, was an external platform over one of the first-floor studios to allow students to sketch views across the city rooftops.

The character of the building is extremely appropriate for its purpose. Rather plain internally, with plastered walls, and mouldings restricted to ceilings and architraves, it nevertheless conveys the lightness and spaciousness suitable for an art school, with the centre space acting as a hub of circulation. Externally, it achieves a sense of order, but within this there is a degree of playfulness. There is a juxtaposition of masses, with the stepped pitched roof, flanked by flat roofs and little gabled rooflights at right angles. A vertical element, the chimney stack serving the boiler flue, pushes up beyond the two pitched roofs at their junction.

It is the incidental details, however, and the use of materials and decoration, that help to provide the balance between the impression of serious academic purpose, and the fact that the building is to be occupied by art students who have a certain freedom born of creative endeavour. The fenestration to the major Anlaby Road façade is dignified and serious, with stone surrounds to the metal casements. These large ground-floor windows are contrasted with areas of unpunctured brickwork above, but relief from unremitting rectangularity is introduced just round the corner in the first floor of the west face, where an elegant elliptical window is introduced.

The wall surface itself is a warm red brick, banded with Ancaster stone in the centre of the south façade, where it breaks back a small distance, and at the corners. As there are only three courses of brickwork between each stone band, the effect is to emphasise the centre portion and still retain further weight for the bay, which is completely of stone. The bay has balconies to its roof and to the headmaster's room at first-floor level, with balustrades executed in elaborately designed wrought-iron work. Where the bay joins the wall, there is stone facing with pilasters. Above the French window

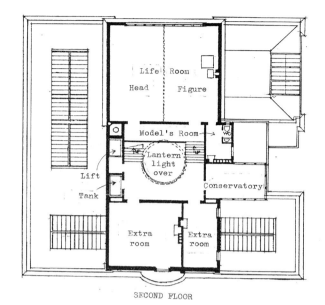

SECOND FLOOR

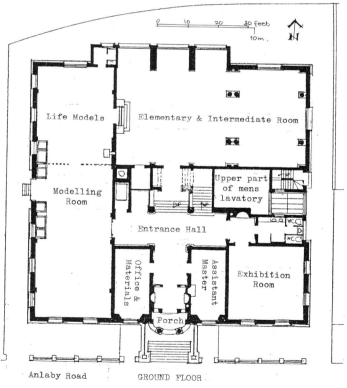

GROUND FLOOR

Anlaby Road

Ground- and second-floor plans of the art college, showing how accommodation is disposed around the stairwell. On the second-floor plan, rooflights to the studios below can be seen, and also the conservatory intended to provide specimens for plant studies, which is entered from the landing.

Chelsea Public Baths

leading from the headmaster's room to the balcony, Rickards placed some typical and delightful sculpture with mermaids supporting the city's coat of arms and the cornice above. This work is by H. C. Fehr, who had previously worked for Lanchester, Stewart and Rickards at Cardiff.

Two more features are of immediate note. The architects added to the rectangular brick chimney to the boiler a fine stone belvedere. This gives the structure extra height, and enhances the play of masses and incident when seen from the south-west. Finally, there is the treatment of the pediment. This contains a colourful glass mosaic, designed by A. G. Jones and executed by the Bromsgrove Guild.

The cost of the building was to be £12,000, but reports on completion talk of 'considerably over £20,000'. This may be expensive in terms of a provincial art school, but is fairly modest for a major civic building, and it seems that the architects made a virtue of the cost limitations in the boldness of the design. Perhaps because of its clear lines and juxtaposition of shapes, it appeals more to the modern eye than more elaborate and highly decorated work. In addition, its warmth, humanity and good humour highlight its role as a place of creativity and enlightenment within the urban fabric of Hull.

It is interesting to note that the Leeds School of Art was built at about the same time as that at Hull, having been designed by Bedford and Kitson, the foremost domestic architects in the city. It was located in a side street, with a steep slope, and included a gymnasium used by the nearby Boys' Modern School. This is in complete contrast to the Hull school on its flat, main road site. The materials are virtually the same, however: red brick with Ancaster stone dressings, and stone banding, although the architectural language is much more direct, expression being given to huge north-facing studio windows to the first and second floors. Apart from heavy cornices, architectural decoration is confined to a fine 'Wrenaissance' doorway and a glass mosaic, bearing the name of the institution and two seated figures, designed by Gerald Moira.

Many thousands of students have passed through both of these institutions, which have served their purpose well throughout the twentieth century. In the case of Leeds, artists of international stature have emerged. In a broader context, they have successfully represented the artistic and educational aspirations of their respective municipalities, which sponsored them with high hopes ninety or more years ago.

1. *A History of the County of York: East Riding*, Victoria County History, Oxford, p.356
2. *Hull News*, 11 Apr. 1903, p.10

The 'Wrenaissance' exterior of the baths provides an appropriately civilised character for a public building in a wealthy borough, adjoining the town hall, despite its relative cheapness and internal austerity.

The first municipal swimming baths in Britain were opened in Liverpool as early as 1828, near to the site where the Cunard building now stands. Before this time, heated, private pools were in existence, and available to subscribers. During the nineteenth century, however, the necessary provision of sanitary facilities for the vast, unwashed urban populations, living in poor-quality housing, became combined with facilities for the enjoyment of exercise, competitive sport and the practical expedient of learning to swim. These seemingly disparate

The ground floor plan of Chelsea Baths illustrates the architectural device of using non-critical areas, in this case waiting lobbies, to reconcile the different axes of the plan, and also highlights the sexual segregation of the building for both swimmers and those intent on personal cleanliness.

Opposite
Sections show how the relatively narrow façade hides the much larger pool spaces behind. The reinforced concrete water storage tank can be seen beneath Manor Road. The men's swimming bath is first class, the ladies', somewhat smaller, is second class.

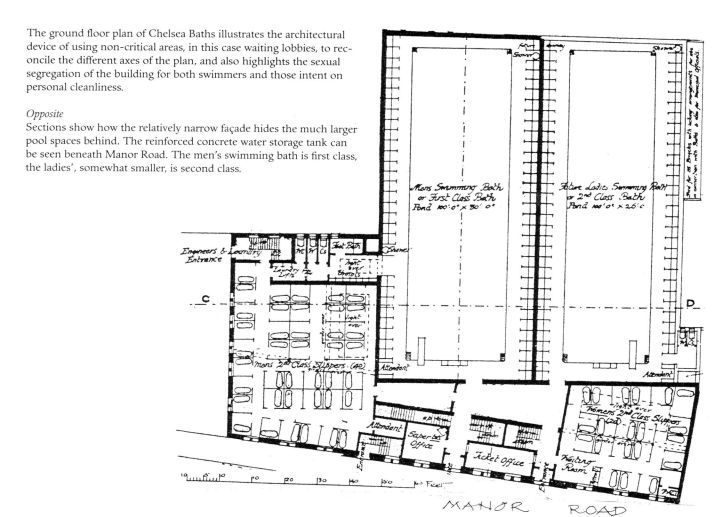

activities may have been combined to economise on plant installed to heat, store and distribute water. The need for such facilities was recognised by central government, and the Public Baths and Washhouses Act was passed in 1846, 'with a view to the promotion of the health, comfort and welfare of the inhabitants of towns and populous districts'. The first metropolitan example was opened near Leicester Square the same year.

Chelsea Public Baths, completed in 1907, was a scaled-down version of a proposal for an extensive scheme incorporating three swimming pools as well as slipper baths on a site between King's Road and Manor Street – now known as Chelsea Manor Street. The less ambitious project which was built was not only half the cost, but allowed for expansion of the adjacent town hall. Although not of a type particular to the Edwardian period, the Chelsea Baths building does address two issues which are relevant: the need to comple-

ment important civic buildings and provide an appropriate face to the community, and the dialogue between engineering technology and architecture, which is here quite sharply delineated.

Two swimming pools were provided, one for men and one for women, together with a laundry and over ninety slipper baths in individual cubicles. Apart from the laundry, all public areas were sexually segregated, and the slipper baths, in addition, according to class. No doubt this ruthless organisation of the building was necessary, if only to forestall any suggestion of impropriety that may have sullied the reputation of a respectable municipality, in a building where a large number of both sexes were naked or near-naked.

Architecturally, the building comprises two major elements: a double 'shed', housing the swimming baths themselves, and a decorated screen wall forming the main façade on the long front of the site, enclosing two levels of accommodation.

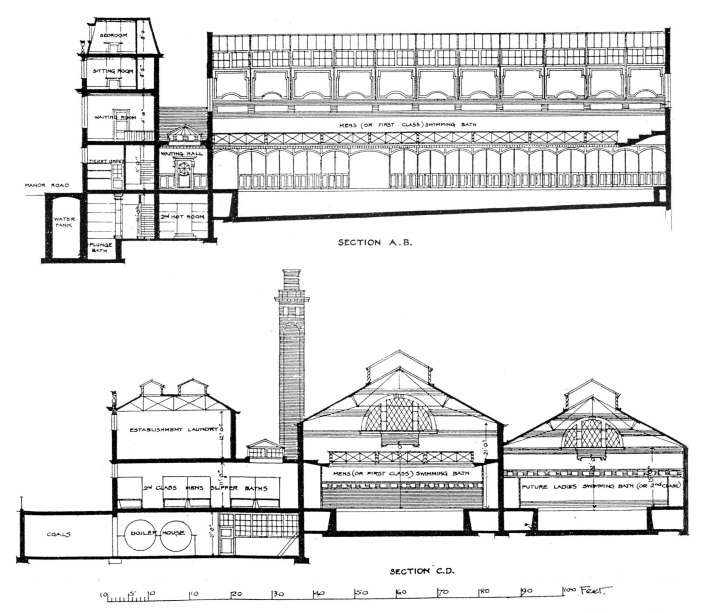

SECTION A.B.

SECTION C.D.

Essentially, this wall is the public face of the building, with architectural enrichments and embellishments, and the public entrances. The 'sheds' are basic, functional enclosures for the pools.

The façade is of red brick with Portland stone dressings, and a balustrade at parapet level. Living accommodation for the caretaker provides a second floor in the middle of the façade, giving the effect of an emphasised central pavilion with side wings. Bedroom accommodation above is lit by dormers in the pitched roof that rises behind the balustrade. The whole composition, with its stone quoins, aproned window-surrounds and swagged bull's-eye windows, gives an agreeable, rather dignified, 'Wrenaissance' character. It is not as interesting as that intended for the larger, superseded scheme, which had an elaborate central block with porticoed entrance, approached up a flight of steps across an 'area' lighting the basement, and a sculpture group above. However,

it does represent an attempt at a scale and character that are appropriate for a civic building in this particular location. Unfortunately, there is a good deal of contrivance necessary to obtain this result. The three symmetrically positioned entrances are given the same weighting, for instance, despite their different tasks: women's and men's entrances, and the door to a small lobby giving access to the private stairs leading up to the caretaker's accommodation. The windows to the second floor, set above a cornice running across from the 'wings' to either side, are also equally weighted, despite the fact that they light a linen store, staircase and sitting room.

Nevertheless, the contrivance is neatly achieved, and even though the modern designer may squirm at the 'dishonesty' involved, the propriety necessary to a public face is accomplished, and many disparate activities are set behind a façade that has a character appropriate to the buildings' wider function.

Internally, the planning of the building is adequately handled, bearing in mind the amount of accommodation required – slipper baths are packed in – and the fact that the swimming 'shed' is parallel with the Manor Gardens front, but at an angle to the main façade. The awkward spaces thus generated are taken up with waiting room and circulation areas, but all the public spaces seem pinched.

The character of the swimming areas is fairly spartan. The men's bath is one hundred feet (30.4 metres) long, and the women's three feet less. The former rises through two storeys, and has a gallery around it at first-floor level. This is of minimal width, and sits on top of the changing cubicles which line the side of the pool. There is no attempt at frivolity here, in either the decoration or the space allowed. The swimmer is either in the water or getting changed; finishes are serviceable but plain, apart from a frieze of brick or tile patterning running around the wall just below the roof. The roof itself is a cheap, lightweight structure, open and undisguised, with strips of patent glazing to either side of the ridge. The aura of physical training, the feeling that healthy exercise is accompanied by an asceticism of approach, is apparent here. It is a characteristic of swimming baths which pervaded most of the century, but which, over the last twenty years, has undergone a complete reversal. Swimming pools now involve immersion in warm water, with sprays, jets, waves, waterfalls and slides – a sybaritic, sensual and shamelessly enjoyable experience.

The technology employed within the building is probably of more note than the building itself. Of particular interest is the storage tank, which is really a reservoir to feed the pool during rapid filling operations. This lies along the entire length of the Manor Street front at basement level, rather like the longitudinal bunkers of a ship. It was constructed of a steel framework, strutted along its length, and covered with concrete on expanded metal. The swimming pools, themselves, were also of this construction.

Within the relatively cheap shell of the building, the plant was extensive and ingenious, relying upon steam generation from two large boilers. Some of the steam produced was used by an engine working a centrifugal pump to transfer water from the storage tank to the baths. A separate engine was used to work machinery in the laundry. Exhaust steam from the engines was taken into calorifiers and used to provide warm water for the slipper baths. The central heating for the building also worked in this way. A well some 470 feet (143 metres) deep was actually sunk on site for the specific purpose of supplying the building, and water was raised by a compressor and fed to the storage tank. Hot water from condensed steam was returned to a sump in the basement floor, and fed into the boilers when required, thereby saving fuel.

Although the total cost was around £30,000, it was a cheap and ingenious solution to the issue of running the facility itself, and to the capital outlay on building structure. A civic building was created on the outside; on the inside was arranged a large amount of functional, if spartan accommodation.

The architects were Wills and Anderson. Although not in the top rank of Edwardian designers, they were involved with many municipal schemes during the period, and won competitions for public libraries and local government buildings. Herbert W. Wills (1864-1937) had wide experience, having at one time worked for McKim, Mead and White, the leading New York architects. He also worked in public practice in Hong Kong and in Canada, before joining in partnership with Anderson in South Wales. His exposure to the foremost American practice must have influenced one of his earliest successes, the rather Beaux-Arts University Registry at Cardiff. Wills does not seem to have been overly committed to this approach, however, and was happy to use 'Wrenaissance' at Chelsea and Baroque detail at Sunderland Law Courts, in conjunction with local architects W. and T. R. Milburn. His earlier experiences resurfaced in the 1920s, when stripped Classicism was de rigueur.

Perhaps Wills and Anderson made a speciality of dealing with difficult cases, providing as much accommodation as possible for as little money as possible for impecunious councils, whilst still managing to introduce decorum and civic scale. The law courts, police and fire station at Sunderland, mentioned above, bears this out. For around £40,000, the architects provided police and quarter-sessions courts with associated rooms, and cells; a police station, and, on a difficult interlocking site, a four-bay fire station with workshops, firemen's houses and dormitory accommodation. Nevertheless, the exterior of the court building was given a fine tower and robust, if not excessive Baroque detailing, all carried out in local stone. The fire station was in brick, with stone dressings, and a balustrade at parapet level. Although from the design of this building it seems to have been a case of shoehorning a large amount of disparate accommodation into a very awkward site, the scheme was not without architectural invention. There was also a modicum of 'Wrenaissance' detail internally, and some specially designed electric light fittings.

Top-rank architects often remain so because, once established, they obtain the best projects, with the most responsive clients and the biggest budgets. Wills and Anderson, on the other hand, represent creative and competent architects who had a harder task, and one that has increasingly been the profession's lot since 1914: that of satisfying difficult conditions and still producing a result that enhances the life of citizens.

Chapter 9
The Artistic House

The Edwardian era was a prime period for domestic architecture, continuing a trend that had begun in the 1890s. 'Domestic', here, does not refer to the country seats of great landowners, a type that dominated the eighteenth century, or to mass housing, which was at its peak of importance in the decades after the Second World War. It refers to the bespoke middle-class house, a place tailored to the particularities of the client and reflecting the personal idiosyncrasies of the architect.

Many architects, particularly in the 1890s, devoted themselves almost exclusively to house design, and even those with greater things in mind were happy to exercise skill and imagination in the production of schemes of relatively modest size. The main proponent of the grand manner, Sir Reginald Blomfield, wrote in his memoirs, 'the design of houses in town and country, is … the most attractive part of an architect's work.'[1] In addition, it may be remembered that Lutyens' early fame rested on his house designs in Surrey and Sussex, and that Voysey did very little architectural work that was not domestic.

One of the reasons for this interest in domestic commissions was that it was in the house for the cultured client that the Arts and Crafts movement was allowed to attain its potential. If the chemistry between patron and designer worked, then the architect could indulge his aesthetic ambitions. Vulgarity and the harshness of modern materials, typical of many Victorian houses, had become distinctly unfashionable by the last few decades of the nineteenth century, and the typical Edwardian house does not strike a jarring note in its surroundings. Indeed, houses were designed to look as though they had been *in situ* for many years, and sometimes as though they had grown from the materials, spirit and history of their sites in the most direct way.

Such was the variety of stimulating work produced, that interest was expressed elsewhere in Europe, most notably in Germany. Hermann Muthesius, a German architect sent to Britain as a diplomatic attaché, was particularly enthusiastic. He had reported on socio-commercial aspects of life in the British Isles, but in a letter to the Grand Duke of Saxe-Weimar in 1897 he stated that he was hoping to start a 'thorough investigation and exposition of the English house' because 'there is nothing as unique and outstanding in English architecture as the development of the home.'[2]

The result was *Das Englische Haus*, which first appeared in three parts in 1904-5 and provided an extensive catalogue of contemporary domestic architects and their buildings. It looked at the origins of the domestic movement in the designs of Philip Webb and Norman Shaw, went on to examine houses by younger architects, such as Voysey and Lutyens, and then tackled the way in which climate and social matters contributed to the essential nature of the English house. The third part was devoted to interiors.

Muthesius was particularly interested in the way in which the design of the house, in the English tradition, was not bound by the formalistic conventions that predominated elsewhere in Europe. The building was a product of many forces that shaped it: response to site and climate; pattern of use and social habits; materials and construction. His only criticisms were concerned with a lack of heavyweight construction – here he must have been thinking about houses in the south of England – and a rather spartan attitude to comfort.

The principles lying behind design parameters noted in Muthesius' book were representative of the mixed social and political thinking of the period. In one way, they represented Morrisian socialism and Arts and Crafts principles, which emphasised the nobility of work and the breaking down of distinctions between artists and craftsmen. On the other hand, they chimed in with the mood of nationalism which was to be found across Europe at the time. This was not a small-minded, 'little England' nationalism, but an attempt to emphasise local roots and traditions: the world was a diverse and interesting place. Arts and Crafts buildings sprang from the soil, adopting the local vernacular.

Lawrence Weaver's popular book *Small Country Houses of Today* emphasised these themes in reviewing over forty examples. Throughout, he promoted the Arts and Crafts ideas which formed the theoretical background to most of the buildings illustrated, whatever their ostensible style. In his introduction, he stated that 'Now, after the lapse of a century devoted to groping experiments and detached eclecticism, there are definite signs of renewing sleeping traditions, not on merely imitative lines, but in the spirit of the old work.'[3] He noted the formative factors affecting the site – soil, views, altitude, protection, slope and contour, neighbourhood and road, accessibility, public services – as helping to determine the setting of the house. Cost was not neglected, and was brought in as a justification for using local materials, rather than those that were mass produced and had spread ubiquitously throughout the kingdom. 'If a home is three miles from a station, instead of nearby,' he said, 'every ton of brick and timber carted will cost about half-a-crown [12½p] more.'

Weaver was interested in the art and practicality of building, in creating a sense of place which made the superficial adoption of a style unnecessary. As one might expect from a commentator writing at this period, he despised Victorian vulgarity, and the pretentiousness and stuffiness that he read into works like Robert Kerr's *The Gentleman's House*, the third edition of which was published in 1871.

A photograph taken shortly after completion of Edward Prior's 'Home Place', one of the most exuberant Edwardian houses.

Most of the buildings illustrated by Weaver were fairly modest, in that they ranged in price from about 6d to 10d [2½p to 4p] per cubic foot. Typically, they had names that reflected either the history of the location or the nature of the site: Walter H. Brierley's 'Bishopsbarns' at York; E. J. May's 'Gilhams Birch', Rotherfield; Horace Field's 'South Hill', near Woking; Alfred Powell's 'Long Copse', Elmhurst.

One of Weaver's main themes was the appropriate use of suitable materials. E. Guy Dawber, for instance, specialised in Cotswold houses, and Weaver prefaced his description of 'Coldicote', Moreton-in-Marsh, by a brief dissertation on the English limestone building tradition. At 'Coldicote', the limestone was in coursed rubble; 'the most suitable treatment for the thin layers in which the local quarries, only two or three miles away, provide the stone.'[4] In a house at Farnham, by Harold Falkner, erstwhile pupil of Reginald Blomfield, green glazed tiles were used internally. These were from the local pottery, originally established in the sixteenth century and working again by the late nineteenth century. The tiles were hand made, and Weaver noted that these, rather than machine-made items, were particularly attractive to architects because they had 'a surface mechanically imperfect, and for this reason delightful.'[5]

Restraint in the use of colour and texture was commended by Weaver. In Ernest Gimson's house at Sapperton, in Gloucestershire, for instance, 'not only is decoration totally absent from the fabric, it is scarcely represented by any of the objects in the [living] room except the one bowl, of flowers.'[6] Indeed, the wide oak floorboards contrasting with the white-washed ceiling, and the play of light from the deeply recessed windows, provided adequate visual stimulation. Sobriety of this kind had been pioneered in the 1890s by Voysey, who had said that simplicity was the end rather than the beginning of design, and that the architect should strictly curb any idea of expressing himself. However, Weaver was firmly of the opinion that too much restraint could give as bad an impression as too little.

Practicality and convenience figured high on Weaver's list, and he noted the disposition of spaces to provide a home that worked well as a functional entity, both in planning terms and in the design and siting of fixtures and fittings. Light, space and cosiness seem to dominate. At 'Coldicote', for instance, 'the billiard room is the main living room, for it has a pleasant bay looking to the south west and doors to a good verandah, while the fireplace is set in a comfortable ingle.'[7] In addition, this house exhibited some of the facilities which were becoming more and more common in the Edwardian home: the stable court containing a garage and engine room 'where electricity is generated for lighting and pumping' as well as loose boxes, a harness room and a coach house.

The spatial disposition of these houses was varied, but quite often the hall formed an important feature. Generally separated from the entrance door by a lobby or outer hall, it provided a pleasant space for sitting and was sometimes arranged with cosy screened fireplace, or built-in window seats. It served also as a circulation space, and smaller houses usually had plans where there were no corridors in the main parts of the house, but all major rooms were accessible from the hall. H. M. Baillie Scott pioneered flexibility of space, and the use of sliding partitions, so that rooms could be combined or separated at will.

Overall plan forms were in many cases compact, with major areas arranged into what amounts to a basic rectangle or 'L' shape, perhaps with an appendage for the kitchen, scullery and servants' areas. If large enough, this could be formed into a service court, with outhouses, garage and stables. The celebrated 'butterfly' plan – canted wings opening out to the south, but enclosing the north – was also used, but its architectural implications seem to have limited its popularity, and costs may have been high when compared to more simple, rectangular types.

Artist craftsmen or members of craft guilds were often employed to work in these houses: G. P. Bankart, who was a specialist in plasterwork, reintroducing Elizabethan techniques in his decorative ceiling designs; or William Aumonier, the carver, asked to produce a suitable lettered motto, or carvings to stone dressings, doorheads or chimney pieces. In addition, artists' work could have included gesso or stencilled friezes above panelling and stained-glass windows. Some walls may have been decorated with wallpaper by Walter Crane or Voysey, a talented designer despite his strictures on purity. In many Arts and Crafts houses, furniture was built-in, comprehensiveness of design being a tenet of the movement. The entire house may have been furnished by one company, such as the Morris concern, or Liberty, which provided a comprehensive range of furnishings and household objects.

Thus, the house was not only a framework for family life, but a place where art, beauty and utility intermingled. Not all were 'precious', but the attitude filtered into most purpose-built, middle-class houses, even if the owner was a hard-headed businessman.

Nor was design confined to the house itself. The garden was made to complement it – to be seen from the house, to be experienced as an outdoor space, and to see the house from.

In Victorian times, gardens had exhibited either contrived whimsicality, or else Italianate, geometrical patterns with garishly coloured plants and bedding-out of hothouse varieties. Towards the end of the nineteenth century, William Robinson promoted the 'natural garden', attempting to create a less formal feeling and to learn from the natural disposition of plant species. Architects tended to favour 'old-fashioned' gardens, modelled on sixteenth- and seventeenth-century examples, where a kind of picturesque restraint was evident,

with parterres, arbours and walks on a fairly small scale, and a limited palette of colours and textures. Two architects, in particular, promoted this type of design. J. P. Sedding, author of *Garden Craft Old and New*, did so up to his untimely death in 1891, and Reginald Blomfield, who wrote *The Formal Garden in England*, established his practice with it, once it became known amongst the gentry.

In true Arts and Crafts fashion, Blomfield pleaded for the design of the garden to be integral with that of the house: 'Is the garden to be considered in relation to the house, and as an integral part which depends for its success on the combined effect of the house and garden; or is the house to be ignored in dealing with the garden?'[8]

Blomfield's position was held by a number of artist architects, and the 'formal garden' became popular, as it could be adopted for large-scale country mansions or fairly modest suburban houses: old-fashioned gardens, with old-fashioned flowers and sober little brick summerhouses. It was Robinson's pupil, Gertrude Jekyll, however, who set the trend for the Edwardian garden. She combined Robinson's 'natural' theme with the architectonic, celebrated in her work with the young Edwin Lutyens from the 1890s onwards. Gardens became 'outdoor rooms', bounded by balustrades, hedges and herbaceous borders, perhaps with a stone-lined channel and a small stream trickling through, but all adjusted to the disposition of the house and its immediate outdoor spaces.

The 'bespoke' Edwardian middle-class house was, therefore, a delightful creation, at once comfortable, romantic, friendly, and at home in its surroundings. It may have been cottagey in style, or have had Tudor or Jacobean overtones. Some houses were plain, a tribute to local building techniques and materials, others had 'Wrenaissance' features. Whatever ostensible style was employed, the Edwardian house continued to exert its influence for many years, though succumbing to an increasing taste for the neo-Georgian. It also had an effect upon speculative builders, and some of its elements are to be seen in inter-war, semi-detached dwellings along the by-passes of Britain.

1. Reginald Blomfield, *Richard Norman Shaw, RA, Architect, 1831-1912: a Study*, London, 1940, p.54
2. Dennis Sharp (ed), *The English House*, London, 1979, p.xv (translation and revision of H. Muthesius, *Das Englische Haus*, Berlin, 1904-5)
3. Lawrence Weaver (ed), *Small Country Houses of Today*, London, 1911, p.xi
4. *ibid* p.38
5. *ibid* p.44
6. *ibid* p.52
7. *ibid* p.42
8. Reginald Blomfield, *The Formal Garden in England*, London, 1892, p.1

Home Place, Norfolk

The terrace and garden front of 'Home Place'. The range of 'natural' materials used, with the consequent textural variety, is very evident. The danger of visual indigestion is increased by the use of a large number of simple patterns built into the walls.

'Home Place', near Holt, in north Norfolk, was built to the designs of Edward S. Prior (1852-1932), an architect whose work can seem extremely eccentric to the modern observer. Despite his small output, however, Prior was one of the most interesting of Arts and Crafts architects. On what might be called the extreme wing of the movement, he was able to take the opportunity to follow some of his beliefs through to their logical conclusions.

At first sight, Prior does not seem the stuff of which eccentrics are made. From an establishment background, he was educated at Cambridge, where his keen intellect was apparent, but where he also succeeded as a sportsman, obtaining an athletics blue. He joined Richard Norman Shaw's office after university, and was one of the band of lively-minded pupils

and assistants who founded what was to become the Art Workers' Guild, a key organisation in the Arts and Crafts movement.

As a young architect he became friendly with Reginald Blomfield, who called him 'a man of considerable ability, and of a thoughtful and original turn of mind.'[1] Blomfield's relationship with Prior seems to have been noisy, for both men liked a good argument, were strong-minded and had similar educational backgrounds. Interestingly, having started off heavily influenced by Norman Shaw, Blomfield became more conservative, restrained and low-key in his work, whilst Prior moved towards an original and idiosyncratic architecture which was ultimately a dead end.

Prior was keen to embrace the Arts and Crafts notion that

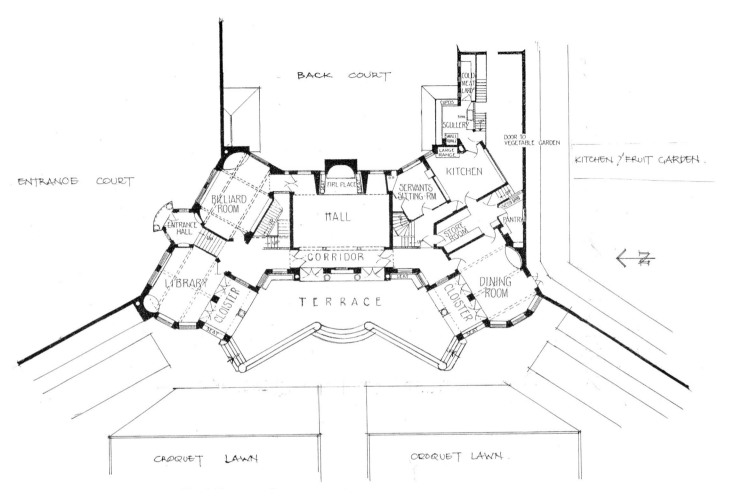

The ground-floor plan of 'Home Place'. The external spaces are part of an integrated plan for the house and its grounds, made more interesting by the 'butterfly' form.

any 'style' that a building had should come automatically from its response to site, use of materials and so on, and should not be historically referential.

During the 1890s he established a theme with a novel symmetrical house plan, which came to be known as the 'butterfly' plan. The centre portion of the building was flanked by wings which splayed outwards, exposing a considerable length of wall to the private areas of the site, usually the sunny south quadrant, and narrowing to the north, where an entrance court could be located. This disposition of elements allowed the architect to control views out and in, to give the best possible orientation to a variety of rooms, and to relate external spaces to internal areas. Prior produced a hypothetical clay model of such a house for the Royal Academy exhibition

in 1895. The following year, he was able to realise his ideas when he designed 'The Barn' at Exmouth, Devon. This rather 'hobbity' building had big thatched roofs with great columnar chimneys pushing through. Continuing the vernacular theme, Prior used local red sandstone to form the main wall surfaces, but here and there it was discontinued, and large, smooth cobbles from a nearby beach were used.

Following 'The Barn', a more elaborate project was shown in wax model form at the 1899 Academy exhibition, but Prior reverted to the earlier plan type, though on a larger scale, for 'Home Place', in Norfolk. This house, first called 'Voewood' and then 'Kelling Place', was built for the Reverend Percy Lloyd and his wife. Work on site began in 1903, but unfortunately in the same year a new hospital building was begun

It was decided that the flower garden should be sunken, and that the materials dug out should be used in the construction of the house. An area one acre in extent and six feet (2 metres) deep was excavated. Pebbles from the excavation were used for facing parts of the walls, gravel for concrete, and sand for general building purposes. The cost of extraction was almost offset by savings on the purchase of materials. In addition, local stone was employed, and much use made of tiles manufactured from Norfolk clay. Oak was obtained locally 'at a cost hardly above that of good deal'.[2]

A general contractor was not employed in the building process. Specialist work for fenestration and plumbing and electrical services was executed by a firm under contract, but the carcass of the house was built in a different way. A. Randall Wells (1877-1942), an architect in his own right, in conjunction with a Mr Blower, supervised the works, employed labour and purchased materials as and when necessary. Wells was an Arts and Crafts architect and, although some twenty-five years younger than Prior, was sympathetic to the view that the process of building and design were inseparable.

Quite a grand house was produced, the splay of the wings exaggerating its size. The area contained within the splay faced on to gardens, but unlike 'The Barn', the outward side of one of the enclosing wings was treated as an entrance front, with a projecting porch. This entrance 'wing' contained the library and billiard room at ground-floor level. The wing to the opposite side contained kitchen and service accommodation, as well as the dining room, and adjoined the fruit and vegetable garden. The 'body' of the house, between the two wings, had a large, rectangular hall rising through two storeys, with a centrally placed inglenook fireplace, and a corridor running at two levels along its length on the garden side. French windows opened out from the corridor on to a terrace above the sunken garden, and to either side, the library and dining room had cloisters with built-in seats, facing on to the terrace.

The wings of the house had basements and two storeys above, but the central block was three storeys, with rooms in the roof. Access to the upper floor was gained by staircases which occupied the awkward space between the centre block and the canted wings.

The morphology of the house does, of course, make for strange views from certain angles, because of roof intersections and changes in height. This could have been played down, and the whole mass given a sober dress. Prior, however, took the opposite line. The patterning and modelling of the wall surface, the colours and textures, are all strongly pronounced. In the patterning, there is reference to a local tradition of Norfolk cottages and farm buildings which

The interior of the hall, looking towards the corridor/gallery which links the two wings of the butterfly plan across the central 'body'. The late medieval character may lead one to expect a timber-framed building.

next door. Mrs Lloyd was concerned about the possibility of contracting tuberculosis from her neighbours, and this very singular house changed hands within a short time.

The construction of the house was the epitome of the Arts and Crafts dream. The site was originally a turnip field. It was developed in stages, various small outbuildings being constructed first, and a vegetable garden established. In 1904 work began on the house itself, ancillary buildings, orchard and flower gardens.

Bishopsbarns, York

display similar, if more subdued, designs. This type of decoration grew up during the nineteenth century and involved the interplay of flint or pebbles, used for general walling, sometimes breaking into diapers or zigzags, with brick quoins and surrounds. Prior did not dream up his seemingly crazy decoration from scratch, therefore. It must also be noted that Detmar Blow had slightly earlier built a smaller holiday house – 'Happisburgh Manor' – along the coast, using similar devices.

There was, in Prior's work, an extraordinary abandon in the use of materials. Tiles were extravagantly employed. They formed the surrounds to first-floor windows, were treated in herringbone fashion at the lintel, and were deployed as decorative bands at eaves level. Tiles or very narrow courses of moulded brick were extensively used for chimney stacks. These huge structures were 'twisted' in Tudor fashion, and at some points paired with rectangular stacks. Tiles also appeared in patterning at the gables and formed the arch over the main entrance door, with the panel above consisting of herringbone tiling interspersed with diamond-shaped pieces of local stone. Elsewhere, stone was used in criss-cross lines, breaking up the pebble surface. The roofs were covered in pantiles. The whole brown, pink and orange composition looks 'hand knitted'. In a sense, it was – from the fabric of the site.

However earthy, though, this was an Edwardian house, and up-to-date features were incorporated. The floors, for instance, were of concrete, reinforced with iron chains. Electrical services were provided – lights, bells, telephones and hot water.

'Home Place' demonstrates both the potential and the limitations of the Arts and Crafts approach. Despite the radical planning, there is none of the magical combination of freedom and control that one finds in Frank Lloyd Wright's houses of the period. The layout and resultant external shapes remind one, if anything, of the Gothic Revival. The freedom is perhaps constrained by social habit and, subconsciously, dare it be said, by historical precedent. On the other hand, it is literally specific to its site. Prior could not have built a similar house in Oxfordshire or Yorkshire. Unfortunately, this approach could only work with houses or smallish buildings in the country. There was little future for such a radical interpretation of the Arts and Crafts movement in the city.

1. Reginald Blomfield, *Memoirs of an Architect*, London, 1932, p.55
2. *Architectural Review*, vol.19, Jan.-June 1906, p.70

The public face of 'Bishopsbarns' is quite private, almost forbidding, despite the fact that the small, unfenced forecourt leads straight off the public thoroughfare.

Built at around the same time as 'Home Place', 'Bishopsbarns' was in complete contrast. Although designed within the same Arts and Crafts tradition, it was restrained, whilst 'Home Place' was exuberant; conservative in planning, whilst 'Home Place' was novel. The main attributes of 'Bishopsbarns' were to do with refinement in the consideration of plan and detail. Overall, a very high quality was achieved, along with a great degree of architectural interest, without resort to stylistic gimmicks.

The house was designed for his own occupation by Walter H. Brierley (1862 - 1926), an architect based in York whose practice was largely confined to the city and to north Yorkshire. He was one of the list of distinguished architects operating regionally at this time. The practice in which he became a partner had, incidentally, been founded by another famous provincial architect of a previous age, John Carr, the celebrated Palladian. It has been implied that although Brierley was a first-rate planner of buildings and a good organiser, he relied upon his assistants, J. H. Tonge – a winner of the Soane Medallion – and J. Rutherford, for aesthetic inspiration. Be that as it may, the work produced by his office is always distinctive and interesting.

The plan of 'Bishopsbarns' is essentially linear. The major rooms, on the ground floor, are situated next to each other on the south side of the house. In the middle is a sitting hall with fireplace, to the east of which is the drawing room, and to the

The private, garden side of the house is more friendly, reducing in scale to welcome its occupants. The roof sweeps down to cover the loggia, or brick parlour, essentially an external room, in a most effective way between the hard edges of the drawing room and dining room projections.

west a dining room. A corridor, in part the 'outer hall', divides them from the staircase, cupboards, lavatory, pantry and entrance lobby on the north side. The only major room here is the study, to the east. At the opposite end of this rectangular arrangement are the kitchen and associated spaces. These can be entered from a separate tradesmen's entrance, which also gives access to outhouses. The whole arrangement is neat and well resolved.

The north side of the house addresses the street directly, for this is a suburban area. It was decided, though, that the site was not deep enough to accommodate a decent front and back garden. A small forecourt was therefore provided, without boundary wall, paved with black and white pebbles from Flamborough on the Yorkshire coast, in a chequerboard pattern. The façade of the house thus imposes itself strongly on to the street. At each end is a gable, and symmetry is almost reached, but then avoided by running a large chimney stack off the eastern gable, and disposing the fenestration to reflect the functions of the rooms behind, rather than providing an artificial regularity.

The north side of the house appears imposing because of its large mass of wall, with relatively small windows and tall gables. In addition, the house is split down its lateral axis, so that to the north there are three storeys of accommodation,

reflecting the low ceilings of the rooms that line this side, whilst to the south, facing the garden, the principal apartments are fairly lofty and there are only two storeys. Here, the roof sweeps down to shelter a loggia, described as the 'brick parlour', leading out from the sitting hall.

The architectural language is non-specific, and is, in part, derived from the materials used. These, in direct contrast to 'Home Place', are kept to a minimum, but are allowed to 'speak out'. There are three: narrow, red, handmade brick; thick, brown, handmade tiles; and oak. The rainwater pipes are lead. This is a house of roofs, chimneys and gables, but with no spurious applied decorative effects. There is no render to be patched and painted, no 'half-timbering', no weatherboarding or tile-hanging to be maintained. There is no need for painting, either, because the window frames and mullions, and the posts supporting the loggia, are of oak. A solid, substantial, but not austere effect is attained. The textures of brick and stone, and the warm colours, give a welcoming, homely feel.

If the name of a historical style has to be applied to this building, 'Tudor' would probably come closest. This is reflected internally in the extensive use of panelling, made from pine, the boarded floors, and the generally cosy atmosphere. In the drawing room is a gently curving ceiling, very reminiscent, though on a much smaller scale, of the treatment of contemporary halls and assembly rooms. It is enriched by decorative plasterwork, designed and executed by G. P. Bankart. At the time of its construction, Brierley was working on the North Yorkshire County Hall at Northallerton, and it may be that this treatment was suggested by the larger building. Hopton Wood stone was used at Northallerton, and also makes an appearance at 'Bishopsbarns' in the stone fireplace in the hall.

As in many Edwardian houses, the design of the garden is carefully considered, and complements the house. It is compartmented by yew hedges and has flower borders with planting devised by Gertrude Jekyll. A bowling green, separated from the building by flower beds, runs the length of the house, and beyond its containing yew hedge to the south of the site is a walk lined with herbaceous borders.

This is a very successful design overall, compact but spacious, modest and conservative, but stimulating in its detail and materials. It has continued in use as a house, with its features little altered.

The ground-floor plan of 'Bishopsbarns' illustrates the compact nature of Brierley's design, and also shows, in part, how the gardens are set out as a series of external spaces, complementing those inside.

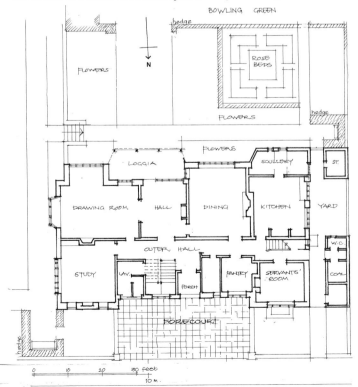

If 'Bishopsbarns' has a certain external austerity, this is mitigated by the warmth of the materials. York, after all, lies in a flat and fertile region. Fifty miles to the south-west, in the Pennine foothills, the climate is not so benign and the materials are more coarse.

Stretching towards Halifax from Huddersfield, a town grown rich on the fine woollen industry during the nineteenth century, a road was constructed which became lined with large, heavy Victorian houses to accommodate mill owners and other businessmen. In 1899, a successful local accountant, William H. Armitage, bought a plot off the east side of the road in Edgerton. There, the following year, he commissioned the Manchester architect Edgar Wood (1860-1935) to provide a design for his new house. When it was completed, in 1902, 'Banney Royd' presented itself as a strange combination of local vernacular and pronounced Arts and Crafts decoration, in many ways similar to the celebrated domestic work of H. M. Baillie Scott, the Manx architect, and Charles Rennie Mackintosh in Glasgow.

Wood was no stranger to Huddersfield, as his mother's family came from the town, and his uncle, James Nield Sykes, had been an early client. As a youngster, Wood had wanted to be a fine artist, but was forced to compromise by the practical concerns of his mill-owning father, and settled for a career in architecture. He was drawn to the Arts and Crafts movement, and was one of the founders of the Northern Art Workers' Guild. He seems never to have lost his desire to adopt the mantle of an artist, affecting flamboyant, artistic dress, and eventually retiring to Italy to paint. However, at the time at which 'Banney Royd', his largest house, was built he was undoubtedly a competent professional as well as an innovative designer. Within a few years, he was to enter into association with the practical J. Henry Sellers.

The house, conventionally, took its theme from sixteenth- and early-seventeenth-century domestic architecture, though it is of a different character from the squat, black, yeomen's houses that occur in the district. It was built in the local sandstone, squared and coursed, with ashlar treatment in places. The roof was covered with sandstone slates. These materials are commonly found in Huddersfield, which is a stone town, and many variants on the 'Banney Royd' theme were subsequently built in the more select residential areas. The stone makes for a robust aesthetic, as it is not easy to carve or shape because of its heavy grain. This is entirely suitable for an area where strong winds, stagnant, moisture-laden days and sharp frosts quickly dispose of more feeble materials and inappropriate constructional techniques.

Contrasted with this austerity is Wood's wilful and idiosyncratic decorative style. His work is very mannered, and almost

A view of 'Banney Royd', looking from the rose garden to the terrace, shows the stark character of the local stone and the blunt, straightforward constructional detailing to which it gives rise. In real life, the scene is less grim and much more welcoming than it appears in the photograph.

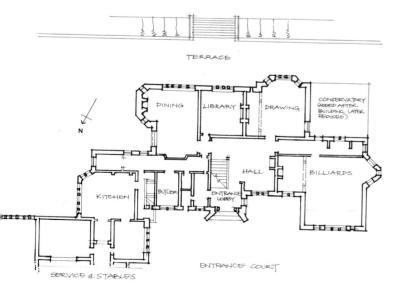

The ground floor plan of 'Banney Royd' is centred on the fine entrance hall, from which access corridors lead. The hall has a pleasant window alcove, an elaborately carved fireplace, and at one time possessed a painted allegorical frieze on the wall above the panelling, facing the entrance lobby.

as exaggerated as that of Mackintosh. Externally, this is evident in the battering, or sloping back, of the canted piers on either side of the ashlar entrance bay, the exaggerated carved keystone to the archway leading to the doors, and the curved copings to the pier heads. Internally, there is a mixture between this type of design and the more conventional panelled manor house style. Above the panelling in the hall, Wood incorporated a frieze painted by Frederick W. Jackson. This was typical of Arts and Crafts pictorial work, obviously with allegorical or historical subject matter; it has unfortunately been lost.

Wood reserved his most idiosyncratic decoration for the fireplaces and some areas of timber carving, such as the staircase newels and the posts supporting the alcove arches in the billiard and drawing rooms. The fireplaces in the hall, dining room and billiard room were all elaborately carved, a less grainy sandstone being employed. Sculptured figures were featured. Appropriately for Huddersfield, that in the dining room was the Angel of the Rains.

These ethereal figures, swirling carving, the battering to the billiard room fireplace and the cabbage-like carving to timber posts all remind one of Mackintosh to such an extent that it may be that Wood had decided to try his hand at the Glasgow style in this house. The decoration is rather at odds with the character of the rest of the building.

The plan of the house is straightforward in essence, the main block lying to the south, with stables, coach house, cottages and laundry forming an open court to the north. This stretches north-east beyond the entrance front of the

Ditton Place, Balcombe, Sussex

Internally, Wood makes good use of alcoves and cosy sitting areas. He also incorporates Arts and Crafts carving of an extreme, almost Art Nouveau, nature in timber and stone. The Angel of the Rains, for instance, enhances the dining room fireplace.

house. The entrance lobby leads into a sizeable hall, in the centre of the plan, from which the staircase rises and also from which short corridors lead to the principal rooms. There is nothing unusual about this layout, but Wood has contrived to introduce alcoves and cosy sitting areas where possible, notably in the hall, dining room, drawing room and billiard room, by separating these zones with arched openings. Upstairs, bedrooms occupy available perimeter wall space, and are served by a central corridor, running from the staircase.

So, in many respects, Wood produced a comfortable, spacious and welcoming house typical of its period. The eruptions of wilful decoration add interest, but are not essential to the success of the house, which achieves much of its character by architectural means. At about the same time that it was built, the architect was able to indulge his idiosyncrasies to a great extent in the design of a nearby clock tower at Lindley, commissioned by James Nield Sykes, which seems to leap out of an illustration to some children's fantasy storybook.

Wood's design themes would have been regarded as rather degenerate in London circles, and verging on Continental Art Nouveau. Looking, too, at Baillie Scott and Mackintosh, one wonders if, perhaps, the farther north one went, the easier it was to get away with such excesses.

'Ditton Place' is distinguished from the other houses so far described in that it is representative of the 'Wrenaissance' style, which gradually became commonplace for country mansions after the turn of the century. The style, as we have seen, particularly with reference to Reginald Blomfield's work, sought to introduce a sophisticated, quiet, controlled effect, free from the hyperactivity of some late-nineteenth-century buildings and the gloom of neo-Tudor. At the same time, it provided opportunities for the artist craftsman, as latter-day Grinling Gibbons, and a relatively light, elegant environment.

'Ditton Place' was built by Cecil Brewer and Arnold Dunbar Smith for Alderson Burnell Horne at Balcombe, in Sussex, in 1904. Horne was a theatrical gentleman. A one-time associate of Johnston Forbes-Robertson, he was an actor manager and owner of the Westminster Theatre. He seems to have spent his life playing roles, for he had two aliases besides his real name: 'Anmer Hall' was used in theatrical business circles, and 'Waldo Wright' when acting.

Horne had his house built on the site of a smaller Victorian dwelling, preserving the formal garden that had been laid out in the mid-1890s by Blomfield. Included on the site is a large tennis lawn in the south-west segment, which is overlooked by a loggia and terrace enclosed by the wings on the west front of the house. This feature gives some clue to the main function of the building, for tennis was one of the owner's chief recreations. In addition, the provision of seven guest bedrooms, some lavish in size with *en suite* dressing rooms, exclusive of Horne's own suite and the nursery bedroom, seems to lead to the conclusion that the primary purpose of the house was entertainment. Perhaps Horne stayed in his Albany apartment during the week, and relaxed at weekends in the country, inviting house parties down to Balcombe.

Another feature of the house, at ground-floor level, is a long, vaulted gallery running north to south, terminating in the drawing room. At the other end, a broad flight of stairs rises to a half-landing beyond. It is the ideal setting for a grand entry by those of a theatrical bent. The gallery must have been a perfect resort for guests on wet days, and it is doubled by the loggia, which runs parallel to it. The drawing room allowed for a more formal retreat, as did the two-section library, although this was sub-divided by curtains to allow for the production of amateur performances. Despite the provision of this conventional accommodation, though, it is interesting to note that the gallery occupies a much greater proportion of the floor area than do the sitting halls in the other houses described. Indeed, a lobby and good-sized entrance hall was provided in addition.

The second-floor space, located in the roof, was occupied by a children's playroom and schoolroom. No doubt the large

The entrance front of 'Ditton Place' with its projecting porch and semicircular pediment on the centre line of the main section of the façade.

rooms were delightful for the children to lark around in, but if their presence was thought undesirable, then Horne and his architects had made sure, by this provision, that they were neither seen nor heard. Indeed, all aspects of comfort and convenience were considered, and should chilly weather spoil outside activities, the splendid fireplaces in the main rooms were supplemented by no fewer than forty-seven central-heating radiators. The hot-water supply was generated by a separate boiler from that which provided the central heating, and gave an instantaneous service to baths and basins, as well as heating towel rails.

The interior of the drawing room was finished in light-painted panelling with pilasters, scrollwork and other elements of early-eighteenth-century Classicism, more humble variations on the theme occurring in the entrance hall and gallery. Features from this period also dominated the exterior. The walls were in red brick with Portland stone dressings, including pilasters, niches and the surrounds to the handsome, elliptical, first-floor windows. These surrounds were enriched with carving. A substantial, white-painted, timber cornice had dormers above, and there were tall, rectangular chimneys.

The form of the house was rather like a compression of similar plans found in larger properties. A symmetrical block to the south contained the principal apartments, and was treated in an appropriately grand manner. To the north was the service block, grouped around a central light well, but containing, upstairs, the owner's suite with bedroom, dressing room, bathroom and parlour. This was expressed externally in a more rural, low-key style. The two blocks, however, were pushed together, such that the entrance front had the north terminal pavilion of its symmetrical façade in the service block. On the other side of the house, the distinction was clearer, but none the less upsetting and inconsequential to the purist.

Such architectural scruples are not relevant to a criticism of the house, however. We may allow ourselves to imagine a sunny weekend at 'Ditton Place': gentlemen in flannels and ladies in long white skirts playing tennis on the lawn, against the red and white backdrop of the house; the architecture relaxed and friendly, but providing a traditional ambience. Tables and chairs would be set out within the cool loggia, with its sunshades, and on the terrace in front. From inside the house would come peals of laughter as the younger guests amused themselves in the gallery. It would have been a de-

The west front of 'Ditton Place', an Edwardian interpretation of the late seventeenth century, with loggia and terrace, overlooking the tennis lawn. Photographed in 1907.

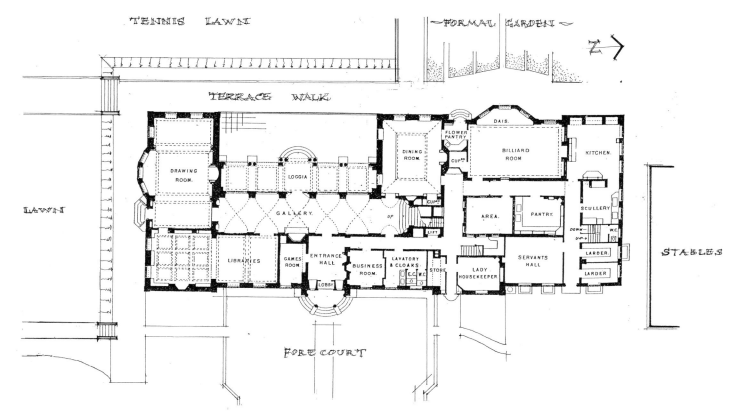

The ground floor plan of 'Ditton Place', showing the overlap between the service area and the house proper, so that the north pavilion of the symmetrical east front is part of the service block. The billiard room and the owner's bedroom suite are also incorporated into the block, which has a more rustic appearance on its west side.

lightful scene, and typically Edwardian, complemented by the early-eighteenth-century architectural language of the house, with its paired Doric columns supporting the entablature of the loggia, and the semicircular pediment looming above on the centre line of the composition.

This fine house is typical of the light-hearted aspects of Edwardian times. It lacks the intensity or wilfulness of some other examples, and was clearly built for pleasure and ease. Perhaps it represents the period so well because it captures the nuances of life amongst a wealthy set during the decade before the Great War, and encapsulates them in its style and form.

The architects of the building, Cecil Brewer and Arnold Dunbar Smith, had formed a partnership in 1895, and won the competition for the design of the Passmore Edwards Settlement in Tavistock Place, Bloomsbury, the following year. This building, now Mary Ward House, was a study in 'artiness' and asymmetry. Internally, it included work by leading Arts and Crafts architects. After its completion, Smith and Brewer went on to design houses for Mrs Ward's estate. It is instructive, therefore, to note that they followed fashion, and not only conceived the later 'Ditton Place' as a 'Wrenaissance' house, but went on to produce the much more severe Classic-

The gallery, running parallel with the loggia and forming a spine to the house, part corridor and part informal social area.

ism of the National Museum of Wales in 1910, its rather dry Beaux Arts style contrasting with Lanchester, Stewart and Rickards' exuberant Baroque city hall next door. Apparently, Dunbar Smith was a talented organiser of buildings, and the Museum of Wales represents his capabilities at their peak. Unfortunately, because of the intervention of the First World War, the first phase of the museum was not completed until 1927, six years before Smith's death, and nine years after Brewer's early demise.

Conclusion

The salon of the liner RMS *Franconia*, 1910, designed by the Liverpool architects Willink and Thicknesse. They went on to design the interiors of many more Cunarders, as well as the company's headquarters in association with Mewès and Davis.

At the end of this survey of Edwardian architecture, it seems as difficult to produce a neat summary of what the term 'Edwardian' means as it did at the beginning. Questions as to whether it is any more than a convenient label to describe the tail end of the Victorian era, or whether it represents a period of transition characterised by growth and change, have been raised, and ambiguous answers found. In addition, whether it should simply cover the years up to the outbreak of the First World War from the turn of the century, or whether it should be expanded to include the 1890s, is another problem. The themes that run through the period are not easy to define, nor are they exclusive to Edwardian architecture, by themselves. Taken together, though, they help to provide as firm an outline as possible for an age of individuality and diversity.

One prominent feature is the importance accorded to buildings by the large diversity of clients commissioning architects to produce anything from modest private houses to universities, and from public libraries to the headquarters of large national companies. Buildings were symbolic of status and civic pride. A great deal of thought was put into their design, and durable, high-quality materials were chosen as a matter of course. The continuing influence of the Arts and Crafts movement ensured that there was respect for the craft of building itself, which reached a high point during the period. The integration of the work of sculptors, painters, carvers and other craftsmen was expected in almost all public buildings, and in many private houses.

Nearly all Edwardian architects were willing to use the very latest technology to expand the range of expression and the functional capabilities of their buildings. It was only as the period wore on that technological issues began to alter the approach to design, interacting with other factors, as we have seen. An analogy may be made with the ocean liner. Contained within the steel hull, powered by throbbing machinery, are the elegant public spaces that act as a backdrop to social activity. The liner, like buildings in a city, is not merely an artefact, but a social organism.

Edwardian architects were reluctant to divorce themselves from traditional culture, and from conventions and proprieties that laid down codes of behaviour. It was surely rude to be thrust into a public building straight from the street without any of the preparation signified by a flight of steps, a portico, a porch and then an entrance hall. Few architects would terminate a column against a horizontal surface like a ceiling without an intermediate capital and entablature to effect the transition politely. In short, there seems to have been a feeling that despite modern technology, the application of an unfamiliar architectural language based on the opportunities awarded by modern construction was too much to introduce at the time. Revolutionary ideas were largely rejected. Perhaps, for many, the intensities of the Gothic Revival were still unpleasantly close.

In *Towards a New Architecture*, published in 1923, Le Corbusier condemns the moribund stylism of established architects and makes a plea for a new architecture, responsive to the directness and honesty of the engineer's aesthetic. His book is full of examples of the admirable work of the unselfconscious designers of grain silos, motor cars, aeroplanes and ships. Indeed, there are no fewer than six illustrations of one great liner, the *Aquitania*, the 'ship beautiful'. As we have seen, she was sister to the landlocked Cunard building on the Pier Head in Liverpool. Both ship and building were examples of the latest in Edwardian technology, and contained design by the same architects. What Corbusier admired, of course, was not the classical detail of the liner's interior, but the grace of hull and superstructure, though even this was designed to

look good, and was not simply the direct result of scientific calculations.

Le Corbusier spoke for the twentieth century, the world after the Great War. As society changed, the marble-clad lobby, the panelled board room, the Louis Quinze dining room, and the Baroque hall with its massive chandeliers all became less relevant. The great ships perished, sometimes in appalling circumstances. Much Edwardian architecture remained, however, and, despite its anachronisms, is fondly regarded by those who come into contact with it during the daily round.

There is, though, little point in trying to return to the manners of a bygone age, or to attempt to create an Edwardian style. Such architecture could not have continued in its own time, anyway, because it lacked a strong root of theory from which to grow. When this was eventually obtained from the academicism of the new, full-time schools of architecture, it was at the expense of the spontaneity, sensuality and evocative charm which lay at its heart. Even those architects who espoused the Arts and Crafts approach were doomed, for their notion of honesty in construction and materials, which may seem progressive, led them away from the country crafts which they loved towards the banal realities of the steel and concrete frame. Many of them subsequently retreated in despair from the practice of architecture.

Unfortunately for present-day architects, the building is no longer the status symbol that it was in Edwardian times; indeed the question of whether business activity needs a specific location at all or will take place on the intangible electronic highway is constantly asked. The same applies to entertainment and, to some extent, leisure activities. Perhaps one of the main purposes of buildings now is to remind citizens of the physical and social world. A return to Edwardian values would help to bring this about, not in a facile copying of images, but by celebrating materials, form and space, and by incorporating the work of artists and designers into all parts of the building; by bringing back into buildings wit, good humour, and a sense of experience and occasion.

Bibliography

A wide variety of sources has been consulted in the production of this work. References in the text have been confined to quotations, and it was decided that it would be useful to the reader to organise the bibliography into a series of sections relevant to the content of the book.

Chapters 1 and 2
Included in this section are certain books that have been useful throughout. Of particular note are those by A. Stuart Gray, Andrew Saint and Alastair Service. Mr Service's book contains articles about many Edwardian architects with interviews and invaluable contemporary comments.

Allwood, J., *The Great Exhibitions*, London, 1977

Aslet, C., *The Last Country Houses*, New Haven and London, 1982

Beattie, S., *The New Sculpture*, New Haven and London, 1983

Bingham, N. (ed), *The Education of the Architect*, Proceedings of the 22nd Annual Symposium of the Society of Architectural Historians of Great Britain, 1993, London, 1993

Blomfield, Sir R., *Memoirs of an Architect*, London, 1932

Brinnin, J. M., *The Sway of the Grand Saloon*, New York, 1971, London, 1972

Budden, L. B. (ed), *The Book of the Liverpool School of Architecture*, Liverpool and London, 1932

Crook, J. Mordaunt, *The Dilemma of Style: architectural Ideas from the picturesque to the post modern*, London, 1987

Cunningham, C., *Victorian and Edwardian Town Halls*, London, 1981

Cunningham, C. and P. Waterhouse, *Alfred Waterhouse, 1830-1905, Biography of a Practice*, Clarendon Studies in the History of Art, Oxford, 1992

Davey, P., *Arts and Crafts Architecture: the Search for earthly Paradise*, London, 1980

De Haan, H., and I. Haagsman, *Architects in Competition: international architectural competitions of the last two hundred years*, London, 1988

Fellows, R. A., *Sir Reginald Blomfield: an Edwardian Architect*, London, 1985

Gebhard, D., *Charles F. A. Voysey, Architect*, Los Angeles, 1975

Girouard, M., *Sweetness and Light: the 'Queen Anne' Movement, 1860-1900*, Oxford, 1977

Girouard, M., *The English Town*, special edn, London, 1990

Goodhart-Rendel, H. S., *English Architecture since the Regency: an Interpretation*, London, 1953

Gray, A. Stuart, *Edwardian Architecture: a biographical Dictionary*, London, 1985

Hobhouse, H. (ed), *County Hall*, Survey of London, Monograph 17, London, 1991

Houfe, S., *Sir Albert Richardson, the Professor*, Luton, 1980

Macleod, R., *Style and Society: architectural Ideology in Britain 1835-1914*, London, 1971

Postgate, R. W., *The Builders' History*, London, 1923

Reilly, C. H., *Representative British Architects of the present Day*, London, 1931

Reilly, C. H., *Scaffolding in the Sky: a semi-architectural Autobiography*, London, 1938

Saint, A., *Richard Norman Shaw*, New Haven and London, 1976

Service, A. (ed), *Edwardian Architecture and its Origins*, London, 1975

Summerson, Sir J., *The Turn of the Century: Architecture in Britain around 1900*, W. A. Cargill Memorial Lectures in Fine Art, Glasgow, 1976

Chapter 3
A number of excellent academic theses and articles were consulted for this chapter.

Beatty, C. J. P. (ed), *The Architectural Notebook of Thomas Hardy*, Dorchester, 1966

Bowyer, J., *History of Building*, London, 1973

Cusack, P., 'Reinforced concrete in Britain: 1897-1908', unpublished PhD thesis, University of Edinburgh, 1981

Cusack, P., 'Architects and the reinforced concrete specialist in Britain, 1905-1908', *Architectural History*, vol.29, 1986, p.183

Lawrence, J. C., 'Steel frame architecture versus the London Building Regulations: Selfridges, the Ritz, and American Technology', *Construction History*, vol.6, 1990, p.23

Lethaby, W. R., *Philip Webb and his Work*, Oxford, 1935, reissued London, 1979

Locker, F. M., 'The Evolution of Victorian and early twentieth century Office Buildings in Britain', unpublished PhD thesis, University of Edinburgh, 1984

Olley, J., 'Masters of building: the Reform Club', *The Architects' Journal*, vol.181, no.9, 1985, p.34

Olley, J. and C. Wilson, 'Masters of building: the Natural History Museum', *The Architects' Journal*, vol.181, no.13, 1985, p.32

Pevsner, Sir N., *Some architectural Writers of the nineteenth century*, Oxford, 1972

Port, M. H. (ed), *The Houses of Parliament*, New Haven and London, 1976

Strike, J. F., 'The influence of new materials and new methods of construction on architectural design: a historical study, 1700-1970', unpublished MPhil thesis, University of York, 1988

Thompson, P., *William Butterfield*, London, 1971

Watt, K. A., 'Nineteenth century brickmaking innovations in Britain: building and technological change', unpublished DPhil thesis, University of York, 1991

Wilkinson, B., *Ex Terra Lucem*, Leeds, 1983

Chapter 4

Much of the information in this chapter was culled from general reading over many years. I have, however, included a number of specific texts that have informed some of the factual information presented.

Bienefeld, M. A., *Working Hours in British Industry: an economic History*, LSE Research Monographs, London, 1972

Ensor, R. C. K., *England 1870-1914*, 1936, reprinted 1968

Fraser, W. Hamish, *The Coming of the Mass Market 1850-1914*, London and Basingstoke, 1981

Gaskell, S. Martin, *Model Housing from the Great Exhibition to the Festival of Britain*, London and New York, 1986

Jackson, F., *Sir Raymond Unwin, Architect, Planner and Visionary*, London, 1985

Keith-Lucas, B., and P. G. Richards, *A History of local Government in the twentieth century*, London, 1978

Laybourn, K., *The changing Face of Edwardian Philanthropy: the Guild of Help and the new Philanthropy, c.1903-1914*, University of Huddersfield, 1993

Magnus, P., *King Edward the Seventh*, London, 1964

Nowell-Smith, Simon (ed), *Edwardian England, 1901-1914*, London, 1964

Physick, John, *The Victoria and Albert Museum: the History of its Building*, Oxford, 1982

Service, A., *Edwardian Interiors: inside the Homes of the Poor, the Average and the Wealthy*, London, 1982

Supple, Barry (ed), *Essays in British Business History*, Oxford, 1977

Thompson, P., *The Edwardians: the Remaking of British Society*, London, 1975

Part Two

The second part of the book discusses a number of examples, and the bibliography is thus categorised according to the buildings which have been chosen.

The works of Gray and Service have provided background information, and in many cases some kind of archive material – drawings, documents relating to the building process or contemporary descriptions – has been used. Publications by local authorities and by building owners and enthusiasts have been an excellent source of material.

Abbreviations used are: *AR: The Architectural Review*; *B: The Builder*; *BN: Building News*; *CL: Country Life*; *RIBAJ: Journal of the Royal Institute of British Architects*.

Cardiff City Hall

AR, vol.20, Jul.-Dec. 1906, p.233

Chappell, E. L., *Cardiff's Civic Centre*, Cardiff, 1946

Purchon, W. S., 'The public buildings of Cardiff', *RIBAJ*, vol.29, no.13, p.385.

Cardiff City Council, *Official Programme for Opening the new City Hall and Law Courts, Cathays Park, Monday, October 29, 1906*

Cartwright Hall

B, vol.87, 5.11.1904, 26.11.1904

Bradford Art Galleries and Museums, *Cartwright Hall: a guide to the Building and its Architecture*, Bradford, 1987

Linstrum, D., *West Yorkshire Architects and Architecture*, London, 1978

Waterfield, G. (ed), *Palaces of Art: Art Galleries in Britain 1790-1990*, London, 1991

North Eastern Railway HQ

Irving, R. J., *The North Eastern Railway Company, 1870-1914: an economic History*, Leicester, 1976

Rankin, S., *A huge Palace of Business*, York, 1979

United Kingdom Provident Institution

AR, vol.22, Jul.-Dec. 1907, p.125

B, vol.93, 10.8.07

The Cunard Building

AR, vol.41, Jan.-June 1917, p.87; vol.43, Jan.-June 1918

Billinge, A., *A Century of Practice: the Gilling Dod Partnership*, private publication, Liverpool, 1982

Cunard Steamship Company, *The New Cunard Building*, commemorative programme for the opening, Liverpool, undated (1917?)

King Edward VII Sanatorium

AR, vol.19, Jan.-June 1906, p.278

Taylor, J., *Hospital and Asylum Architecture in England 1840-1914: building for Health Care*, London, 1991

Birmingham University

B, vol.82, 3.5.02; vol.92, 18.5.07; vol.93, 13.7.07

Cheesewright, M., *Mirror to a Mermaid*, Birmingham, 1975

Vincent, E. W. and P. Hinton, *The University of Birmingham: its History and Significance*, Birmingham, 1947

Wolverhampton Public Library

Champneys, A. L., *Public Libraries: a Treatise on their Design, Construction and Fittings*, London, 1907

Dewe, M. D., 'Henry Thomas Hare (1860-1921): an Edwardian public library architect and his work', unpublished MA thesis, University of Strathclyde, 1981

Latham, C.J., 'Wolverhampton Central Library: an architectural study', Open University A305 project, 1975

Munford, W.A., *Penny Rate: Aspects of British Public Library History, 1850-1950*, London, 1951

RIBAJ ser.III, vol.14, no.10, 23.4.07; ser.III, vol.28, 22.1.1921

Hull School of Art

AR, vol.18, Jul.-Dec. 1905, p.265; vol.15, no.86, Jan.-June 1904, p.164

B, vol.84, 25.4.03

BN, vol.89, 13.10.05, p.506

A History of the County of York: East Riding, Victoria County History, Oxford

Chelsea Public Baths

AR, vol.22, Jul.-Dec.1907, p.30

B, vol.87, 3.12.04

The Artistic House

Sharp, D. (ed), *The English House*, London, 1979; translation and revision of H.Muthesius, *Das Englische Haus*, Berlin, 1904-5

Stamp, G., and A.Goulancourt, *The English House 1860-1914: the Flowering of English domestic Architecture*, London, 1986

Weaver, L. (ed), *Small Country Houses of Today*, London, 1911

Home Place

AR, vol.19, Jan.-June 1906, p.70

Bishopsbarns

B, vol.96, 20.3.09, p.347

Nuttgens, P., *Brierley in Yorkshire: the Architecture of the Turn of the Century*, York, 1984

Banney Royd

Banney Royd Study Group, *Banney Royd, 'An Agreeable House'*, Huddersfield, 1991

Ditton Place

AR, vol.22, Jul.-Dec.1907, p.187

CL, vol.30, 1.7.1911, p.18

Index

London 25
County Hall, London 28, 34, 76; *76*
Creswell, H. Bulkeley 26
Cunard Building, Liverpool 108 - 14; *109, 111, 112, 113*
Currey, Henry 52, 70

Davis, Arthur J. 14, 40; *see also* Mewès and Davis
Dawber, E. Guy 142
Denell, R. A. 44
Devey, George 16
Ditton Place, Balcombe, Sussex 151 - 4; *152, 153, 154*
Doyle, J. Francis 21, 63 - 4, 109
Dronsfield Bros, Oldham *54*
Dunn, William 54, 59, 72

Edwards, J. Passmore 80, 128
Electra House, Moorgate, London 69, 96; *79*
Elliot, John 129 - 30
Elm Street School, Middleton 77; *55*

Falkner, Harold 142
Fehr, H. C. 90, 137
Field, Horace 102, 105, 142; *101, 103, 104*
Forsyth, J. Dudley 107
Frampton, George 96
Frith, William 125

General Post Office, King Edward Street, London 55 - 9; *56, 58*
George, Ernest 7, 9, 12, 14, 16, 26, 36; *11, 24*
Gimson, Ernest 142
Ginham, Percy 28
'Gothic Revival' 7, 9 - 10, 16, 46, 52, 92 - 3, 147, 156
Green, William Curtis 46; *46*
Gueritte, T. J. 102

Hall, E. T. 116
Hardy, Thomas 52, 70
Hare, Henry Thomas 21 - 2, 34, 42, 105 - 8, 128 - 34; *106, 107, 108, 129, 131, 133*
Harrington Gardens, South Kensington, London *11*
Harris, E. Vincent 46, 92
heating and ventilation 52, 69 - 73, 78, 96 - 9, 102 - 4, 114, 120, 128 - 9, 132, 140, 152
Henman and Cooper 71 - 2
Hennebique system (reinforced concrete) 53 - 4, 57, 59
Holden, Charles 14, 46, 115 - 20; *115, 117, 119*
Holland, Hannen and Cubitt 28, 114
Home Place, Norfolk 28, 144 - 7; *142, 144, 145, 146*
Horsley, Gerald 70; *71*
Howard, Ebenezer 82 - 3
Hull School of Art 24, 134 - 7; *127, 135, 136*

Institute of Chartered Accountants, Moorgate, London 12 - 13, 105; *15*

Jackson, Frederick W. 150
Jekyll, Gertrude 120, 143, 149
Jenkins, F. Lynn 107
Jenney, William le Baron 63
Joass, J. J. 16, 22, 48
Jones, A. G. 137

Kahn system (reinforced concrete) 59, 112
Keay, Lancelot 46
King Edward VII Sanatorium, Midhurst 115 - 20; *115, 117, 119*
Knott, Ralph 14, 28, 34, 76; *76*

Lanchester, Henry V *see* Lanchester, Stewart and Rickards
Lanchester, Stewart and Rickards 24, 28, 87 - 93, 134 - 7, 154; *51, 63, 87, 89, 90, 91, 127, 135, 136*
Leeds School of Art 137; *127*
Leitch, Archibald 80
Letchworth Garden City 78, 82 - 3; *78*

Abercrombie, Patrick 32, 36; *46*
Adams, H. Percy 116, 120
Adams, Maurice B. 130
Admiralty Arch, London 34 - 5; *35*
Adshead, Stanley 27, 32
Aldwych Competition 32 - 4; *32*
Allen, E. Milner J. 95
Alliance Assurance Offices, St James's Street, London 21, 72; *20*
Architects' Journal 40
Architectural Association 14, 26, 37, 39, 45, 116, 132
Architectural Review, 40, 114
Art Workers' Guild 10 - 14, 40, 96, 102, 144
'Arts and Crafts' 9 - 12, 16, 19 - 21, 28, 39, 53, 55, 115, 118 - 20, 132, 134, 141, 143 - 7, 149 - 50, 154 - 6
Ashton Memorial, Lancaster 22; *22*
Atkinson, R. Frank 64
Atkinson, Robert 45
Aumonier, William 107, 133, 143
Ayrton, Maxwell 95

Bankart, G. P. 89, 92, 125, 143, 149; *90*
Banney Royd, Huddersfield 149 - 51; *150, 151*
'Baroque, English' 18 - 26, 35, 42, 74, 79, 88, 93, 95, 105, 132, 140, 154
Barry, Charles 52
Bates, Harry 13
'Beaux Arts' 30 - 2, 36, 39 - 43, 48, 60, 64, 84, 110, 114, 140, 154
Bedford and Kitson 137; *127*
Belcher, John 9, 12 - 16, 20 - 2, 26, 67, 69, 96, 105; *13, 15, 16, 21, 22, 23, 47, 79*
Bell, Edward Ingress 121
Bell, Robert Anning 125
Bell, William 72, 102, 105
Bentley, J. F. 21, 85, 125
Birmingham University 121 - 6; *121, 122, 123, 124, 125*
Bishopsbarns, York 142, 147 - 9; *147, 148, 149*
Blackpool 81 - 2; *81*
Blomfield, Arthur 16, 26, 52
Blomfield, Reginald 12, 16 - 21, 26 - 7, 34, 36, 38 - 40, 48, 53, 141 - 4, 151; *18*
Blow, Detmar 147
Board of Architectural Education 38 - 9
Brewer, Cecil *see* Smith and Brewer
Brierley, Walter H. 71, 142, 147 - 9; *147, 148, 149*
British Museum, London 42; *41*
Broadbent, Abraham M. 96
Brock, Thomas 34
Bromsgrove Guild 13, 107, 125
Brydon, J. M. 16, 21, 75, 130
Burges, William 87, 92
Burnet, John James 40 - 2
Burnham, Daniel H. 32, 42, 63, 64
Butterfield, William 52
Bylander, Sven 44, 64, 67
'Byzantine' 21, 26, 125

Cadbury, George 30, 79, 82
Cardiff City Hall 28, 87 - 92, 154; *87, 89, 90, 91*
Carnegie, Andrew 62, 80, 122, 128
Cartwright Hall, Bradford 29, 94 - 9; *94, 97, 98, 99*
Chambers, William 36
Chelsea Public Baths, London 137 - 40; *137, 138, 139*
Coignet, E. 53 - 4
Coignet, François 53
Colchester Town Hall 21 - 2; *21*
Corbusier, Le 84, 156
Country Life offices, Tavistock Street,

Lethaby, William Richard 10, 19, 38, 46, 53, 125
Lever, William Hesketh 30, 32, 79, 82; *83*
lifts 72, 114, 118
Lindsay (W. H.) and Company 132
Lister, Samuel Cunliffe 95, 99; *50*
Liverpool School of Architecture 37, 39 - 40
London County Council 27 - 8, 32 - 4, 46, 64 - 7, 72, 76 - 8
Lucas, F. J. 60, 62, 93
Lutyens, Edwin 9, 12, 16, 30, 36, 48, 96, 120, 133, 141, 143; *25*

Macartney, Mervyn 20, 38, 40
McKim, Charles F. 42, 45
McKim, Mead and White 42, 140
Mackintosh, Charles Rennie 9, 149 - 51
Manchester Town Hall 76; *75*
Manningham Mill, Bradford *50*
Mappin House, Oxford Street, London 22; *47*
Marsh, Charles F. 54, 72
Maufe, Edward *46*
Mewès, Charles *see* Mewès and Davis
Mewès and Davis 42, 44, 59, 64, 67 - 8, 108, 109; *38, 43, 64, 65, 66, 67*
Millbank Estate 28, 78; *77*
'Modern movement' 30, 46 - 8, 62, 114, 115, 120
Moira, Gerald 107 - 8, 137
Montford, Paul 90
Moorcrag, Windermere *17*
Mouchel, L. G. 54, 57, 72, 102
Moundsmere Manor, Hampshire *18*
Mountford, Edward W. 22, 42
Muthesius, Hermann 45, 141

New Scotland Yard, Westminster, London *10*
New Theatre, Manchester *45*
Newton, Ernest 21, 72
North Eastern Railway Headquarters, York 101 - 5; *101, 103, 104*
Nuvacuumette system 70 - 1

'Old English' 7, 12, 16
Omsted, F. L. 32

Parker and Unwin 83
Parr's Bank, Liverpool 21; *62*
Pascal, Jean-Louis 39, 42, 48
Peach, C. Stanley 80
Pegram, Henry 125
Pickenham Hall, Norfolk 69
Pite, Arthur Beresford 14 - 16
Pleghard and Haefeli 62
Poole, Henry 90, 92, 107
Port Sunlight, London 82; *83*
Prior, Edward S. 14, 28, 144 - 7; *142, 144, 145, 146*

Quadrant, Regent Street, London 19, 21, 35 - 6; *37*
Queen Alexandra Sanatorium, Davos 62
'Queen Anne' 7, 12, 16, 133

Reilly, Charles H. 14, 26, 32, 37, 39 - 40, 42, 109; *46*
reinforced concrete 53 - 62, 67 - 8, 72, 84, 112
Richardson, Albert 14, 40, 42, 44 - 5; *46*
Richardson and Gill *33, 45*
Rickards, Edwin 9, 42; *see also* Lanchester, Stewart and Rickards
Riley, W. E. 28
Ritz Hotel, Piccadilly, London 44, 64, 67; *38*
RMS Franconia 109; *155*
Robinson, William 143
Royal Academy 12, 14, 19, 26, 36, 39 - 40, 96, 122, 145
Royal Academy of Music, Marylebone Road, London 24
Royal Automobile Club, Pall Mall, London 44, 67 - 8; *43, 64, 65, 66, 67*
Royal Institute of British Architects 12, 19, 36 - 8, 42, 44, 53 - 4, 57, 67, 71 - 2, 80, 132, 134
Royal Liver Building, Liverpool 59, 110; *61*

Royal London House, Finsbury Square, London 22; *23*
Royal Naval College, Dartmouth 26

Sachs, Edwin Otto 54, 72 - 3
St Paul's Girls' School, Hammersmith, London 70; *71*
St Thomas's Hospital, London 52, 70
San Francisco 32; *31*
Schenck, F. E. E. 107
Schultz, R. Weir 69
Scott, George Gilbert 30
Scott, Giles Gilbert 14, 46, 85
Scott, H. M. Baillie 143, 149, 151
Sedding, J. P. 143
Selfridges, Oxford Street, London 64, 67, 80; *64*
Sellers, J. Henry 55, 149; *54 see also* Wood and Sellers
Shaw, Richard Norman 7, 9 - 12, 14, 18 - 22, 28, 35 - 6, 53, 63, 70, 72, 102 - 5, 108 - 9, 141, 144; *10, 20, 37, 62*
Simpson, Frederick M. 37, 40
Simpson, John William 95; *94, 97, 98, 99*
Singer, Messrs J. W. 92
Slater, John 72
Smirke, Robert 42, 49 - 50, 94
Smith, Arnold Dunbar *see* Smith and Brewer
Smith and Brewer 92, 151 - 4; *152, 153, 154*
Stable court *13*
steel 42, 44, 62 - 8, 84, 88
Stewart, James S. *see* Lanchester, Stewart and Rickards
Stokes, Leonard 80
Sunderland Law Courts 140

Tanner, Henry 54, 57 - 9; *56, 58*
Thicknesse, Philip C. *see* Willink and Thicknesse
Thomas, Alfred Brumwell 22
Thomas, W. Aubrey 59, 110
Thornycroft, Hamo 13
Trafalgar Square, London *33*
Turner (E.) and Sons 28, 92

United Kingdom Provident Institution, Strand, London 105 - 8; *106, 107, 108*

ventilation *see* Heating and ventilation
Victoria and Albert Museum, London 24, 80, 95, 125; *27*
Victoria Memorial, London 34; *34*
Vietch and Fenn 92
Viollet-le-Duc, Eugène Emmanuel 52 - 3
Voysey, Charles F. A. 16 - 19, 141 - 3; *17*

War Office, Whitehall, London 75; *74*
Waring White Building Company 44, 126
Waterhouse, Alfred 9, 22, 39, 76, 79 - 80, 92, 95, 108, 130; *75*
Weaver, Lawrence 83, 141 - 2
Webb, Aston 14, 19, 21, 24 - 8, 34 - 5, 38, 48, 73, 80, 95, 96, 121 - 6; *26, 27, 29, 34, 35, 121, 122, 123, 124, 125*
Webb, Philip 9 - 10, 19, 28, 141
Wells, A. Randall 146
Wesleyan Hall, Westminster, London *51, 63*
Westminster Cathedral, London 21, 85, 125
Willink, William E. *see* Willink and Thicknesse
Willink and Thicknesse 21, 108 - 14; *62, 109, 111, 112, 113, 155*
Wills, G. Berkeley 26 - 7
Wills, Herbert W. *see* Wills and Anderson
Wills and Anderson 137 - 40; *137, 138, 139*
Wolverhampton Public Library 128 - 34; *129, 131, 133*
Wood, Edgar 55, 149 - 51; *150, 151 see also* Wood and Sellers
Wood and Sellers 77; *55*
Woodhouse, Corbett and Dean 59; *59, 60*
'Wrenaissance' 16 - 24, 34, 42, 92, 102 - 5, 127, 137, 139 - 40, 151, 154

YMCA, Manchester 59; *59, 60*
Young, William 75; *74*